D0752971

ASTORIAN ADVENTURE

ASTORIAN ADVENTURE

The Journal of Alfred Seton
1811–1815

edited by

ROBERT F. JONES

Fordham University Press
New York
1993

Library of Congress Cataloging-in-Publication Data

Seton, Alfred, 1793–1859
    Astorian Adventure: the journal of Alfred Seton, 1811–1815/edited by
Robert F. Jones.
    p.   cm.
    Includes bibliographical references and index
    ISBN 0-8232-1503-2 (cloth) : $25.00
    1. Astoria (Or.)—History.   2. Fur Trade—Northwest, Pacific—
History.   3. Northwest, Pacific, Description and travel.   4. Northwest,
Pacific—History.   5. Hawaii—Description and travel.   6. Seton, Alfred,
1793–1859—Diaries.   I. Jones, Robert Francis, 1935–   .   II. Title.
F884.A8S48   1993
979.5'46—dc20   93-2067
                                                                      CIP

Printed in the United States of America

For Ann and Chris,
Rob,
Ken and Kathy,
Tim,
and Bill—
helpers always

CONTENTS

Illustrations following page 86.

LIST OF ILLUSTRATIONS

INTRODUCTION

THE FUR TRADE AND JOHN JACOB ASTOR are linked in the minds of most students of American history through his American Fur Company, whose trappers roamed the West in the 1820s and 1830s. This is in spite of Washington Irving's masterly rendering of the history of an earlier venture of Astor's, the Pacific Fur Company, in *Astoria, or, Anecdotes of an Enterprise Beyond the Rocky Mountains* (1836), which led to the founding of a post on the Columbia River in 1811. Not only was the Pacific Fur Company a bold effort in continental and international trade, it also aimed to strengthen the United States' claim to a share of the Pacific coast of North America and to head off a move by the Montreal-based North West Company into the Columbia basin. Although the Pacific Fur Company was not a commercial success, it cannot be said to have failed in its other goals, as the post at Astoria did bolster the American hand in subsequent negotiations and the geographical knowledge of the Oregon country brought back by the Astorians encouraged eventual American settlement. Astor, the Pacific Fur Company, Irving and his history, are all linked in the journal presented in these pages, as its author, Alfred Seton, a young New Yorker, enjoyed (or at least thought he did) a privileged relationship with Mr. Astor when he signed on as a clerk with the company, and Seton's journal later served as a source for *Astoria*. This journal, and Duncan McDougall's Astoria journal (at the Rosenbach Library, Philadelphia), are apparently the only ones written at the time which survive today. Neither has been published. Since the Seton journal is largely unknown to scholars, it is appropriate to give the reader an idea of its author and of the enterprise in which he enlisted.

Alfred Seton was eighteen years old in 1811 when he signed on for what was expected to be a five-year tour of duty as a clerk with the Pacific Fur Company on the Columbia River. In the normal run of things, he would almost certainly not have entered commercial life in such an arduous, not to say dangerous, way, but the early nineteenth century was not normal in New York, even for a young man from Seton's privileged background. His family was relatively new to America, his grandfather, William Seton, having emigrated in 1763 from Scotland. William Seton was a merchant in New York City when the tensions between the colonies and the mother country exploded into open warfare in 1775. Along with many other colonial Americans, Seton chose loyalty to the Crown and served as assistant superintendent of the port of New York during the British occupation, 1776–1783.[1] When the British evacuated the city in November 1783, Seton remained for a time as a deputy to Hector St. Jean de Crèvecoeur, who was managing a line of packet ships as well as acting as French consul in New York.[2] When the Bank of New York was organized in 1784, Seton became cashier, in effect the chief executive officer of the bank in charge of its daily operations. Prior to the organization of the Bank of the United States in 1792, he also acted as the fiscal agent for the United States government in New York.[3] In 1794, he left the bank and organized the mercantile firm of Seton, Maitland & Co., with a branch in London and correspondents in Germany, the Mediterranean, and the West Indies. For a time, the firm did well, and Seton was obviously established in the upper rungs of New York society. He had married Rebecca Curzon of Baltimore in 1767, by whom he had four sons and three daughters; when she died in 1776, he married her sister, Anna-Maria, by whom he had eight additional children. His two oldest sons, William Magee and James (Alfred's father), carried on the business when the elder Seton died unexpectedly in 1798. Until then, life had been good for the Setons, who enjoyed not only a pleasant home in the city, but a country estate, "Cragdon," in the village of Bloomingdale (around 110th Street in modern terms) on the East River during the summer.[4]

Perhaps William Magee Seton was not the businessman his father had been, or ill health (tuberculosis), or the difficult economic times brought on by the Wars of the French Revolution, or possibly a combination of all of these, brought down Seton, Maitland in 1801. With the death of William Magee in 1803, James became head of the family.[5] Whatever the problems caused by the failure,

James seems to have been able to soldier through, keeping his family of two boys and four girls in a three-story house on Greenwich Street and paying the bills through a brokerage in marine insurance. In 1809, he moved the family to Pearl Street and set up as a commission merchant and auctioneer, dealing mainly in imported goods. When Alfred signed up with the Pacific Fur Company in 1811, the family was living on Cedar Street.[6] The moves indicate that James rented the family's quarters, and Alfred's lament that his father was "reduced" owing to the difficult economic situation of the country reflected genuine difficulties (p. 29). These difficulties certainly increased for James when his wife, the former Mary Hoffman, died in 1807.[7]

In addition to the stress of business and personal losses, James Seton also had to deal with family tensions caused by the 1805 conversion to Catholicism of his brother's widow, Elizabeth Bayley Seton, tensions increased by the later conversions of two of his half-sisters, one of whom, Cecilia, lived with him. Although James's wife, Mary, took the conversions very hard, she was reconciled with both Elizabeth and Cecilia during her final illness, as was James.[8] Memories of the discord and distress caused by all this were no doubt instrumental in convincing Alfred not to propose marriage to a young Spanish-American Catholic woman in California in 1814 (pp. 166–68). Not all the Seton family were reconciled with Elizabeth; their anger with her was one of the principal influences leading her to move to Baltimore in 1808, then to Emmittsburg, Maryland, the following year. There she helped to found the Sisters of Charity in the United States, a Roman Catholic order of religious women devoted primarily to education. Her personal life and her work with the Sisters of Charity led to her canonization in 1975 as the first American-born saint of the Catholic church.

Alfred's mother, Mary Hoffman, also came from a well-connected, and less distressed, family, active in both mercantile and legal life in New York City. Through her, he was related to Matilda Hoffman, his first cousin, and Washington Irving's intended wife. Matilda died when only seventeen, to Irving's lifelong regret.[9] More important to Alfred's immediate prospects were his maternal uncles Josiah Ogden and Martin Hoffman, both of whom gave him letters of recommendation when he joined Astor's company (pp. 83, 98–99).[10]

Alfred was the first-born of his parents, probably sometime early in 1793, as they had married in March 1792. He says little in his journal about his early education, but it was certainly thorough and effective, as the journal shows. The writing is not inspired, but it is usually clear and, on occasion, gives a strong, vivid impression. He sometimes frets about the possibility that his surroundings are de-civilizing him, using as evidence his "bad spelling, frequent repetitions, & bad orthography" (p. 116). He dropped out of Columbia College,[11] where he had spent two years, to join the fur company. He shows a familiarity with nautical terms and maritime usages, which is not surprising for someone from a family engaged in trade.

One can say little of Alfred physically, as no portrait, sketch, or photograph apparently survives. In Oregon, the Canadian *voyageurs* called him "la tete blanche" (p. 141), literally, "white head"; thus, he probably had blond hair and its accompanying fair complexion. He may have been relatively slight, as he did not feel able to take on an obnoxious fellow clerk during a shipboard argument other than with the stylized violence of the *code duello* (pp. 00ff.), although his reluctance may have been an attempt to assert his status as a "Gentleman," a term he usually capitalized. He did not lack physical toughness, as three years in Oregon, during which he seems generally to have been healthy, proved, as well his survival of a siege of malaria while making his way home in 1814–1815 (pp. 172ff.).

Temperamentally, Alfred was certainly something of a snob, as his concern with genteel status indicates. No one on the expedition measured up to his standards, and he was careful to note his companions' lack of gentlemanly character, particularly the French Canadians and Spanish Californians. He began the journey, and the journal, pious to a fault, especially in his reaction to the loss of two sailors on the voyage out (pp. 51–52). However, the general knocking about, as well as some instances of real physical danger, bred a more tolerant attitude, as witness his calm resignation to the last rites of the Catholic Church, when he seemed near death from malaria in Mexico. His tolerance had its limits, as he could not resist noting that the ritual "appears more like the preparation for some puppet show than the most sacred office, that man can be engaged in" (p. 173–74), an appearance probably bolstered by his ignorance of both the Spanish of the priest and the Latin of the service. Also, his journal shows him beginning the trip as deeply introspective, always examining his motives for actions both serious and trivial. By the end of his time, he is clearly more comfortable with himself, although he still tends to protest his virtue and good faith a bit too much. Finally, Wilson Price Hunt, the ranking Pacific Fur Company partner on the scene, felt it necessary to caution him to moderate his "haughtiness of disposition" (p. 99), a caution Seton admitted was justified. Hunt's advice was not caused by disappointment with Seton, as he was one of only two clerks to receive a $500 bonus when the post was broken up in 1814; he had obviously given satisfaction as a clerk (p. 166).[12]

The title of clerk did not indicate clearly the status of the young men who enjoyed it. They were what one might call lower-rank officers, coming just under the partners. Although they did clerkly things, such as writing letters, keeping ledgers, marking packs of furs, and the like, they could also be called on to lead expeditions to search out new sources of furs, take charge of small posts for extended periods of time, see to the safe carriage of furs, and trade goods from one point to another—in brief, the duties of the partners to whose status they aspired.[13] Clerk status was a kind of executive training program. Seton hoped, after serving his five-year contract, "the sacrifice of a few years more would enable me to return to my Country in an independant situation" (p. 30).

He had been led to take such a difficult course to securing a competency by, as he termed it, "the distressing emergencies of the times" (p. 29), especially his father's business reverses. The years after the resumption of war in Europe in 1803 were anything but normal for American commerce, and the efforts of Presidents Thomas Jefferson and James Madison (1801–1817) to deny American goods and markets to the principal antagonists, Great Britain and France, who interfered with American neutral traders, served only to complicate the situation further. If James Seton was having trouble making ends meet (and he probably was), he was not alone. With five younger children at home for whom his father had to care, Alfred's signing on with Astor was both generous and prudent. He also may have felt a need to get away to examine his priorities:

> In N York I was acquiring habits of expence, which my Father's affairs did not justify, & which I believe would insensibly have got the better of me & perhaps at this time if I had there remained I would have found myself overwhelmed with debts, in bad Company, & with little hopes of raising myself to a respectable situation in life. [p. 130]

In today's language, he seems to have been telling himself to "Get a life!"

However he may have been enriched in character and experience, he arrived back in New York sometime in 1815 still recovering from malaria and "as poor as a Starved Rat" (p. 175). Little is known about Alfred's life for the next several years. He must have been doing reasonably well, as he married Frances Barnewall in 1819.[14] The following year, he was in New York City and, with fellow Astorian Gabriel Franchère, attested to the correctness of a letter which Astor was using in an attempt to prove the fraudulent character of the sale of Astoria in 1813. He was working for the mercantile firm of G. G. and S. Howland at the time. While he was with Howlands', he traveled on their behalf, revisiting the "isolated regions of Kamtachatak, the Kodiac whaling grounds," going on to "Japan, the Indies, and South America," and Europe. In 1822, a cousin mentioned his return from "Angostura [now Ciudad Bolivar, on the Orinoco River in Venezuela] where he is doing it appears extremely well in the way of business." So well that he was considering bringing his wife and two children down there. He certainly spent a bit of time there, for he later contributed to an article on the fur trade which appeared in Benjamin Silliman's *American Journal of Science and Arts*, informing the anonymous author on, among other things, the fur trade with South America.[15]

By 1828, Seton had set himself up as a fur merchant, with an establishment on Water Street in Manhattan.[16] Irving lists him as one of the principal backers of Captain Benjamin Bonneville's 1832–1835 fur hunting expedition in the West, chronicled by Irving in *The Rocky Mountains; or, Scenes, Incidents, and Adventures in the Far West* (1837), more familiarly known as *The Adventures of Captain Bonneville*. Seton's involvement in Bonneville's effort furnishes an interesting parallel to his earlier involvement with the Pacific Fur Company, for both enterprises apparently shared trade and political goals—goals which, in their immediate sequels, neither achieved. However, if both Astor and Bonneville wished to help the United States secure the West, their efforts did eventually contribute to that goal.[17] Seton's association with Bonneville may have had another, probably unexpected, effect. It may have reminded him of his youthful adventures on the Oregon and during his visits to the Russian-American Company's outpost at Sitka. Alternatively, his memories could have been jogged by John Jacob Astor's recruiting, in the fall of 1834, Washington Irving to write *Astoria*, a task which took most of Irving's time and energies through February 1836.[18] Seton mentions the personal character of his journal in several places in it. To my mind, it is doubtful that he simply handed it over to Astor on his return to New York as part of the Pacific Fur Company's papers. Rather, he probably kept it until this time, when either Astor or Irving asked him for help.[19] This request may have moved him to write of Astoria and Alaska. Whatever the cause, in 1835 and again in 1837, he sat down to write what might be called new and improved versions of his experiences with the Pacific Fur Company. Two installments, entitled "Life on the Oregon," which appeared in *The American Monthly Magazine* (May and July 1835), edited by Seton's cousin, Charles F. Hoffman, chronicle trips upcountry with a partner of the company. He signed the articles simply as "A." Incidents, some extraordinarily colorful and exciting, are described in them which do not appear in the journal. They are included here as Appendix A. Two years later, still using only "A.," Seton told, with great gusto and verve, his adventures at Sitka, especially the drinking bouts that seemed to have been an obligatory accompaniment to doing business with Count Alexander Baranov,[20] the Russian-American Company's governor. Given the graphic title "Astorian Reminiscences: The Carousals of Count Baranoff," it appeared in the New York *Mirror* (XV, 84–85) on September 9, 1837. Although the drinking, etc., are mentioned in the journal, the account given in the *Mirror* is much more circumstantial, with a wealth of vivid detail. Perhaps, as with old army or college stories, things seemed a good bit more exciting—and funnier—in the retelling. Seton's retrospective version of these drinking stories is given here as Appendix B. It should be noted that Seton shared the material in *The American Monthly* with Irving, for Irving copies dialogue directly from Seton, especially his version of Donald McKenzie's confrontation with some truculent, thieving natives.[21]

One further point might be made about them. Moving from the journal to the later writing, one is struck by the very different style and even content. In the latter case, the style is much more self-conscious, with many more allusions to literary characters and sites and more elaborate sentence-structure; the writer is striving for effect, and it shows. In the journal, Seton generally used a simpler and clearer style; when he described something, it was done in an almost functional way as if he were writing a kind of field journal. As to the content, there is no way of judging which, the journal or the later essays, is more authentic, but it may be noted that the later writing includes a number of exciting incidents which Seton did not note down at the time of his original writing and which no other Astorian seems to have bothered to record.[22] These differences make Seton's journal, along with the McDougall journal, all the more valuable as the only contemporary records of Astoria to survive.

Seton left the fur business in 1841 when he got together with a number of other New Yorkers to found the Sun Mutual Insurance Company, writing marine insurance. From then until 1859, he served as the company's vice president, from time to time also serving as an officer of New York's Board of Underwriters. The company prospered, becoming the third largest firm of its kind in New York before 1860. Around 1850, he moved to a country home at Throg's Neck in what was then lower Westchester County (the present-day Bronx) and from which he commuted into the city. He died at home on Sunday, May 22, 1859.[23]

****

John Jacob Astor, the man directly responsible for bringing Seton halfway around the world to Astoria, was born in Germany in 1763, just about the time Alfred's grandfather was getting to New

York. After a period of time in London, working for a relative in the musical instrument business, Astor also moved on to New York, and probably for much the same reason that had inspired William Seton: to do better. Young Astor arrived in 1784 with a small parcel of instruments to sell and a large ambition. On the way over, he had talked about the fur business with several other travelers and had apparently become relatively well informed about something of which he had had little knowledge previously.[24]

Astor would need a good bit more than information to succeed in the fur business in the 1780s. The entire world of Anglo-American trade was going to have to be extensively revised to take account of the effects of American independence. Pushed from the relatively warm and certain world of the old British Empire by their success-ful assertion of independence, Britain's former colonies were feel-ing their way toward a new relationship in international trade, both with their old colonial mistress and with their new trading partners throughout the world. The fur trade was complicated by this new status, in that some of the richest fur sources lay astride the still incompletely determined boundary between the United States and Canada. Jay's Treaty of 1795 dealt successfully with some of the problems of Anglo-American trade, but left the boundary, espe-cially the northwest corner of it, still undefined. Little of this both-ered Astor for some years, as he made his way up in the mercantile world of New York, moving from one area to another as the possi-bility of profit presented itself. Increasingly, however, he came to specialize in the fur trade and in trade with China. However dis-similar they may seem at first glance, these pursuits were related, in that Europe and America had relatively little that China would trade in exchange for its much-valued tea and manufactured luxury goods, especially dishes ("china"), furniture, and textiles. At first, Westerners could give the Chinese only coin and ginseng, obtained in the eastern United States and widely valued in China for its supposed curative and aphrodisiacal powers. American traders added to these goods in the 1780s when they began carrying trade goods to the west coast of North America and trading them with the natives for furs which they then took to Canton, the principal Chi-nese trading port. Later, they added Hawaiian sandalwood to this brief list of exports. This trade was well developed by the time

Astor involved himself with it through an interest in the *Severn* and its cargo in 1800. Once involved, he moved quickly into the trade, ordering the ship *Beaver* built in New York City in 1805, designed for the special demands of the China trade.[25]

Astor did not allow this new and exotic trade to distract him away from the places where he had first entered the fur trade, New York and Canada. He continued to travel frequently to Montreal and to interest himself in the operations of the companies working out of that city. He professed to be increasingly bothered by the fact that many of the furs which he purchased in Montreal had been obtained in American territory in the upper Midwest, either directly by Canadian trappers or indirectly by Candadian traders who crossed the border, wherever it might lie.[26] At that time, American trappers and traders worked principally out of St. Louis, where Astor had correspondents and interests. The Louisiana Purchase, made by the Jefferson administration in 1803, had given the United States title to an undefined area west of the Mississippi River and north of Spain's colonial borderlands in Mexico. The activities of these traders and trappers would certainly influence where the boundary between the United States and Canada would eventually be placed. Also present in these mixed considerations of trade and politics was the possibility that the United States would push its way into a share of the western coast of North America. American ship captains and traders had been active on that coast, especially in the area of present-day Oregon, Washington, and British Columbia, since 1790 and the first voyage of Robert Gray. In 1792, Gray had been the first European known to have sailed into the Columbia River, which was named for his vessel, and thus he became the official discoverer of the river, at least to Western notions of discovery and conquest. The subsequent explorations of Meriwether Lewis and William Clark, 1804–1806, an official activity of the United States government, had reinforced the American claim to some share of the coast. This claim would be contested not only by the British and the Canadians, but also by the Spanish, present in upper California since the 1770s, and the Russians, who had established a settlement on Kodiak Island in 1784.

Spain, declining since the seventeenth century, did little more than defend, and feebly at that, its colonial possessions. Turned back by the British from an assertion of control in the Northwest at the time of the Nootka Sound Controversy in 1789–1790, it retreated to its settlement at San Francisco Bay. But it did not formally renounce its pretensions. Not so with the Russians. The Russian-American Company, chartered at St. Petersburg in 1799, moved aggressively in Alaska under Count Alexander Baranov, already mentioned, who would govern the company's affairs there until his death in 1818. He even moved into the vacuum created by the Spanish withdrawal after Nootka, and placed a Russian post tentatively at Fort Ross, about seventy miles north of San Francisco, a post which Seton visited after his carousal with Baranov (pp. 163–64). All was not well with the Russians, however. The distance across the Eurasian continent from St. Petersburg to the Bering Strait created what would prove to be insuperable supply problems. They not only had difficulty getting furs west to the Russian capital; they also had problems getting supplies for the post east to Alaska. Part of the market for their furs, especially sea otter skins, was in China, and they lacked the shipping to get them there. Nor was their residence in Alaska accepted easily by all the natives. The harsh, cruel practices followed by the first trappers to go into the area had throughly cowed the Aleuts, but had failed to impress the Tlingit Indians of the mainland and those who lived on Kodiak Island. They continued hostile to the Russians, resisting when they could, and even in Seton's time, Baranov's post at Sitka resembled nothing so much as a far northern version of a frontier stockade with a prodigious moat (p. 156; Appendix B, pp. 203–204). Tlingit resistance was made much more effective by muskets, shot, and powder, traded to them by American and British captains, especially American. Russian efforts to get the United States government to intervene in this murderous trade were unavailing.[27]

None of these problems—the United States–Canadian rivalry for furs, the United States-British disagreement over the northwest boundary, Spain's pretensions in the area, or the growling of the Russian bear, Baranov—was near resolution in the early nineteenth century as John Jacob Astor surveyed the state of both the international trade in furs and affairs on the northwest coast of North America. Alexander Ross, one of Seton's fellow clerks at Astoria, later commented that Astor possessed a "comprehensive mind," by which he meant an ability to see an underlying unity in an apparently diverse set of conditions.[28] This ability is clearly seen in his first plans for what would become the Pacific Fur Company, plans he laid out to DeWitt Clinton, the scion of the New York political family, who was then serving as mayor of New York City. In these plans he proposed a trade network carrying European goods through St. Louis to a chain of trading posts along the Lewis and Clark route as well as vessels carrying goods to trading posts on the Columbia and elsewhere on the northwest coast. These same vessels would supply the Russians in Alaska and carry furs from both their posts and the northwest posts both to a market in China and back to the northeastern United States and Europe.[29]

Astor had written Clinton because of his influence in New York politics. Knowing the large demands his enterprise would have for capital, he wanted to incorporate it, an act requiring the special consent of the state legislature, a measure which he hoped Clinton would support. He also realized the political implications of what he was proposing and he wanted some kind of a connection with the federal government, another area where Clinton might be helpful, as his uncle, George Clinton, the former governor of New York, was then serving as vice president.

The charter of incorporation was the first hurdle surmounted. In April 1808, it passed the legislature easily, creating the American Fur Company, capitalized at $1,000,000 (with a possible expansion to $2,000,000), to last for twenty-five years. The money was needed "to support a fair competition with foreigners who are at present almost in the exclusive possession of the fur trade." The company would be "of great public utility, by serving to conciliate and secure the good will and affections" of the western Indians toward the United States. The charter held nothing of the larger purposes Astor saw the company serving.[30]

Astor had already begun trying to enlist administration support directly by writing to President Thomas Jefferson in February. He presented his project in the most inoffensive terms possible, never breathing a hint of his encompassing all the fur trade, as he had to Clinton. What he was clear about was that he wanted "the countenance and good wishes of the executive of the United States." Without the government's "approbation," the enterprise would fail and not achieve the advantages for the country its success would ensure. He was asking Jefferson to approve a very vaguely described proposal, put forward by someone whom he had never met. Actually, Jefferson had already answered the question, although it had been put in a somewhat different form. In 1806, he had approved Meriwether Lewis's suggestion of an American trading post on the Columbia, noting to Senator William Plumer of New Hampshire that, while trade would follow government-sponsored exploration, the traders would still be on their own. Jefferson replied to Astor's query on April 13, indicating his pleasure that American merchants were thinking of operating in the area, an area whose immense size would certainly demand the participation of a number of companies, to which "every reasonable patronage and facility in the power of the executive" would be given. Not at all what Astor had wanted.[31]

He followed up the initial letter with a visit to Washington sometime in April 1808, a visit during which he was able to meet with the president, together with Secretary of State James Madison, Secretary of the Treasury Albert Gallatin, and Secretary of War Henry Dearborn. The only record of the meeting is an 1813 letter of Astor's in which he insisted that the president had promised government protection in the event of interference with his company by the British government, " 'that to Prevent this Som protection from government might become neccessarry which was promisd in the most Desided & explicit manner' " by Jefferson. Such a promise is very unlikely. Gentle, vague words of support and approval were about the most Astor could have gotten.[32]

Although Astor wanted President Jefferson (and his successor, James Madison) to think that he had American interests only at heart, in Montreal, he made several proposals in 1808–1809 to buy a share of the North West Company. These proposals were eventually rejected by the partners in Montreal, but accepted grudgingly (and ineffectively) by the "wintering partners," that is, those who stayed in the West at Fort William, on the northwestern corner of Lake Superior (p. 107n71), running the company's operations. Not knowing of Montreal's refusal to accept Astor's offer, in 1810 the winterers sent a party west to cooperate, up to a point, with the Americans in the Columbia country. Expecting a favorable decision, Astor organized the Pacific Fur Company as a simple partnership in March 1810, first recruiting the Canadian partners, Alexander McKay, Donald Mackenzie, and Duncan McDougall. Astor held half of the one hundred shares; the partners, five shares each. Obviously, additional partners were to be added. (Under certain conditions, Astor could assign his share in the concern to the American Fur Company.[33]) If the North West Company agreed to cooperate, the stock would be increased to two hundred shares and the Canadians would buy one-third of the total; thus, Astor would retain ultimate control. Before knowing of the eventual decision of the North Westers, Astor continued organizing the Pacific Fur Company, adding four American partners in June: Wilson Price Hunt, Ramsay Crooks, Robert McClellan, and Joseph Miller. He also began the work of recruiting clerks, *voyageurs*, trappers, hunters—all the various types of men needed to make such a venture work.[34]

Astor planned three divisions for his grand effort in the Northwest. One, headed by Wilson Price Hunt, who was to be the ranking partner at Astoria, was to go overland from St. Louis. Along the way, they were to select sites for fur trading posts on the eastern side of the Rocky Mountains. Another division was to go out on the ship *Tonquin*, newly purchased by Astor and commanded by Captain Jonathan Thorn, on leave from the United States Navy. It would carry the heavier trade goods and provisions and was scheduled to arrive some months before the overland party. Thorn was accurately described by Gabriel Franchère, a clerk recruited in Montreal, as a "precise and rigid man, naturally hot-tempered, expecting instant obedience."[35] Even before the *Tonquin* left the port of New York, there was a quarrel between Thorn and Alexander McKay, the ranking partner aboard, over space assignments on the overcrowded vessel. Unfortunately, the quarrel was the first of many, and the voyage which lasted from September 1810 to March 1811, with a layover in the Hawaiian Islands, was an especially tense one.[36] When they arrived at the mouth of the Columbia, both Thorn and the Pacific Fur Company people were eager to be rid of each other, and that as quickly as possible.

As the *Tonquin* was making its unhappy way around the Horn, Astor was working on a third aspect of his comprehensive plan, the development of a trading relationship with the Russians at Sitka. Dealing with Andrei Dashkov, Russian *chargé d'affaires* in Washington, Astor sketched out a tentative plan to give himself a trading monopoly with the Russian-American Company, supplying them with provisions and trading goods and carrying some of their furs to the most profitable market, Canton, China. It was expected that this would make voyages by other American captains into the area unprofitable and thus end the trade in guns, shot, and powder with the Tlingits and other tribes. Astor's son-in-law, Adrian Bentson, went to St. Petersburg where his efforts to get a firm contract with the Russians foundered on the questions of where the respective boundaries between the two countries' claims were and whether or not Astor could import furs into Russia. Finally, in May 1812, a tentative agreement was signed by which the two companies promised not to trade in the other's territory, the boundaries of which were left undefined. The Pacific Fur Company received a trading monopoly at Sitka and promised not to trade weapons with the Indians and to carry the Russian company's furs to Canton. By the time Astor signed the agreement in December 1812, the British-American war, which would seriously damage the Pacific Fur Company's chances for survival, let alone profit, was already six months old.[37]

While Thorn and the seagoing Astorians were arguing their way around Cape Horn on the *Tonquin*, Hunt was experiencing equally heavy weather making his way across the continent. Setting out from Montreal in July 1810, Hunt was already at a disadvantage because of his late start, about two months later than was preferred. Along the way, stopping at Mackinac, he tried to recruit more men—Americans, if he could get them. He could not. Moving on to St. Louis, reached in early September, Hunt continued to experience difficulty in recruiting men. Astor's name was not well known there, and the effort to go through to the Pacific did not sit well with trappers who knew where skins could be obtained east of the mountains. Recruiting and securing the necessary supplies consumed too much time for a start for the Pacific to be practical that year. Hunt decided to winter on the Nodaway River, five hundred miles above St. Louis on the Missouri (fittingly enough in the neighborhood of present-day Oregon, Missouri). After getting the men comfortably settled there, Hunt returned to St. Louis where he learned, via a letter from Astor, that there was no longer any hope of working with the North West Company and that it was now illegal by federal statute for non-citizens to trade on American soil. Astor dealt with this by ending the rough parity that had been the case between Hunt and Mackenzie, putting Hunt clearly in charge. Hunt spent January and February recruiting a few more men, leaving St. Louis on March 12, 1811. He reached the winter camp after traveling for about a month. On April 20, the party set out for the Pacific. The trip would consume all the rest of the year. Its rigors and the reasons for them, aside from the unavoidable difficulty of traveling through what was, literally, an uncharted wilderness, are well described in a number of places.[38] It must suffice here to note that Hunt found it necessary for survival to break up the party into several different groups, each of which was to try a different route through the mountains. His party was one of the last to reach Astoria, finally arriving on February 15, 1812.

That there was an Astoria to arrive at was a blessing which the overlanders very much needed. When the *Tonquin* had arrived almost a year earlier, Captain Thorn had been eager to drop the fur traders off and to set off on the coastal trading voyage ordered by Astor. Duncan McDougall, the ranking partner present, and the men were just as eager to embark from the ship and set about building a post. Even the selection of a site was accompanied by a good bit of acrimony, with Thorn ordering the cargo unloaded on the north shore of the Columbia when McDougall did not settle on a location soon enough. Although it was far from perfect, a site east of Young's Bay, about ten miles from the mouth of the river on the south shore, was selected. Some of the cargo was unloaded, and the men began a task for which they had very little experience and surprisingly few suitable tools. With much labor, the site was cleared, and buildings, surrounded by a log palisade, constructed. Gardens were planted and the livestock which had been purchased in Hawaii either set to grazing or, in the case of the hogs, set free (to become a serious nuisance within a short time). The gardens, tended by Hawaiian natives taken on in the islands, did well, especially turnips and potatoes. The livestock never contributed much to the men's diet and they subsisted mainly on game and the yearly run of salmon and other fish from the river.[39]

The neighboring Indians soon began to visit Astoria where their different ideas of propriety and property soon made them a nuisance, but a necessary one. The local tribe was Chinook, a people relatively experienced in trading with the vessels that had been calling along the coast since 1790. Its chief was Comcomly, in the view of the Astorians an especially crafty old villain who convinced the outlying tribes that they had to trade through him. Finally, McDougall gave the chief a large gift, signifying his local control, and other tribes began to show up at the post. McDougall would go even further than this and marry Comcomly's daughter in July 1813, a step that presumably guaranteed peace with the tribe (p. 226).

Once they were established at Astoria, the Pacific traders went into the interior, both trapping animals themselves and also setting up posts to trade furs with the area tribes. Eventually they moved up the Columbia and branched off into the Willamette, the Snake, the Clearwater, the Palouse, and the Okanogan rivers. Posts were set up as far inland as the present state of Idaho. Once the fact of the Montreal partners' rejection of Astor's offer had reached the winterers at Fort William, the North West Company mounted a counterattack. Although they did not defeat the North Westers' move into the Columbia basin, the Pacific adventurers, for a time, competed hard and strong, and with a fair degree of success. The North Westers also sent representatives to London to try to secure a monopoly of all non-Hudson's Bay Company territory and the right to trade with China, then a monopoly of the East India Company. They failed in these latter efforts.[40]

Captain Thorn took the *Tonquin* out beyond the troublesome sandbar at the mouth of the Columbia River on the 5th of June, in so much of a hurry to be rid of his sailing companions that not all the cargo consigned to the post had yet been unloaded. He was to trade for furs along the west coast of Vancouver Island, stopping back at Astoria in late summer, before sailing for Canton. Alexander McKay, a partner, went with him to look after the company's interest and give the benefit of his experience. Unfortunately for the *Tonquin* and her crew, Captain Thorn's experience, judgment, and will were the only ones that mattered to Captain Thorn. While trading with a tribe led by an especially belligerent chief, Wickananish, in Clayoquot Bay (above Nootka Sound on the west coast of Vancouver Island), Thorn became angry at a chief's complaint on the low prices being paid, and threw the skins in his face. The most elementary precautions had apparently not been followed, such as rigging boarding nettings and limiting the number of natives allowed on board at any one time. Hence, the *Tonquin* was wide open to the chief's vengeance several days later, when he returned with two canoe-loads of warriors; finally growing suspicious, Thorn ordered the vessel to get under way. Before the sailors could do that, the Indians, about forty in number, attacked the crew. In the immediate event, only Jack Ramsay, the Indian interpreter, escaped, eventually making his way back to Astoria in 1813; all the rest, except for one or two who hid themselves, were killed. The next day, natives crowded on board the *Tonquin*, looting and celebrating their victory. A crew member (or members) who had hidden in the powder magazine exploded it and the entire vessel, along with everyone on it, blew up. Rumors of the tragedy reached Astoria by early July. The full event was not confirmed until the arrival of the *Beaver* in May 1812, long after the Astorians had begun to act on the supposition that the vessel had been lost. Astoria's course was not changed remarkably by the loss of the *Tonquin*, although the settlement was, to all intents and purposes, isolated until the *Beaver*'s arrival.[41]

The *Beaver*, carrying several more of the company's partners, supplies, and more clerks, including Alfred Seton, had left New York City in October 1811. With an easier-tempered captain and good luck, the voyage was relatively uneventful and, after the usual layover at the Hawaiian Islands (where Seton and the others heard an all-too-clear confirmation of the fate of the *Tonquin*), Captain Cornelius Sowle dropped anchor inside the Columbia River bar on May 9, 1812. Seton was soon put to the work for which he had been hired and which he describes in this journal. Although he is often at pains to note the physical discomfort and labor of his duties, he never notes the responsibilities he was being asked to take on, frequently directing the labors of men vastly more skilled in woodcraft and trapping lore than he was. He also assumes his superiority to both his French Canadian associates and the native inhabitants with whom he dealt. This unconscious assumption of superiority probably assisted him to taking on the responsibilities noted. These comments aside, it seems best to allow him to take over from here, with an occasional assist in a footnote.

Although Alfred Seton can fairly be given the task of chronicling the labors of the Astorians, he could hardly be expected to assess the significance of the failed effort which had brought him to the northwest coast. Commercially, the Pacific Fur Company cannot be said to have been the wave of the future. Even Astor's American Fur Company would be conducted on a more modest scale, east of the Rocky Mountains, when the fur trade regained its momentum after the War of 1812. And Astor withdrew from the trade in the mid-1830s, both because of ill health and a conviction that the trade's time was past, a conviction concurred in by the anonymous author of the 1834 article in *The American Journal of Science and Arts*. Seton, it may be recalled, assisted in the preparation of the article and may have agreed with its conclusion. That he began his business career in the largely unexplored wilderness of the northwestern United States, trading with Indians and drinking with half-mad old Russians, and ended it as an insurance company executive, commuting from The Bronx to Manhattan, may be a fair analogy to the course of the fur trade during the same period.

Even the contribution Astoria made to the United States' acquisition of the Oregon country seems to have been a minor one. It was the fall of 1818 before American authorities arrived at Fort George (the North Westers' name for Astoria) and raised the American flag there. But it was also agreed to allow the Canadians to remain in possession of the actual post. This duplicated the terms of the Convention of 1818 (transacted almost simultaneously with the American ceremony) which permitted both American citizens and British subjects full range of the Oregon country, from 54° 40' on the north to 42° on the south.[42] This prompted an anguished outcry from Astor to his friend Albert Gallatin, who had helped to negotiate the agreement. But Astor also noted that his age kept him from renewing the effort and he claimed, somewhat prematurely, that he was "withdrawing from all business as fast as I can."[43] He did not live to see the settlement of the boundary along the present

49° line in June 1846. Astoria, by then a few logs moldering in a still largely unsettled wilderness, was within the bounds of the United States.

****

The journal presented here is an unprepossessing document; it is a cardboard-bound copybook, originally containing somewhat less than 300 pages, each 7½" by 9½". At some point in the past, the original covers were covered with morocco leather. As noted above (p. 7), it is not known formally how the notebook came into Irving's hands originally. Almost certainly, Seton lent it to him when Irving was composing *Astoria*, 1834–1836, and it was never returned. The notebook was found in a cupboard at "Sunnyside," Irving's Tarrytown, New York, home in 1947, after the house had been acquired by Sleepy Hollow Restorations (now Historic Hudson Valley). The journal had been badly damaged by mice and water and could hardly be handled without further deterioration.[44] It was restored in 1976 by Carolyn Horton Associates of New York City. This restoration included de-acidifying and stabilizing the pages and rebinding them in morocco leather. The journal is currently in the safekeeping of the Rockefeller Archives, Pocantico Hills, New York.

Following its restoration, work began on preparing the journal for publication. A partial transcription had already been made by Lawrence Leder. This was taken up and completed, with a good bit of the necessary editorial apparatus added by Stephen W. Sears, Andrew Breen Myers, Alvin M. Josephy, Jr., Jacob Judd, and Peter Malia. Then, for various reasons, work on the project was suspended. In the spring of 1991, Saverio Procario, Director of Fordham University Press, asked me if I would be interested in taking up the task. I agreed and began to supplement the work done previously with my own research. I have found the incomplete notes originally prepared by Dr. Myers and Mr. Sears and the comments upon those notes prepared by Mr. Josephy to be especially helpful. My work has also been aided by Professor Robert Carriker of Gonzaga University and Professor T. B. Barry of Trinity College, Dublin. The librarians of the New-York Historical Society, the

New York Genealogical Society, the New York Public Library, and Fordham University Library have given abundant evidence of the reason why "service" appears prominently in librarians' job descriptions. The generous enthusiasm of Mr. Procario and of the Executive Editor of Fordham University Press, Dr. Mary Beatrice Schulte, has also spurred me on in my work. I must also note that the documentary editing procedures used in the preparation of the text were decided upon by me; they and any errors in the text or notes are my responsibility.

ROBERT F. JONES

Fordham University

NOTES

1. Monsignor [Robert] Seton, *An Old Family, or, The Setons of Scotland and America* (New York: Brentano, 1899), pp. 260–61; hereafter, Seton, *Old Family*.

2. Allen Gay Wilson and Roger Anselineau, *St. John de Crèvecoeur: The Life of an American Farmer* (New York: Viking, 1987), p. 110.

3. Allan Nevins, *History of the Bank of New York and Trust Company, 1784 to 1934* (New York: Arno; 1935; repr., 1976), p. 13; for an instance of Seton's service to the federal treasury, see Alexander Hamilton to William Seton, March 25, 1792, in Harold C. Syrett, ed., *The Papers of Alexander Hamilton*, 27 vols. (New York: Columbia University Press, 1961–1987), XI, 190–91.

4. Seton, *Old Family*, pp. 267–68. The name "Cragdon" was later given to an estate in Eastchester, New York, owned by Elizabeth Bayley Seton's son, William, in the mid to late nineteenth century. Ibid., chap. 19, passim; Annabelle M. Melville, *Elizabeth Bayley Seton, 1774–1821* (New York: Scribner's, 1951), pp. 29–30, 36; hereafter, Melville, *Seton*.

5. Melville, *Seton*, pp. 36–37, 69.

6. *Longworth's American Almanac, New York Register, and City Directory*, 1809, 1811; hereafter, *City Directory*.

7. Melville, *Seton*, p. 123.

8. Ibid., pp. 94–95, 123–24.

9. Stanley T. Williams, *The Life of Washington Irving*, 2 vols. (New York: Oxford University Press, 1935), I, 103–107.

10. Eugene A. Hoffman, *Genealogy of the Hoffman Family: Descendants of Martin Hoffman* (New York: Dodd, Mead, 1899), p. 12; hereafter, Hoffman, *Hoffman Genealogy*.

11. *Columbia University Alumni Register, 1754–1931* (New York: Columbia University Press, 1932), p. 788.

12. Alexander Ross, *Adventures of the First Settlers on the Oregon or Columbia*

River, ed. Milo Milton Quaife (Chicago: Donnelly [1923]), pp. 296–97; hereafter, Ross, *Adventures*.

13. James P. Ronda, *Astoria and Empire* (Lincoln: University of Nebraska Press, 1990), pp. 210–11; hereafter, Ronda, *Astoria*; Kenneth W. Porter, *John Jacob Astor: Business Man*, 2 vols. (Cambridge: Harvard University Press, 1931), I, 475–78, for the articles of agreement signed by Seton and the other clerks; hereafter, Porter, *Astor*.

14. Hoffman, *Hoffman Genealogy*, p. 234.

15. "Notarial Certificate, January 12, 1818, John C. Halsey, Alfred Seton," *U.S. Dept. of State, Message from the President of the United States . . . Relating to an Establishment Made at the Mouth of the Columbia River (January 23, 1823)* (Washington, D.C.: Gales & Seaton, 1823), pp. 16, 65; "Biographical Sketch of the Late Alfred Seton, Esq.," *The United States Insurance Gazette*, N.S., 9, No. 49 (June 1859) 65–68, hereafter, "Biographical Sketch"; Walter Barrett [Joseph Scoville, pseud.], *The Old Merchants of New York*, 5 vols. (New York: Carlton, 1863), I, 305, 308.

16. *City Directory*, 1828.

17. Washington Irving, *The Adventures of Captain Bonneville*, edd. Robert A. Rees and Alan Sandy (Boston: Twayne, 1977), pp. xxxv–xxxix.

18. Washington Irving, *Astoria, or, Anecdotes of an Enterprise Beyond the Rocky Mountains*, ed. Richard Dilworth Rust (Boston: Twayne, 1976), pp. xxii–xxiv; hereafter, Irving, *Astoria*. I have used this edition for all references to the text of *Astoria*; however, I have also used the editorial apparatus of the Edgeley W. Todd edition of *Astoria* (Norman: University of Oklahoma Press, 1976). All such references will be given as Irving, *Astoria* (Todd).

19. There are several studies of Washington Irving as author and historian; two that are relevant to this study are Andrew Breen Myers's "Washington Irving, Fur Trade Chronicler: An Analysis of *Astoria*, with Notes for a Corrected Edition," Ph.D. diss., Columbia University, 1964, and Wayne Raymond Kime's "Washington Irving's *Astoria*: A Critical Study," Ph.D. diss., University of Delaware, 1968. Myers describes the circumstances under which the Seton journal was found and the extensive use of it by Irving (pp. 96–146); he also notes the likelihood of conversations with Seton and other Astorians who either were then living in New York or had passed through during the time Irving was writing. Kime's is a more general study; he had not seen the Seton journal at the time he wrote it (p. 245). Both writers give Irving high marks as an historian.

20. The nineteenth-century transliteration of the Count's name, normally spelled in the Cyrillic alphabet, was Baranoff. I have used the preferred modern transliteration of Baranov, retaining the older one wherever it was used by Seton and friends; hence, the disparity in spelling.

21. Irving, *Astoria*, pp. 318–19.

22. Ross Cox, Gabriel Franchère, and Alexander Ross were the other Astorians who wrote of their adventures with the Pacific Fur Company.

23. *First Annual Report of Superintendent of the Insurance Department of the*

State of New York: (Albany: Insurance Department, 1860), pp. 325–26; "Biographical Sketch," 65–66.

24. Porter, *Astor*, I, 6–24. See also John Denis Haeger, *John Jacob Astor: Business and Finance in the Early Republic* (Detroit: Wayne State University Press, 1991), especially his excellent discussion in chap. 1 of the various studies of Astor done over the years. Astoria is covered in chaps. 4 and 5. His interpretation of Astoria does not differ in important respects from either Porter's or Ronda's, although it is more compact than both.

25. Foster Rhea Dulles, *The Old China Trade* (Boston: Houghton Mifflin, 1930), especially chaps. 3, 4, 5; Philip Chadwick Foster Smith, *The Empress of China* (Philadelphia: Philadelphia Maritime Museum, 1984), passim; Porter, *Astor*, I, chaps. 5, 6.

26. Porter, *Astor*, I, 164–65.

27. Hector Chevigny, *Russian America: The Great Alaskan Adventure, 1791–1867* (New York: Viking, 1965), pp. 32, 55, 86–88, 93, 96–97, 100–101, 116.

28. Ross, *Adventures*, p. 36.

29. Ronda, *Astoria*, chap. 3; J. J. Astor to DeWitt Clinton, January 25, 1808, DeWitt Clinton Papers, 4:5–6, Butler Library, Columbia University, New York City.

30. "An Act to incorporate the American fur company, Passed April 6th, 1808," in Porter, *Astor*, I, 413–20.

31. Ronda, *Astoria*, pp. 40–44; Everett S. Brown, ed., *William Plumer's Memorandum of Proceedings in the United States Senate* (New York: DaCapo, 1923; repr. 1969), p. 520. In 1813, Jefferson praised Astoria as " 'the germ of a great, free, and independent empire,' " which would help to ensure the establishment of liberty and self-government over the entire continent; Thomas Jefferson to J. J. Astor, November 9, 1813, in Richard W. Van Alstyne, *The Rising American Empire* (Chicago: Quadrangle, 1960; repr., 1965), p. 93. But the words of a former president meant little.

32. J. J. Astor to James Madison, July 27, 1813, in Dorothy Wildes Bridgewater, ed., "John Jacob Aster [*sic*] Relative to His Settlement on the Columbia River," *Yale University Library Gazette*, 24, No. 2 (October 1949), 62.

33. Porter, *Astor*, I, 182.

34. Ronda, *Astoria*, pp. 55–65.

35. Gabriel Franchère, *Journal of a Voyage on the North West Coast of North America* . . ., ed. W. Kaye Lamb, trans. Wessie Tipping Lamb (Toronto: The Champlain Society, 1969), p. 55; hereafter, Franchère, *Voyage*.

36. Irving, *Astoria*, chaps. 4–7; none of the modern authors pays much attention to the voyage of the *Tonquin*; as Seton was on the *Beaver*, his journal contains nothing of the other vessel's trip out, just its tragic end.

37. Ronda, *Astoria*, chap. 3.

38. Ibid. Chaps. 5 and 6 are the most recent treatments of the journey.

39. Ibid., pp. 196–220.

40. Ibid., pp. 245–48.

41. Ibid., pp. 235–37; Irving, *Astoria*, pp. 62, 72–79; Seton's description of the tragedy (see below, pp. 91–93), was a major source for Irving's rendering of it. See Wayne R. Kime, "Alfred Seton's Journal: A Source for Irving's *Tonquin* Disaster Account," *Oregon Historical Quarterly*, 81, No. 4 (December 1970), 309–24. Myers, "Washington Irving, Fur Trade Chronicler," cites several other uses of the Seton journal or conversations with its author in the preparation of *Astoria*; see pp. 97, 144–46, 152. Myers concludes: "For all the old-fashioned Romantic characteristics of *Astoria*, it is still an irreplaceable volume in any library about the history of the Far West" (p. 262).

42. An American agent reclaimed Astoria on October 6; the Convention was signed in London on October 20, 1818.

43. Frederick Merk, "Essay I, The Genesis of the Oregon Question," *The Oregon Question: Essays in Anglo-American Diplomacy and Politics* (Cambridge: Harvard University Press, 1967) pp. 1–29, esp. 25–27; John Jacob Astor to Albert Gallatin, December 30, 1818, Albert Gallatin Papers, New-York Historical Society, New York City. The ceremony at Astoria occurred on March 6, 1818; the Convention was signed on March 20th. Merk sees the British failure to register in writing a reservation of title when the United States reclaimed Astoria as a fatal blow to their claim to any territory south of the Columbia River. After 1818, Britain did not assert any such claim in the negotiations on the Oregon question.

44. The circumstances of its finding and the condition of the journal at that time are given by Myers, "Washington Irving, Fur Trade Chronicler," pp. 96–97.

EDITORIAL PROCEDURES & GUIDELINES

IT HAS BEEN MY INTENTION to present the Seton journal as a readable document with the assistance and within the constraints of sound scholarship. The expanded method of historical editing, which aims at presenting a readable text with the fewest possible changes, has been used, with the following rules and adaptations. (The expanded method is described briefly in Oscar Handlin, et al., *Harvard Guide to American History* [Cambridge: Harvard University Press, 1955.])

1. Spelling, capitalization, and punctuation appear as in the original document, with the exception of capitals being supplied at the beginning of sentences and periods at the end, where they are lacking.

2. Author's dashes at the end of sentences are replaced by a period.

3. Abbreviations and contractions are generally spelled out, except for those still in common use (months, proper names, titles) and those readily intelligible from the context.

4. Superior letters are brought down to the line of text, i.e., wch appears as which; C^{apt} appears as Capt. No punctuation is added.

5. The ampersand—&—remains.

6. Missing or illegible matter in the manuscript appears as . . . Because of the journal's poor condition, many words are wholly or partially missing or are obscured by stains. Where the context or a portion of the word(s) clearly or strongly indicates what the missing word(s) is, it is supplied in brackets. Any words in brackets are part of the original journal. Where necessary information is lacking in the manuscript—a first name or part of a date, for example—the omission is made good in a footnote, not in brackets within the text.

All text which can be read has been included, even if it does not form a complete sentence or a word, except for letter combinations not suggestive of a word.

7. Interlineations are brought down to the line of text where indicated by the writer.

8. Canceled passages, sentences, and words are as in the manuscript.

9. The appendices are presented as they were printed, save the addition of footnotes.

The Voyage Out

Journal of a voyage to Columbia River on the North West coast of America made by Alfred Seton on board the Ship Beaver, Cornelius Sowle, Master.[1]

It is the intention of the writer of the following pages to note down the little occurrences that happenned to himself & his companions during the voyage alluded to above, & to state the object [&] pursuits of it, & the causes that induced him [to] undertake it, with the hope that (if it shou[ld] please Providence to permit his return [some] future day in the Bosom of his friends & fa[mily] he may peruse these lines & call to mind t[he] sensations he then experienced.

The obj[ect of] our voyage to so remote & a[lmos]t unkn[own a part] of the world is to ass[ist] . . . trade with the natives . . . [The compa]ny was formed in. . . .[2] . . . of whom under the direction of Mr. Wilson P. Hunt left Montreal in July of 1809[3] to form the establishment at the mouth of the Columbia. Another party sailed last year[4] from New York in the Ship Tonquin under the direction of one of the Partners,[5] & a third is now on its way there on board the Ship Beaver under [t]he direction of John Clark Esqr.[6] of Montreal, & of this party I am a member being engaged [in] the service of the Company as a clerke.

[T]he [in]ducements that determined me to undertake [so] long & dangerous a voyage & to remain for [suc]h a length of time among uncivilized natives, [deprive]d of the pleasures of society & friends, are . . . in the first place the distressing emer[gen]cies of the times prevented me from encoura[gi]ng any sanguine expectations of acquiring a [com]petency in [time] to enjoy it at Home; in [the seco]nd pla[ce,] my Father had been reduced . . .[7] licence

---

[1] This opening entry was apparently written on board the *Beaver* on Sunday, October 27, 1811, ten days after clearing New York Harbor.

[2] Most of the next two and one-half lines are missing; Seton seems to have discussed the purpose of Astor's Pacific Fur Company.

[3] The correct year is 1810.

[4] They sailed on September 6, 1810.

[5] Duncan McDougall, who carried Astor's power of attorney when he sailed aboard the *Tonquin*.

[6] Seton regularly misspelled Clarke's name.

[7] The "distressing emergencies of the times" that left Seton's father "reduced"

& having a large . . . expensive of them . . . myself would be . . .
[considera]ble [bur]then; added to this, the prospect of becoming
a par[tner] in the establishment after the expiration of my time (five
years) & the certainty then, that the sacrifice of a few years more
would enable me to return to my Country in an independant situation. These alltogether determined me to leave the comforts of a
home & a fireside for at least ten years, a long long time. Ten days
have scarcely past & it has appeared almost an age since my eyes
were blessed with the sight of my dear Friends; wha[t] then must
be my feelings at the prospect of n[ot] seeing them for 10 years.
How many changes [must], necessarily, happen, those whom I
have now [left] in the high day of youth & happiness may before
. . . time be numbered with the dead. These thou[ghts] are too
distressing. God, Grant that they [may] enjoy peace & happiness
& that I may return & find them comfortable & c[ont]ented.

    I now commence a nar[rative] of the dai[ly] occurrences that
happened.

    On Thursday [October 17, 1811][8] we weighed an[chor] . . .
with a fair Wind from the N.W., & the Pilot left us out side of
Sandy Hook at 1/2 past 8 in the Evening. Mr. Clark then read over
the names of his party consisting of 26 persons, viz. 5 clerks, 15
mechanics & 6 Canadians, & the Captain divided us into messes.
Messrs. Nicholl, Clapp, Halsey, Cox[9] & myself, clerks, mess with

---

probably refer to the economic troubles caused by the 1807–1809 Embargo,
imposed by the Jefferson administration in a vain attempt to secure United States
foreign policy objectives through the denial of American goods and markets to
Great Britain and France. The same basic policy of commercial coercion was
continued under Jefferson's successor, James Madison, but in a weaker form.
James Seton (1770–1834?) lived by overseas trade, first with the family firm of
Seton, Maitland & Company, then as a marine insurance broker, and, after
1808, as an auctioneer and commission merchant. Seton, *Old Family*, p. 267;
City Directory.

    [8] Although the *Beaver* left her berth on the 13th, she did not get a favorable
wind until the 17th. Porter, *Astor*, I, 200.

    [9] Charles A. Nicoll, Benjamin Clapp, John C. Halsey, and Ross Cox. Of the
clerks, only Ross Cox and Seton left accounts of their adventures. Cox's was first
published as *Adventures on the Columbia River* in London in 1831; it was printed
in the United States the following year as *The Columbia River*. The University
of Oklahoma Press edition of 1957, edited by Edgar I. and Jane R. Stewart, has
been used for these notes; hereafter, Cox, *Columbia*. See "Articles of Agreement

him in the Cabin, & the mechanics & Canadians in the Steerage
with the Boatswain. Our mess at present consists of [ele]ven persons, Mr. Clark & the 5 clerks, the Captn. [and] three officers, &
the Captns clerke, George Ehnin[g]er, a nephew of Mr. Astor's.[10]

[Friday October] 18th. The wind continues fair, overtook the . . .
ship that sailed in company with us. [T]he narration of the circumstances that happen any day on board [s]hip is pretty nearly the
narration of all.

[Si]ckness & other causes have prevented me from [wr]iting the
dai[ly o]ccurrences & am obliged to commence [ane]w on
Thurs[day] 14th Novr. 1811, exactly one mon[th] . . . from New
York. During this . . .[11] to judge something of . . . [per]sons with
whom I assoc[iate] . . . ple[as]ant. They have all of them faults,
but as yet we have agreed pretty well. Mr. N.[12] is rather too
[crossed out: officious].

This day the weather commences fair & with a fine breeze & we
find ourselves in N Lat 6° & Long 21° 15'.[13] We have been becalmed for the two last days & this wind therefore is particularly
gratefull. During the calm there were some Bonetas[14] playing about
us. The Captn. & third officer each took one from the Gib boom
end with a Hook & line & at supp[er] we had chowder, a mess
made with Fish & . . . stewed together. Some of our officers refused
eating [it] as they have known several instances where . . . have
been poisoned. This did not deter our [Captn,] Mr. Clark & some
others from eating, & they have [ex]perienced no bad effects. We
likewise saw a shark & threw over a piece of pork which he s[oon]

. . . , October 8, 1811" for the first names and pay of these clerks. Seton received
$200 a year, $50 more than the other clerks mentioned here. Porter, *Astor*, I,
475–76.

[10] Ehninger was a son of Astor's sister Catherine. Porter *Astor*, I, 200.

[11] Most of three lines is missing; remaining fragments ("to judge something
of . . . persons with whom I associate") indicate that Seton was assessing his
fellow passengers.

[12] Charles A. Nicoll.

[13] Off the bulge of Africa, south of the Cape Verde Islands.

[14] Bonita, a mackeral-like fish, of genus Sardus.

devoured; on a shark Hook we [pu]t a larger pie[ce] but the rascal was too cu[nni]ng for us. [We] are well provided with fish. . . . no doubt catch a . . . passage.

Friday 15th Nov. 1811. Th[e] weath[er] . . . four knot breeze, our fish have all deserted us, which we attribute to our copper bottom, as no dirt can attach itself to us, which is the only inducement for Fish to remain with you.

We contrive to kill an hour or two in the Evening with music. Mr. Nicoll plays on the drum & Mr. Clapp & Mr. Cox on the Fifes. Last evening we had a concerto of this kind. It was a fine moonlight night, with a gentle breeze. We were all collected in different attitudes about the performers, 15 or 16 of the settlers & sailors were setting [tog]ether on the deck, the performers with Mr. Clark [on] the lee Hencoop, Halsey, Ehninger & myself on [a] t[r]unk facing them, all together a motley mixture.

I have no doubt we all experienced the [soo]thing effects of music; eight o clock is the [hou]r when all music must stop & all lights be [pu]t out, & eight o clock soon interrupted our [pl]easure.

Friday morng. Nov. 29th 1811. South lat 25°—W. Long 33° 5'.[15] A variety of cir[cu]mstances have [pre]vented me from writing up . . . [w]rite what has happened . . . SE trade winds a day . . . ate & they have conti[nued] yesterday & have driven us rapidly on our passage. We are within a fortnights sail of Cape Horn.

The other afternoon they were some Birds flying about the ship. I put a bullett through one at the distance of fifty yards with my rifle, which was thought a tolerable good shot. We expect in a day or two to have fine sport shooting at Boobies[16] & albatrosses from the ship as we are near the Lat where they are generally seen in large numbe[rs].

Old sailors generally think it a privile[ge] to duck & shave those who for the first tim[e] cross the Equator. They wished to exercise

---

[15] Off the Brazilian coast, approximately opposite Rio de Janeiro.
[16] A tropical sea bird which resembles the gannet.

th[at] this passage, but our Captn. forbid it, but [let] them have their forfeits, viz a bottle of Rum [for] each person. With this they were satisfied, & w[ere] for a day or two drunk enough.

We h[ave] been all anxiously expecting [to] see some vesse[ls] by whom we could let our f[rien]ds know that we were well, but have not . . . [fallen] in with any until . . . the cry of S[ail Ho].
. . . made us a . . . the glass on the fore top mast Head & in a few minutes gave the word to bear away after her. We soon got out our top gallant stteering sails & sky sails & gave chace to her, expecting her to be a Yankee bound Home, but she in a little time put an end to these Hopes by showing Portugeuse colors. We continued to overhaul her fast & she seeing that it was impossible to escape, backed her Main topsail & lay to.[17] We luffed up to windward of her & our Captn. [ha]iled, "What Brig is that." We could not [un]derstand them, but fortunately having a [Por]tuguese sailor on board, he told them that [we] only wanted to put some letters on board [and as]ked him to lay too, till we boarded him. [The] second officer in the jolly boat then wen[t a]long side & found she was 30 days out from Rio Grand bou[nd] to Pernambuco[18] in the Bra[zil]s. The [ma]ster of her a large Negro. . . . they ever are of the letters and on . . . some Captn. bound . . . [Fa]ther & Edward[19]. . . . they ever receive the Letters, but as Captn. S.[20] does not expect to fall in with any vessel before we get to the Sandwich Isles,[21] I thought I had better embrace the opportunity, especially as there was nothing of importance in them. The Captn. of the Brig by all appearances was very much afraid of us. After our Boat had left his Brig, he continued to lay to untill we made sail & took in

---

[17] The commerce-destroying and trade regulations of the belligerents in the Napoleonic Wars caused any vessel, of whatever nation, to be wary of such encounters on the high seas.

[18] These are both port cities in Brazil; Pernambuco is known today as Recife.

[19] Edward A. Seton (b. 1790), Alfred's uncle. Seton, *Old Family*, p. 268.

[20] Captain Sowle.

[21] This was the contemporary name for the Hawaiian Islands. Seton (and probably others) must have given the Portuguese captain letters to be mailed when he touched port. He was obviously not very confident that they would ever be received.

our colours. We certainly must have had a very rakish appearance bearing down before the wind [with] all sail set. Every now & then the ship yawed to & showed her broadside,[22] & the Portuguese I believe are generally more easily frig[htened] than any other nation.

This meeting [afforded] us some subject to talk of for three or four [hours] & we had just returned to our common occupation (sleeping) when [crossed out: the] another [cry of] Sail Ho, started us again. We . . . the deck on our lee[ward] . . . to speak an . . . point or two. She . . . & put . . . about. . . .

Saturday Morning Novr. 30th 1811. S Lat. 26° 54'. W Long 33° 8'. Our favorable winds which have conducted us so far rapidly & pleasantly, have at length deserted us & with them has likewise gone our fair weather. This day commences with a SSW wind, & boisterous rainy weather. So unpleasant, that we [crossed out: we] can not keep the Deck, but are all obliged to stay below in the Hot cabin. I do not believe there is any situation that [is] so trying [to] a mans temper, as to be on board ship. Here, then are six Young Men pretty nearly [the] same age, & all pretty violent in their tempers [con]fined together in a ship for six Months. [It] would be strange indeed if there was not [so]metimes some disputes, between one or the [ot]her, yet no open quarrel has broke out till [t]his day, w[hen Ha]lsey & Cox had a clinch in [t]he c[abin] . . . about their Hammocks. . . . immediately, Nicholl . . . this had fought . . . [wi]th no particular damage to either. There will be I expect [more] fighting before we reach Columbia River although except that affray all had been peace & quietness.

There has been a very heavy Sea going all night with a gale of Wind. We have been ploughing through it, under close reefed topsails & courses, as close to the wind as we could lie. This wind will no doubt change our weather a little. As yet we have suffered all the inconveniencies of a vertical sun, it has been so warm that it has melted the Pitch on our decks, but there is a sensible difference in the atmosp[here] this morning. It feels quite cold & raw & w[e] begin to think about our warm Jackets.

---

[22] The *Beaver* mounted twenty cannon. See the frontispiece.

Our friend[s] at Home have no doubt mounted theirs long ago, f[or] the first of Decr. generally brings along with i[t] cold weather at New Y[ork]. . . . Lat we must ex[pect] weather, & if we cold enough off . . . [wee]ks will convince us, whether it is so, or not. If it is, thanks to the kindness of my friends I am prepared to meet it.

Sunday Morng. December 1st 1811. S. Lat. 27° 35'.

This morning commences with pleasant weather although our Head wind continues yet & we do not advance very fast on our voyage, but we can not expect always to be fortunate. As yet thank God, we have been rapidly propelled on [ou]r destined voyage & we are at this time 45 [da]ys from N York considerably to the Southward of Rio Janeiro, [w]hich is without doubt a good run. One inconvenience attending this course [w]hich the Captn. very much dreads is the chance [of] our falling in with a British cruiser, of which [he] says there is a great probability; they will [n]o doubt give us considerable trouble & may perhaps detain u[s for] some time,[23] but for all this I s[hould] have no objection of meeting with . . . thing would be pleasing . . . [Lan]d Lobbers, beside this . . . [u]p three or four . . . is a great thing for me,[24] for there is great lack of material on board ship for filling up the Pages of one's [jour]nal as whoever will take the trouble to read this will easily discover; but a Journal must be kept, & something must be written, & whether it is Sense or nonsense is not of much consequence. It serves to kill an hour or two every day & it may be a Source of amusement at some future day.

All Sailors hail Saturday nights with joy. It is then that seated

---

[23] Seton is referring to the British practice of stopping neutral vessels, especially American, on the high seas, in search of British subjects to impress into the Royal Navy. Since Britain did not recognize United States' naturalization, and Royal Navy officers frequently, whether by mistake or on purpose, also took native-born American citizens as well as British subjects, the practice was quite objectionable to the United States. It was not satisfactorily resolved until the increasing strength of the United States in the nineteenth century and the changed conditions of service in the Royal Navy made it anachronistic.

[24] Apparently Seton would have seen an encounter with a British cruiser as an enjoyable break from the tedium of the voyage, provided he was not impressed.

round their can of Grog the[y] pledge their Sweethearts & wives.
Every thing is regular on board ship, & we (the clerks) on Saturday
nights drink to our Sweethearts & absent fri[ends] [crossed out:
in] a full bumper of Madeira, this is [the] pleasantest hour in the
week to us & it is celebra[ted] with sincere joy. The last night's did
not pass ov[er] as pleasantly as it usually do[es]. The air was co[ld]
& raw, & we were obliged to ta[ke] our [glass belo]w in the cabin.
This is the first [Satu]rda[y nigh]t too that we have not had a . . .
all turned in about. . . .

However, this finds . . . [in] good spirits, we look forward to
dinner time [with] no small degree of pleasure, for the Butcher has
this morning sacrificed a Pig, & a piece of Roast pig, is no contem-
tible dish either on shore or at sea.

Monday morng Decr. 2d 1811. South Lat. 27° 10'.[25]
   This day commences with calm & pleasant weather. The Captns.
dread of falling with a cruiser has not yet been realised, although
we were a little alarmed yesterday afternoon. After [di]nner I generally go to Mast Head for exercise. While on the main top gallant
Yard yesterday I spied a sail on our Lee bow & sung [out] as lustily
as [crossed out: only] any old Sailor, Sail Ho. [Where] away? said
the officer of the deck. Two points on the Lee bow.
   The Captn. came on deck [w]ith his glass & said she was an
English Brig [r]unnin[g] down before the wind & bound he supposed for some p[or]t in the Brazils. She passed us at the . . . three
miles to leeward. . . . it was more than . . . shall see a Man of
War, as we are near the S American shore & near their cruising
ground, which is from the River Plate[26] along the whole extent of
the shore.
   We fared sumptuously yesterday on our roast pig. There was but
one thing wanted to make it a most delicious dinner, viz currant
jelly. This luxury I supplied as long as my stores lasted, which was

---

[25] Seton must have erred in taking down this position, for the *Beaver* could
not have moved backward since the previous day; a south latitude of about
28°10'is more likely.
[26] The River Plate (Rio de la Plata) forms the great estuary between Uruguay
and Argentina where those two countries and the Atlantic Ocean meet.

for a considerable time. None of us have any left now except Mr.
Clark, & he it seems intends to keep it. After partaking with us of
our little, nick nacks, it is rather ungenerous in him to keep his up
now. From what I have seen of him, he has not proved to be the
Gentleman I expected to find him. A certain selfishness marks his
whole conduct, & one c[an] easily perceive that he has not been
much accus[to]med to company. He is likewise most astonishingly
fond of talking of himself & his exploits in the north, & there has
not been an a[ne]cdote told of an[y] great man, since we have
[been] on board ship, but he has matched . . . of his own. Nay, if
we were to . . . strength & courage of . . . the skill & prudence of
a Washington, of these qualities we have not any other vouchers
than his own word & one is apt to be a little suspicious when he
hears another continually bragging of his courage & prowess although this may be owing to Mr. C ignorance of the world, & it is
possible that he may possess the qualities he attributes to himself. I
only say, that when one hears so much, he is apt to suspect a Captain
Bobadil.[27] Time will determine what he is, & it is probable that
[crossed out: the] some of the succeeding pages of this Journal will
be filled up with the character he bears among his companions in
the North.[28]

Clapp is [s]inging out on deck for Seton to bring his [ri]fle as
there is a whale playing under our bows.

I have just been on deck with my rifle, but the whale had disappeared, he swam about the ship [on]ce or twice & then disappeared. He w[as a y]oung on[e] about 12 feet long & came within
7 or 8 [feet of the ve]ssel, it is a perfect plan & . . . not see him,
but the . . . his coming along side again.

Tuesday Morning, Decr. 3, 1811.

South Lat. 29° Long. about 39° / 47 days out. Our calm &
pleasant weather continues with us yet & we do not anticipate any

---

[27] Captain Bobadil is the shallow braggart in Ben Johnson's *Every Man in His
Humour* (1598).

[28] Seton may have influenced Irving's description of Clarke as "somewhat
given to pomp and circumstance . . . , a firm believer in the doctrine of intimi-
dation." Irving, *Astoria*, pp. 320–21.

change, yet a while, although it would be better if we could have a breeze, for a person does not seem at home at sea, without a wind.

It seems that Fortune is determined to make us amends for not seeing vessels when we first came out, for there is now scarcely a day passes over, but we are alarmed with the cry of Sail Ho. Yesterday morning before dinner a man on the Main Yard sung out that there was a sail on our Weather beam. When we could see her with our glasses from the deck, we perceived by [the] cut & whiteness of her canvass, that she was an American. It was nearly calm & we rounded too & hoisted our colours, hoping [tha]t whe[n] she saw them she would bear down . . . she was too far too win[dward] as . . . for us to overtake . . . with the intention . . . but when she came within about 3 miles, so that we could plainly perceive she was an American Schooner, she hauled her wind & stood away from us. We could not account for this in any other way, but that she was afraid of us & took us for a cruiser & as she was a flyer & had the weather guage she knew that it would give us considerable trouble to catch her. This was a great disappointment to us, as we were all employed in writing home by her, for by her course we judged she was from the River Plate bound to some American port. She showed her colours which were American [& p]assed away from us. We very much wished the [C]aptn. to fire a gun & bring her to, but he would [n]ot consent to it, & although he was anxious to speak her, yet he said her Captn. behaved perfect[ly r]ight.

No British frigate yet, but the wind . . . [u]s in towards the shore & w[e]. . . . their cruising ground . . . it from one of . . . would be a good joke indeed, if they were to detain us & send us into some of their ports, a thing not altogether improbable, for I am certain our case would be a new one to them & I do not know how they would like a parcel of Yankees going to make an establishment in their territories (I think they claim the NW coast of America) & the Captn. I suspect fears something of the same kind, or he would not be so fearfull of falling in with one & I understand from him that had any British cruisers been off our Hook when we left New York our Frigates would have attended us untill we were out of their reach—a day or two will determine either what their conduct will be to us, or it wi[ll] take us safe from them. The River le Plate is the most Southern Lat that they cruise in & two days of fair wind will [b]ear us to the Southward of that.

[I] saw [somet]hing more of our whale ye[sterday]. . . . this afternoon they were som[e] . . . about. Clapp got his Gun . . . but c[ou]ld not get a shot at the rascals. [crossed out: Clapp] We will now tho very soon have fine sport among the albatrosses, which are a large bird about ten feet from wing to wing & you meet with them [crossed out: with them] in great quantities in about 36° or 37° of South Lat. We are all prepared for them & will no doubt give a good account of them. We look forward to our falling in with them, [crossed out: with them] with a great deal of pleasure, for there is now really so little to employ or amuse us on board ship, that any occupation which will kill an hour or two is hailed with pleasure. We get tired with reading, tired of writing, of [e]ating, drinking, sleeping, thinking & in fact get [m]ost completely tired of [t]he society of each other. Yet a third of the voyage is scarcely completed, & how [t]he remainder of the time is to pass [only] God . . . knows, it is a trial of patience ind[eed.]

Wednesday Morning Decr. [4, 1811.] Lat 30° 33'; Long. 40°. 48 days out. [This day comm]ences with a fine six knot breeze & very pleasant weather, & we are advancing rapidly. Two weeks such wind as this will bring us to the Cape & three days will carry us out of the track of the cruisers. Yesterday passed away without seeing a sail, although we were in momentary expectation of falling in with one & there was a man on the Fore top Gallant Mast Head looking out the whole time. It is the opinion of every one on board that we will fall in with a cruiser this day. Whether we do, or not as I have said before it is immaterial to me, & for my single self I would have no objection to take a trip to Rio Janeiro where I suppose they would order us. It is ten o clock now & no sail has yet appeared & I very much doubt if we will see one to day or not.

There happened nothing [yester]day that will serve to fill a single [page in a] journal. There were no fish or . . . or [n]o sails in sight, & we sp[ent the time] reading and lounging about. . . . produce something worthy of insertion. It is so excessively hot, that it is almost impossible to stay below, so that I must go on deck & make a finish of my days work.

Thursday morning, Decr. 5th 1811. S Lat 32° 40' Long. 42°. Out 49 days from New York.

Yesterday passed away as the foregoing one did in spite of the Captns. prophecies that we would see a British Man of War, & this day commences with a stiff breeze from the Westward, which is fair for us. We were running off 9 1/2 knots this morning with top Gallant steering sails & royals out, when by a sudden flaw we carried away our weather main [to]p sail yard arm, so that we cannot take as [m]uch advantage of this breeze as we would if this accident had not happened, & what is more unlucky we have not a new Yard ready to go aloft but the [car]penter & all hands are now busily preparin[g] . . . in hopes that our Main topsail will . . . to morrow.

This is a rainy . . . [with] a heavy swell going. [It] makes one . . . [pl]easures of a home . . . once, but now a wanderer from Home & the joys that a House produces. I must be content to sacrifice these, & many other comforts; yet in my present uncomfortable situation, I have one consolation left, that the blessings & well wishes of my friends attend me wherever I go, & that they appreciate the motive that induced me to leave them. This consolation is no trivial one & has already eased me of many hours of sorrow. Sorrow in spite of all my philosophy, will sometimes exercise her dominion over me, when I think of the pleasures that might have been mine, and which now have entirely fled. But this is not a life of joy. The Cup of Some is fuller than that of others, & we have only to be content with the station in life where it has pleased Providence to place us.

[I] wish to God, I could act in this case as . . . but when I consider that thre[e] short months ago I was in the society of [all] that my Heart held dear, for I enjoyed t[he co]mp[a]ny of Sarah & of my Sis[ters]. . . . many months & years will roll . . . again so blessed, when I . . . [t]hings I am sorry to say, that my feelings get the better of my judgement, & I give way to unavailing Sorrow. Sometimes I think that if I had not been so hasty in this undertaking, I might have been blessed with S. at home. My God! Have I then been so foolish to sacrifice so much happiness? Have I stupidly thrown it away. No Sarah, for although I love you as sincerely as ever woman was loved, & the greatest happiness I can conceive, would be, to spend my life with thee, yet I had a greater duty to perform. I had a Father & Sisters, whose situation claimed some exertion from his Son. I have made the exertion and sacrificed my present happiness.

My prayers for [yo]u my beloved S. will never cease. I am convin[ced] the Almighty Father will not suffer so much [crossed out: so much] innocence & goodness to be thrown away upon o[ne] unworthy of them, & that he who . . . to obtain your affections, will know . . . them,[29] that he may. & that . . . [ha]ppy as your goodness deserves, . . . c[o]nstant prayer of. . . .

Friday morning, Decr. 6th, 1811. S. Lat 34° 5'.[30] Out 50 days from New York.

The unpleasant & disagreeable weather that commenced yesterday, cleared away towards noon & the after part of the day was very pleasant. Our long expected pleasure of shooting at the Albatrosses was enjoyed for the first time this day, & we shot at an average about eighty balls at them, but none of them struck the mark, except one shot made by the Captn., Nicholl, Clapp, Halsey, Ehninger, Mr. Clark & myself were alike unsuccessfull. These birds present a very fair mark. They fly within fifteen or twenty yar[ds] of the ship, but the rolling of the vessel make[s] it almost impossible, to one who is not accustomed to it, to strike them . . . ball. In two or three days more [they will,] from all accounts be more plenty [full & we all] agreed to reserve our powder till [then. In] fact, we have but five pounds [remaining] to shoot . . . which thanks to the kindness of my friend Edward I brought on board. I have this day divided it among us, & have kept for myself one cannister & a half.

We experience here as much variety of weather as one very well can. The wind seldom blows two hours from the same point of compass. This morning when I got up we were knocking it off 8 or 9 knots with steering sails out. Now we are braced up as sharp

---

[29] Seton's beloved, for whom he was feeling such self-pitying pangs, was a second cousin, Sarah Hoffman. However much he may have missed her at that time, he married Frances Barnewall in 1819; Sarah never married. Hoffman, *Hoffman Genealogy*, pp. 24, 234.

[30] The *Beaver* was now about 300 miles east of the Rio de la Plata.

as we can be & not going within two or three points of our course. An hour ago there was not a cloud to be seen, & now [i]t is quite thick & foggy with a cold & damp air. From what I at present see & feel, I am sensible that our passage round Cape Horn will be extrem[ely] uncomfortable, & somewhat danger[ous. We will] be uncomfortable, inasmuch as it is mo [st miserab]ly cold & we have no fire in our . . . [to] retreat to. There will be a very high [sea] going & if we stay in the cabin, its almost certain that we will be sick. Here is our choice between freezing & sickness and whichever it may be, I am certain that we will be most uncomfortable.

It will be somewhat dangerous because you experience there the most boisterous weather in the world, & let your ship & crew be ever so good, you will sometimes meet with too hard weather for her. This is not exactly the case with us. Our Ship is as good a one as ever crossed the Ocean, but our officers complain most bitterly of the crew. There are in fact, but five Sailors on board, the rest are boys & green hands, & the safety of yr. ship depends very much on the activity & skill of her crew.

I do not make these reflections because I an[ticipa]te any accident but only as a memento of . . . [the] situation. I cherish the [hope that] I may read these pages in my native [land] . . . [if t]his should not be allowed [to] me . . . will see what my feelings & thoughts were, for I have freely wrote down & will continue to do so, these thoughts, that are [crossed out: most] uppermost in my mind, & as this is intended for no other eye than my own, (except in case of accident to me) there can no bad consequences result from it.

I am convinced though that indulging too much in thoughts of the happiness that once was yours, & which has now fled, will not only make one extremely unhappy, but will injure his health materially. It is for this reason, that I check myself, when I find my thoughts straying to the many hours that [I] spent, Sarah, in your company at M—hours that will never, never return. Fate has inhumanly [par]ted me from the only Girl I ever love[d] . . . [&] perhaps I might have been equally belov[ed]. . . . thoughts will carry me too far, . . . the comforts of Life to my . . . S.

Saturday morning Decr. 7th, 1811. S Lat. about 36°—out 51 days.
Here commences another dismal day, it is thundering & raining

& we have the prospect of being confined in the cabin all day. I never had an idea that the weather had so great an effect upon ones spirits. On such a day as this is, my thoughts wander to my Home, & to my friends there. What Edward now occupies you, tis ten oclock here, & half after eight at NY. You & Sam have just come [crossed out: got to] down in the Parlour & there you find old Matthew has made you a good fire. Your Pancakes I suppose will soon be done, & perhaps Murray or Bill Farquhar has come [to] breakfast with you.[31] I hope you will [find it good] & that you may think of your absent friend.

You my beloved Sisters[32] . . . are seated around the breakfast table . . . [with] Father enjoying the happiness of a. . . . It is a situation where I wish I could join you, but Fate has determined it otherwise. By her decrees we are sepperated, but I hope it will be for the best, & although I feel now the most poignant sorrow at the seperation, yet Hope whispers that we shall meet again in happiness. It is now after being accustomed to your Society for such a length of time, that this absence bears the heaviest on me. I am sensible that Time has power to cure the most severe wounds of the Heart, of this we have had experience. We lost our Mother, my Dear Sisters at an age when [you] most wanted her maternal instruction.[33] Time has in a great measure healed this most severe wound. We can talk of her without fe[eling that] excess of sorrow that once actuated us; . . . Mother can never be forgot. She . . . the fruits of her labour on Earth, & . . . resigned in being certain that she . . . ; [if time] had power to heal this wound, the most heart breaking we ever experienced, the pangs of seperation must

[31] Seton's "friends" were all relatives. Edward (see p. 33) and Sam were uncles, the latter being Samuel W. Seton (1789–1869), his father's half-brothers and his near contemporaries in age. Murray was a first cousin, David Murray Hoffman (1791–1878), the son of his mother's brother. Bill Farquhar was the son of his father's aunt. Matthew was probably a servant. Seton, *Old Family*, pp. 267–68; Hoffman, *Hoffman Genealogy*, p. 25; J. Hall Pleasants, *The Curzon Family of New York and Baltimore* (Baltimore: Privately printed, 1919), pp. 46–47; hereafter, Pleasants, *Curzon Family*.

[32] Alfred had four younger sisters. Hoffman, *Hoffman Genealogy*, p. 234.

[33] Mary Hoffman Seton had died in 1807, at thirty-four years of age. Melville, *Seton*, p. 123.

[crossed out: in time] be less than what they are now. I console myself with the idea that you are happy, & I have no doubt I shall be so in time.

Sunday Morning Decr. 8th 1811. S Lat. 37° 9'. W Long. 47° 32'. Out 52 days.

Yesterday did not pass away so gloomy & heavy as I expected in the morning it would. It rained very hard untill 12 oclock when the wind got round to the S.W. & soon dispersed the clouds. This wind answers to our N.W. & is similar in its effects. The wind from the S. makes it extremely cold, while that fr[om] the N. has a contrary effect. This I suppose may be accounted for, that [in the] S. Latitudes the wind passes over great [masses] of Ice, [crossed out: & of course] near the Poles & [the closer we] get to the S the more of course we feel its effects.

Last night we felt [crossed out: them] its [effects] . . . & went to get our Pea Jackets on. According to its custom it did not last long, for this morning it blows a gentle breeze from its opposite point the N.E. & we feel the cheerfull effects of a warm Sun. We have not advanced as rapidly as we expected for the last ten or twelve days. We have had calms or gales of wind alternately the whole time. We now have taken a breeze though which the Captn. thinks will hold on.

I feel so stupid this morning that I cannot arrange a sentence grammatically, & have got a Headache hanging about me.[34]

Wednesday Morning Decr. 11th 1811. South Lat 39° 10'. Long about 51° 20'. 55 days out.

Monda[y] [was a ra]w & disagreeable day & so dark & [dismal it wa]s impossible to write in the cabin. [Passed] [of]f though tolerable well, notwit[hstandi]ng Nicoll's prophecy, that [t]hat there would [be a] quarr[el.] The Lat. on that day was, 38° 48'. S.

Tuesday morning commenced with calm & pleasant weather. This day we got our new main top Sail Yard up, & had our sail

---

[34] Seton may have been suffering a hangover from the regular shipboard Saturday-night drinks ("a full bumper of Madeira") he described on December 1st.

bent, & all hands busily preparing the ship for hard weather. We expect it now soon, as we are in the vicinity of the Cape. The Captn. requested we would all lend our assistance as he did not know when we would have another calm day, & we all turned to accordingly. Got our Guns stowed away in the Hold, & the carriages lashed on deck. The Sailors sent down our royal masts & yards & got all our heavy spars from off the gallows lashed on deck. We have now a very snug ship & in the Captns. opinion fit to weather <u>any</u> storm. [There is no dou]bt about our ship, but [I do not] believe that there ever was a vessel . . . so long a voyage so poorly manned.

We were well recompensed for our trouble by a good dinner of <u>Sea pye</u>; as we do not have this treat often, we think much more of it, & in fact I do not believe any <u>alderman</u> ever relished his Turtle Soup & venison better than we do our <u>Humble</u> pot pye. I really wish some of our delicate young men had to live on board ship for about three months. I am sure it would do them good, it would make them relish much more the good things of this life at home. I have many a time complained of my dinner at Home when there were articles that now I would esteem the [gr]eatest luxurys. I am certain of one thing whether I succeed in my pursuit of wealth or not, th[at is] I shall be a gainer by this voy[age. It w]ill show me something of the worl[d and the ne]cessity there is of [crossed out: not] giving up one . . . & putting yourself to some inconveniences for [the] benefit of others. I do not believe this lesson is any where so well inculcated as on board ship. Here one very soon perceives the necessity of it, & if he has common sense, he will give in to it.

We are now out of the track off all cruisers, & indeed our oracle (the Captn.) did not expect to fall in with any vessel untill we reached the Sandwich Isles, but in this, as many other things, he was mistaken, for yesterday afternoon about 1/2 past 6 there was a cry of <u>Sail Ho</u> from the man at the Helm. Mr. C,[35], Nicoll, Clapp, & myself were playing a hand at whist, but this unexpected cry soon made a finish of our game & I was on de[ck] in an instant. I saw a large ship on our weather bow, seemingly stand[ing on the] same course we were. In a few minutes . . . [we] found out that she was standing . . . & our Captn. said she was a whaler [vessel]

---

[35] John Clarke.

probab[ly] bound Home & . . . he would la[y] an hour or two, till we could write. We hauled up our courses & hoisted our colours & she showed hers which were Yankee & bore down to us. She soon came within hail under our stern & sung out in the usual way—Whū ū ū. Whōō ōō ōō said our Captn. Where are you from, said the Stranger. From New York. Where are you from. Nantucket. How long have you been out? Five months & a half after oil & we are full now & bound Home. What ship is it? The Manilla. What ship is yours. The Beaver of NY. [Can] you give us a few Potatoes, asked the stranger—Aye, Aye. Send your boat on [board.] Hearing this, we went below to let our [families] know where we were & how we. . . . [I wrote] to my Father & I have no [doubt] but he will receive it. . . . The [captain of] the Stranger boarded us in his whale boat & he was welcomed on board the Beaver by our Captn. with no small degree of ceremony. He said they had been after Sea Elephants oil[36] & had been remarkably successfull. They had been in a Bay on the coast & were five days out. He agreed pretty well with our Captn. as to the Lat. & Long. & told us that on the Brazil Banks he had caught plenty of fine Codfish. This was an agreeable piece of news for us, & we anticipate a dinner of fresh fish with much pleasure.

We made one Packet of all our letters & directed them to Mr. J. J. Astor. We then drank to his pleasant passage & after supp[lying] him with a barrel of potatoes bade him [farewell.]

The Manilla is a small [ship of] 250 tons & rigged very snug having no . . . [miz]zen top Guns & Masts, & her main . . . She looked very small along side the Beaver, & it was a fortunate thing for us that we got our royal masts down & our Guns below, for if they had seen any thing suspicious, they would not have come down, & we would have lost this excellent opportunity of writing home. As yet we have not reaped any advantage from looking so extremely warlike. It makes almost every vessel avoid us, & we would have had an opportunity of writing to our friends before this, had it not been for our appearance. Bye & Bye though, when we [ge]t among

---

[36] The so-called elephant seal was found in the Pacific coastal waters of both North and South America.

the Islands, where a warlike appearance is necessary we will find great advanta[ges in] our guns & men.

It is near 12 o c[lock & the s]tewart wants the table for dinner, & as [I have wr]itten a tolerable days work. I will [only] add that this morning was as pleasant [a day] a[s e]ver was, with a fine four knot breeze.

Thursday Morning Decr. 12th 1811. South Lat 39° 46'. This morning commences pleasant but with a head wind & we are making but slow progress. I have now to relate an unpleasant circumstance that happened last night. Mr. Nicoll & Cox were playing whist against Clapp & myself. In the play something happened that occasioned some words between Nicoll & myself, in which I believe I was rather too hasty. Mr. N. struck me, which I returned, but finding him too powerfull for me, I told him so & said that other means must be resorted to. He agreed to it; I applied to Mr. Clapp in the bus[iness to] be my friend.[37] He applied to Ni[coll this] morning who told him that [he wanted] to see me. I went forward on th[e] . . . where N soon came, there He [told] me [he was] sorry that he proceeded so far, & that it was the impulse of the moment that made him give me the blow. I told him that situated as I was on board ship, I was compelled to sacrifice my feelings, & admit the apology, but that had it happened on shore, I would have gone to extremities. He repeated what he had said & that he appreciated the motive, that induced me to accept it.

Here in this depositary of my thoughts I say, that had it not been for Mr. Clapp, the life of Nicoll or myself [w]ould have been the sacrifice for a petty disagreement at cards, for it was my firm intention to [pre]ss the thing & not admit of any apology, . . . I asked Clapp last night to ask N[icoll immediate]ly if he would meet me. This . . . [Clapp re]fused to do, & said he would have [nothing] to [do] in the affair untill this morning, when we would both be cool. Even now after the affair is finished I must confess I feel myself injured & I do sincerely say that had it been possible to bring the affair to an immediate conclusion, I would not on any terms whatever have accepted an apology. I was struck in the pres-

---

[37] That is, to act as his second and deliver a formal challenge to a duel.

ence of the whole Cabin a vile blow. My face burns while I record
it. They though know my willingness to resent it & the situation I
am placed in, which is, that there is no probability of our being on
shore for at least three months, & my absence from all my friends.
These motives though I say again would not have induced me to
admit of his apology had not I felt convinced that [I was] too hasty
in the beginning of the [quarrel]. Clapps prudence has saved the
. . . of us.

Friday Morning Decr. 13th 1811. S Lat 41° 8'. 57 days from New
York.

This morning begins with a gale of wind from the westward
which is nearly ahead & a very heavy sea. All Hands are now taking
the second reef in the Topsails & preparing the ship for a more
severe blow. As the Captn. says, it will blow much harder before it
lessens. It is a fine clear day though & the wind feels something
like our cold NW's at Home. Mr. C.[38] & all the clerks are wrapt
up in their pea jackets on deck, reading, while I came below to
enjoy the [a]dvantage of a little silence to enable me to note down
our present situation, & the little circumstances that happened since
yesterday morning.

N.[39] & myself have not any more conversa[tion about] our dispute. He appears to me to [be sorry f]or what he done & as I
accepted [his apology] I will endeavor to forget the. . . . [Ye]t, I
feel myself injured, and even now when all the effects of passion
must be removed, my Heart burns when I think I have been struck
with impunity. It must be forgot.

The wind continues as variable as ever no two Hours does it blow
from the same point, and when we get a fair wind & just have our
Steering sail booms rigged out, it is certain then to come about. It
has served us so five or six times, and the Captn. declares that let
the wind blow ever so fair, He will not have a boom rigged out
again. This I suppose is only vexation, in fact I have no doubt his
rage at the booms will disappear at the first fair wind. We have not
progressed for the last two weeks as rapidly as was exp[ec]ted, for

---

[38] John Clarke.
[39] Charles A. Nicoll.

at that time we expected [to be o]ff of Cape Horn by this [crossed out: time]. . . . Now [though the] probability of eating our Christmas di[nner] . . . side of the Cape, I . . . say . . . Yet from what I can understand from the Captn., our dinner on that day will not differ from what it does on common days and that we will not observe that almost universal Holy day. My friends at Home though will observe it, & I am certain that amidst their general rejoicing some of them will think of the absent Alfred with sentiments of affection.

The sea is getting so extremely Heavy that it almost rolls the very table from under me & the inkstand has been over once or twice. They have all left the Deck too, & there is a confused noise of dice, music, & talking; I must make a finish for this day.

Fr[iday] Morning January 3, 1812. South [Lat 5]7° 10′ W Long. 68° 5′. Diego R[amirez on the r]ight[40]—calm & pleasant wea[ther. It] is nearly a month now since I have touched my journal. During that time, many circumstances have occurred [crossed out: have occurred], both pleasant and unpleasant.[41]

We progressed very slowly during the week of my last date with variable winds, & a very heavy sea. Tuesday Decr., 17th 1811 we carried away our fore topsail in a gale of wind & the ship laboured excessively in a very heavy sea. This Gale continued until Friday De[c.] 20th when it gradually subsided. Our ship behaved as well as could be expected, & we think that she could weathe[r] more than a common gale of [wi]nd. The Officers call this a t[aste] of Cape Horn but I hope we [may] . . . many more such tas[tes. Friday] Evening ended tolerable pleasant. . . . Weather much more after having storms so long. Saturday morning[42] about 3 oclock the officer of the Deck awoke the Captn. & said there was land on our weather Bow. The Captn. went on deck & true enough the land was seen plainly. This was very unexpected as we did not calculate

---

[40] An island group at the extreme southern tip of South America, sixty miles off Tierra del Fuego.

[41] Seton occasionally lapsed into the form of a daily log, suggesting that he kept running notes which he later wrote into his journal.

[42] December 21, 1811.

to fall in with the land for a day or two, but land there was in sight, & the only difficulty was to ascertain, what land it was; as it was evident there was a strong current setting either to the Eastward or Westward—to the Westw[a]rd was favorable for us, & therefore we conclud[e]d that a current had set us in under [the co]ast of Patagonia—& we were all . . . looking out for the Horsem[en of the H]ills whom Carteret & Byron mention in their voyages but not a sign of an Inhabitant could we see.⁴³ At 12 oclock this was cleared up for we got an observation of the Sun, which had been obscured for three or four days before, & the Coast of Patagonia turned out to be the Faulkland Islands.⁴⁴ This was a disappointment to all of us, to be three or four hundred miles to the Eastward of where we expected we were & when westerly winds prevail 7/8ths of the year was a serious calamity.

The weather though was very pleasant, & we enjoyed some gratification at seeing land after the prospect of sky & water [for s]uch a length of time. The land . . . rugged & barren & the only inh[abitants it] possesses are Seals & Birds. [We could wi]th our [gla]sses discern great numbers of them running & flying about the rocks, and if it had been calm so that we could have gone on shore, we would no doubt have had fine sport among them. We shot though from the ship fifteen or twenty shags,⁴⁵ a bird that greatly resembles some of our species of Wild Duck & which the Captn. says are equally good for eating. It was no satisfaction to kill them, for we were going 8 or 9 knots through the water, & to heave too with a fair wind to get a bird, could not be thought of, so we resolv[ed] to keep our powder & shot untill we coul[d] . . . something for it. We were in sight [of the] Islands all Sunday.⁴⁶ With light . . . [w]inds, the shags came off to us in great numbers, &

---

⁴³ Philip Carteret (d. 1796) and John Byron (1723–1786) were Royal Navy officers who circumnavigated the globe, Byron in 1764–1766 and Carteret in 1766–1767. Byron was shipwrecked off the Chilean coast in 1741 and published an account of his experiences in 1768, experiences which his poet grandson, Lord Byron, used when he was writing "Don Juan." *Dictionary of National Biography*, III, 613–14, 1125.

⁴⁴ The Falklands lie some 300 miles east of the Strait of Magellan.

⁴⁵ Another name for the cormorant.

⁴⁶ December 22, 1811.

Mr. Clarke & one or two of the clerks shot some of them. Sunday Evening we cleared the Islands with a fine breeze at N. & then we did not much regret our Sail round them, for if the wind held on at N. the next day we would fall in with Staten Land.[47] These were our calculations then, but how vain, & uncertain are all Mortal prophecies. Monday[48] Morning it blew very fresh from the same quarter, but as it was favorable for us, we carried to it, & were running under whole topsails & courses, mizen, & fortopmast staysail, jib & spanker. At 12 oclock though it began to blow so hard that we were compelled [to furl] our topsails. All hands but . . . [at] the Helm were aloft on . . . th[en] the flying jib which had been handed the night before broke loosse. Whether it was through the carelessness of the man who handed it last or whether the gaskets broke loose, I cannot say, but the Men being all aloft & the officer of the Deck seeing it flapping about took the wheel himself & sent the two men who were there to furl it, poor fellows! Little did they think they were going to certain death; it was very cold & had been hailing all the morning, & they had their pea jackets & heavy boots on. The men on the foretopsail yard sung out to them that the Gib Boom bent very much th[ey ans]wered that there was no danger. [They had] scarcely spoken th[e w]ords [when the jib b]oom went with a tremendous crack & precipitated them headlong in the foaming deep. The Ship was thrown in the wind as soon as possible & a hen coop put over board, that they might keep themselves above water untill we could round too, but Fate had destined them to a watery grave, for all our exertions (& every exertion in our power was used) were in vain. They were so heavily clothed that they sunk in fifteen minutes after they were in the water. Thus were two Young Men in all the pride of strength, called in the presence of their God without a moments warning, with all their sins unrepented of.

O Merciful God, force on my mind the les[son this] melancholy accident inculca[tes] . . . vanity of Human life, . . . [the] necessity of more strictly keeping thy word & commandments, so that when my race of existence is run, I may be better prepared to appear in

---

[47] The easternmost island off Tierra del Fuego.

[48] December 23, 1811.

thy divine presence, & O merciful Father, hear the prayer of a Sinner for the Souls of those two unfortunate men.

The names of these poor fellows were Peter Valliant & George Washington. Peter was a french Boy whose Father was Captn. of a Frigate in the French service under the unfortunate Louis 16th. His Sisters & himself got away from France about three years ago. They support themselves by keeping a school in New York, & this unfortunate circumstance [will no d]oubt be a heavy blow for them, . . . which were found in the che[st] . . . be very fond of him, & look upon him as the last hope of their once very respectable family. The day that they receive the tidings of his Fate will be a melancholy one indeed. Their dearest Hopes will be blasted & they will rue the day, Poor Peter ever entered on board the Beaver.

George Washington the other sufferer was a native of one of the Society Isles, in the Pacific Ocean whom Captn. Sowle brought away from there Seven Years ago, & who had been with him in the capacity of a Servant since.[49] Captn. S. during the time he has been with him has found him uniformly honest, good natured, kind & obliging & during the time he was on board ship he had supported that character well. He poor Fellow was consoling himself with the idea of once [more beho]lding his family & friends after . . . absence, but his hopes were suddenly . . . this presence of an Almighty God, there to answer for his few very few sins.

The Ship lay too four hours in hopes that they might have reached the Hencoop but they must have drownded in ten or fifteen minutes after they were in the water.

Tuesday morning Decr. 24th 1811. Begins with a very heavy gale of wind from the SW. & a tremendous sea. We carried a close reefed Main topsail, foresail & fore topmast Stay Sail to it, but toward night it blew so excessive heavy that we split our fore top mast Stay sail & had to unbend it. We [lost] this day by the Heavy Seas all our Head railings, & our quarter[bo]ards. The fig[urehea]d though yet stands firm, & we . . . it with us.

Christmas [day dawned] . . . gloomy indeed, strong gales of wind, a heavy sea, & [weather] extremely cold. We were all con-

---

[49] The Society Isles are now known as French Polynesia; in the southwest Pacific, due west of Australia. Tahiti is the largest island in the group.

fined the whole day to the Cabin & it was about as uncomfortable a day as ever I spent. Yet I hope that you my Dear Friends at Home, passed as merry Christmas, as I have been accustomed to witness.

Thursday morg.[50] the gale abated a little & we could carry our close reefed topsails. Our Lat by an obsn. of the Sun this day was 54° 55′ South. We had not seen him for three or four days.

Friday Morg. pleasant weather & a fine wind & we could once more show [our]selves upon deck; it will be a happy day for all Hands when we get [clear] of this stormy Cape. I had heard a . . . of it & it really equals m[y] . . . the hight of the Pale on . . . on deck, & witnessed [crossed out: such] a scene that before I had no idea of; I have read many descriptions of a gale of wind at sea, but no words can express the awful sublimity of the scene. I will not attempt it, but will only say, that it appears most wonderful to me, how such materials as a ship can withstand the shocks of a heavy sea.

Through the Mercy of God though we have weathered the Storm, & I have no doubt that the same Divine Hand, who protected us in this storm, will also guard [us] in a much m[ore] severe one.

Saturday 28th[51] commences moderate b[reeze] and fine [wea]ther, the heavy sea continues. . . . [To]day the Captns. Clerk George Eh[ninger sold] at auction[52] the . . . of . . . for about three times their value.

We have been a week now from Faulklands Islands & have not seen Staten land, which we expected to fall in with the day after we left the Islands. [crossed out: they] It can not be far off, for there is a quantity of <u>Kelp</u> floating about the ship, which proves our vicinity to some land. On Sunday morning[53] at 8 we discovered the land on our lee beam & soon found out it was the long expected Staten Land. At 9 we saw Terra Del Fuego. We stood in towards it untill 12 when the squalls of Hail & snow obliged [u]s to stand

---

[50] December 26, 1811.

[51] December 28, 1811.

[52] It was probably the possessions of Vaillant and Washington that were auctioned.

[53] December 29, 1811.

off. We were detained in [s]ight of this bleak coast for two days. On Janry. 1st 1812 we had a fair win[d that] carried us in sight of the . . . Cape Horn & we were . . . with the prospect of being round this Cape in 48 Hours, but a few moments put to flight these prospects, for the wind suddenly veered to its old quarter the SW. & we obliged to alter our course.

It is now Twenty five days since that time,[54] during which we have experienced as much diversity of weather as was possible. We were becalmed off Cape Horn three days when a breeze of wind took us in sight of Diego Ramirez off which we were likewise becalmed for two days. While Here we observed a great many Penguins and Albatrosses abo[ut] the Ship & for the curiosity of the circumstance [crossed out: of] we lowered away a . . . [j]olly boat & Halsey & Ehninger [and I] . . . guns went after them. We shot one albatross & two penguins & after rowing about for an hour & an half between the Atlantic & Pacific Oceans, we returned on board. The circumstance of being in a small boat in pursuit of pleasure, in one of the most stormy places in the world, was certainly curious & having it in your power to say that you were in a small boat in this place, amply repaid for all the danger you incurred.

The Situation of the Island of Diego Ramires is differently laid down by two Navigators of acknowledged abilities, Cook who traversed this O[ce]an in 1783 & Collnett in 95.[55] We as[cer]tained that Collnett was correct.

The [wind] favoured us here for a day or two, & the[n blew] from its old quarter. . . about until Jany 10th when we found . . . of the Sun & Moon to be 77° 45'[56] & our Lat. 59° 58' & as the wind was favorable for our bearing away, we tacked Ship to N. & West & expected in a day or two to get out of this boisterous Lat & in idea had already got clear of the Gales of Wind & of Cape Horn.

---

[54] Seton apparently wrote this entry on Tuesday, January 28, 1812.

[55] James Cook passed Cape Horn in 1769 and 1774. *Dictionary of National Biography*, IV, 991–95. James Colnett explored the region during a voyage aboard *Rattler* in 1793; he found the island to be entirely barren, except for seals and birds described as "white crows." James Colnett, *A Voyage to the South Atlantic* . . . (London: The Author, 1798), pp. 17–18.

[56] That is, longitude.

But our expectations have been disappointed, for since bearing away, we have experienced three tremendous gales. One indeed was much more severe than any on board ever met with, & if it had not been of as short duration as it was, it is the opinion of the Officers, that we could not have weather[e]d it. It commenced Sunday Morning Jany. [19]th about 9 oclock & continued with unabating . . . until 1 oclock the next morning, [when] it moderated. We carried a[way] . . . [fo]re sail while laying too under it. . . . & mizen staysails. The Foretopmast Staysail followed the Foresail in a few minutes after, & the only sail we could show for the remainder of the gale was the mizen Staysail. This fortunately was a new sail & the Ship lay too tolerable well under it.

We continued with variable winds & unpleasant weather untill Jany. 26 when Henry Willetts, one of our men, who had been complaining for a month or six weeks, died. He was a young man about nineteen years of age, from New York & engaged in the service of t[he] Company for five years. We com[mit]ted his body to the deep on Monday [Jany.] 27th.

The Captn, Mr. Clark & every [b]ody on board paid him as much attention . . . [in] their power & he would no [doubt have rec]overed, if he had not impr[udently eaten a] quanity of the paste of a sea pye, which lay so heavy on his stomach, that he had not strength enough to digest it.[57]

Thursday Morng. 30th[58] commences with a fine fair breese & we are rapidly approaching Massafuero.[59] This day we were all employed preparing our Fishing lines, & guns for going on shore, running bulletts &c. &c.

We were all disturbed though with the unusual cry of Sail Ho from the man at the H[elm] & a large ship on our weather bow was pla[in]ly to be seen. She was running down before [the w]ind, & we bore away to speak her, but [whe]n we came within about

---

[57] Cox diagnosed Willetts' fatal illness as the "black scurvy," and suggested that he probably brought it aboard with him, as no one else on board the *Beaver* suffered from it. Cox, *Columbia*, p. 19.

[58] January 30, 1812.

[59] Mas Afuera, in the Juan Fernandez Islands, about 400 miles west of Santiago, Chile.

three miles, the Cap[tn. said] she was a Spaniard & as no info[rmation could] be procured from her we . . . on our course & passed her about three or four miles to windward.

During the whole of Friday our favourable wind drove us on rapidly toward our Island & this day at 12 oclock Saturday Feby. 1st we find ourselves in S Lat. 36° 32′ & W Long. 82° 5′ dist. from Massafuero, 160 miles. We have a favourable five knot breese & expect to enjoy our legs once more to morrow or next day.

Sunday afternoon, 2d 1812.[60] Our fair wind has stuck to us yet, & [crossed out: yet] no land in sight by our obsn. at 12 oclock. We find ourselves in [S Lat] 34° 43′ & dist. from Massafuero 58 mi[les.] The Crew are all busy bending a cab[le an]chor & mounting the guns & the ship is a g[ene]ral scene of confusion. [It] is pleasing though, . . . it looks like preparations for going on . . . thing conducive to that . . . to persons who have been confined better than three months & an half to ship board. The Land on which we anticipate so much pleasure is a barren, uninhabited, Island with a few wild goats on & its shores abounding with fish, but if it was a mere rock, the idea of being on shore would be pleasing—Land Ho is the cry.

Monday afternoon 3d.[61] I was interrupted yesterday with the joyful cry Land & could just distinguish it from Mast Head, rig[ht] ahead. We were going five knot & expected to be up with it before night & this morning [to] go on shore, but this is one of the [nume]rous disappointments we have met with this [voy]age, for by 5 oclock instead of [the expec]ted Island of Massafuero, it [proved to be the] Isle of Juan. . . . the Spaniards who, our Oracle[62] says are so inhospitable that they will not permit weary & almost worn out wanderers to touch at their shores. The Distance of this Isle from Massafuero is only ninety miles, but it is dead to leeward of it & from the winds which generally prevail here this season, if you fall to leeward, it will take you considerable time to

---

[60] February 2, 1812.
[61] February 3, 1812.
[62] Captain Sowle.

beat up. This is exactly our case now, & we have been all persuading our Captn. to try Juan Fernandes, & four of us have offered to row the Boat on shore, while the ship lay off. . . . He has not as yet determined what he [will] do, but says to morrow if the wind still [holds] us off, that perhaps he will make a[n] ex[per]iment with the Spaniards.[63] I hope he . . . f[rom] an acct. of the place from . . . board (wh[ich] has been on the . . . it is an excellent spot to touch at for refreshmts. Fresh Beef, Hogs, Potatoes, Yams, Oranges, Limes &c, are to be procured here in great abundance. Although we have been weaned for a considerable time of these good things, yet they would not come unacceptable. To morrow or next day will determine whether it is intended for us to enjoy these Luxuries. 'Till then we must rest contented.

This has been a thick cloudy calm day & we have not seen the Island. It [is c]learing away a little now & no doubt before [the] "Sable Curtain is drawn," we will once more [behold] it.

Tuesday afternoon.[64] This morning at 6 o clock the import[ant] island of Masafuero was seen . . . [at a] distance about 24 miles. The wind . . . night and we suppose . . . us on a little. We have all been asking our Captn. to lend us the jolly boat so that we might reach shore to night, but all our intreaties have been in vain, for he will not permit the Boat to be absent from the Ship a night, & I do not know but what he is correct. We are going now about 2 Knots p Hour, & the land I suppose is nearly 15 miles from us, so that, we enjoy a good prospect of being on Shore to morrow. What our occupations will be there will be the subject of another days [entry].

The day is very warm & pleasant [with] a light breeze from the S. our Lat . . . was S. 33° 52′ & Long. p Lunar 80° 44′.

It is now determined [we will] not enjoy the Luxuries of J[uan Fernandez] but I willingly resign them. . . . on shore, which we

---

[63] Cox presented the more reasonable view that Sowle's reluctance to land at Juan Fernandez was to avoid "the inquisitive and jealous eye of the Spanish authorities," that every vessel touching there "was subjected to a rigorous search; and from the number of our guns, joined to great quantities of warlike stores on board, the captain did not deem it prudent to run the risk of an inquisitorial inspection." Cox, *Columbia*, p. 22.

[64] February 4, 1812.

will enjoy on Masafuero & which from all accts. the Spaniards
would not allow at their Island. Masafuero, though is not without
its good things, for its shores abound with excellent fish, & Lob-
sters, & its Hills with Wild goats, for both of these we are prepared, & I have no doubt to morrow we will be able to give a good
acct. of both.

Thursday afternoon 6th.[65] Yesterday we enjoyed the [long] anticipated pleasure of being on shore. Owing [to] the lightness of the
wind on Tuesday night, [the] Ship was not as near shore as could
be wished, but as the day was pleasant . . . [we were] called at 4
oclock to lower [the pinnace and the] Jolly boat & to get. . . . We
started 8 men in the Jolly Boat ahead towing the Pinnace which had
14 men in & had 22 empty water casks fast to it. I was one of the
8 in the jolly boat. The Land we supposed to be distant about 6
miles & after three hours very fatiguing rowing we reached the
shore. There our boat was sent along the beach to look out a proper
place for landing. We found one about the middle of the island, &
close to a fine stream of water. Although the surf ran much less here
than on any other part [of the] Shore, yet we had to go in the
[water] about the depth of a mans ar[m.] As we landed we discovered a [crossed out: fine] large [he]rd of goats near two hundred
yards from [us.] [C]lark & Myself approached with our [guns,
but they] no sooner saw us, than . . . they disappeared though in a
few minutes among the crags & rocks of this dreary isle. Mr. C.
& myself followed up a gulch between two immense mountains
whose [crossed out: whose] craggy tops, overhanging, seemed to
threaten the Traveller below with instant destruction. We came at
lenght to a water fall of 20 or 30 feet & endeavoured to ascend its
perpendicular sides, but in this we could not succeed, & there was
but one way left of reaching the top of th[e] mountain, which was
by drawing yourself [up by] the trees. This was extremely dangerous for if [one] of the trees had given away, a person would [prob-
ably] have broken his neck, but dangerous [as it was], we attempted it & as Mr. C. was more [accustomed to] such travelling
than I . . . [considera]ble distance. I was loaded likewise heavy,

---

[65] February 6, 1812.

with my rifle, Pistols, powder & balls & after reaching half way up the mountain, I found myself so excessively fatigued, that I was obliged to lay down. I fired my gun first as a signal to Mr. C. & as he did not answer it, I thought he had penetrated higher up than I was. I rested in this spot about half an hour, & then thought of returning, & after an hour & an half most laborious & dangerous work, I was overjoyed to find myself again at the water fall. From this place to the beach, it was comparitively level, & three quarters of an hour brought me [there. I] found Mr. C. & all hands dining on some . . . fish [crossed out: they] Ehninger & Mr. Dean had ca[ught] & joined them with a great deal of pleasure.

I learned from Mr. [C.] that he did not go [as high as] I thought he had been, that . . . almost as soon as he lost . . . as he [did] not perceive me, he concluded that I had already gone down, & that he had been there about an hour & an half. After finishing our Dinners, Clapp & Mr. C. agreed to proceed along the right hand shore down to the extreme point & see all that was to be seen. Nicoll, Cox, & Halsey were to go on the opposite side exploring, & I who had seen enough of the Island agreed to join the fishing party. It was [crossed out: about] about half past two, when we commenced our respective employments. In the boat the grapling was cast about 40 yards [from t]he shore in about three fathom water, where we [co]uld see numbers of very fine fish swimming a[bout.] We enjoyed most excellent sport here, untill [near] 5 oclock when we perceived two of the [Travellers] returned, and as the Boat was hailed [(I was in the jolly] boat,) leaving George E & D[66] in [the pinnace,] I skulled her to the shore. There I found Mr. C & Clapp returned. They had been very lucky, having fallen in with a large [crossed out: flock] herd of goats, out which they had the good fortune to kill two. These they dispatched two men for, & Clapp resolved to join us in the fishing party. It was getting late now, & Mr. Rhodes[67] (the first officer of the Ship) told me to send Dean ashore in the jolly boat to assist in getting the water casks off, while we were to remain fishing in the Pinnace. At 1/2 past 6 when we left off we had two Hundred & twenty fish, the average weight

---

[66] George Ehninger and the Second Mate, Dean.

[67] Benjamin Rhodes.

of which was at least t[hree &] an half pounds p [crossed out: piece] fish. I could not [se]e any difference either in the appearance [or tas]te of these fish, from our Sound Black [fish] at NY. They are certainly equally as good, . . . of catching them to a person w[ho] . . . fishing, is beyond any thing . . . , as m[ay] appear from the number that was caught in four hours. At 7 oclock we had 16 water casks full along side, & every thing prepared for starting for the ship, which was at least 5 miles off. The Boats were loaded down very deep, especially the Pinnace which had at least 700 wt. of fish on board, half full of wood, & at the lowest calculation 1/3 full of water, 13 men added to this made our boat almost too deep for safety. There were nine men ahead in the jolly boat towing us in the same order as we came off. I had lost my [place in] the Head boat by not attending & as our boat made [a] great deal of water it kept two of us co[nstantly] bailing.

About a mile from shore, [we] perceived the weather getting thic[k] . . . [a]ppearance of squalls. At this time, [the ship fired] a gun & hoisted a light [&] we . . . & Mr. R. made me signal repeater. The weather was now so very thick, that we could but barely distinguish the ship, & there was a very thick squall to windward. We were all conscious that if the squall struck us hard, that there would be no safety for us in the pinnace. There was a chance for the head boat, being so much lighter & stronger than we were. At half past eight it began to rain violently with some wind & the weather excessively thick & [heavy], so much so that we could scarcely distinguish any thing but the flashes from the guns of the ship as [they] were discharged every five minutes. We were convinced by this that they were exces[sively] anxious for our safety, & indeed I must co[nfess] that the prospect before us was dreadfull. . . . over ladened boat in the Pacific . . . ten o[clo]ck at night with every . . . to burst upon us & in consequence to overwhelm us, with thirteen fagged out men, was not the either the most comfortable or safe situation. Yet the same Gracious Providence who has conducted us so far & through so many difficulties & dangers, has through his divine mercy preserved us in this, the most severe one we have as yet experienced. God Grant that I may be sufficiently thankfull for this & all other mercies, that I daily experience.

I kept myself emp[loyed] the whole time in keeping my gun &

powder [s]ecure from the rain, (which was pouring upon us [the] whole distance) & loading & firing in answer to [t]heir signals. We reached the ship at [abou]t half past eleven oclock & relieved . . . a great deal of anxiety. I . . . as much more. We had been exposed to a continual rain for more [than] three hours & an half & every person on board the boats were almost ready to give up. We had been very lucky with our water, having only lost one cask & at half past one had all our water on deck & boats in—& turned in in our births which [crossed out: had] at one time we had almost despaired of enjoying that night.

This has been a thick foggy day & although we can not be more than 9 or 10 miles from the Land, yet it is not visible.

Friday aftern[oo]n 7th.[68] This day commences clear & pleasant [with a] light breeze of wind. The Land in si[ght] distant near 9 miles. As we did not [complete] all our water the day before yesterday, the day has been devoted to that purpose. The . . . this morng. at 9 & have not ye[t]. . . . [A]ll asked to get on shore [but] . . . one of us to go. The reason that he[69] is so disobliging is, I expect, that he thinks we have not treated him as well as we ought to have done. Nicoll, a young of a fiery disposition imagines himself agrieved by Capt. S. & has persuaded Cox & Halsey to think themselves also.

Capt. S. had pasted up in a conspicuous part of the cabin two regulations about the light burning in the evening & about whistling & singing.[70] One of them, I know, Nicoll *tore* down, the other was likewise destroyed. . . . on shore the Captn. discovered that they were [g]one, & instantly pasted some regulations muc[h more] severe. When we came on board I observed that he did not accost us with his [usual fam]iliarity, & during the whole of y[esterday he only] spoke to one of us. I . . . for any imaginary insult N received, so immediately told the Capt. that I had no con-

---

[68] February 7, 1812.

[69] Captain Sowle.

[70] These rules were in consideration of the ship's officers, who slept in the cabin when off watch. The clerks, who did not stand watch, were reasonably expected to follow them.

cern & no wish to show my contempt of this authority & hoped that he did not think me guilty of it. He said he did not, but that untill he discovered who had so insulted him, that he would not allow us any of the little privileges we had hitherto enjoyed. In my opinion in this business he has conducted himself perfectly right, but in this I have the misfortune to differ from our Major Domo Mr. Clark, who, I likewise think, encourages these petty little insults too much. In fact, I [he]ard that Mr. C. himself tore down one [of t]he papers. This has not been ascertained, & [I wou]ld not wish to strengthen the report.

[Ni]coll carried his animosity against the Captn. . . . that he made a serious proposition . . . [to the] cl[er]ks to remain on shore. . . . I told him, that, so far from feeling myself insulted during the passage on board ship, by the Capt., I was very well pleased with the treatmt. I had experienced & even if I had been aggrieved that I could not reconcile to myself leaving the ship & the employment I had engaged in, [crossed out: in] in such a clandestine manner, & accordingly positively declined having any thing to do with it. Clapp hesitated, more I believe from the fear of giving N. offence by immediately rejecting his proposal, than from any serious cons[ideratio]n [crossed out: of the proposal]. Cox & Halsey agreed if the [plan] [w]as practicable to remain with N. But so [incon]stant & so fleeting in his disposition is N. tha[t] the three officers in the ship knew . . . himself & of consequence it . . . of this he gave . . . from the ship & I expect did not much care if two or three had remained on shore.

After we had been on shore three or four hours & had returned from our *survey* of the Island, I understood from Halsey that He, N. & Cox had determined to remain. I told him he had better consider well what he was doing, & what his friends would say if he should ever return home. He made me no answer to this. I was very much surprised a few moments after to hear N. in the course of conversation about the Captn. with Mr. Clark, say, that we had all determined to remain on shore to . . . of the Capts. insults, but that we f[ound t]he thing impracticable.

I was not [the on]ly person surprised here for Cox & Halsey the per[son]s with whom he had a few moments before mad[e] . . . to remain were very much as to . . . the circumstance to Mr. . . . to

stay. What surprised me was to hear him say that we all had determined, when Clapp & myself had told him expressly that we would
not have any thing to do with it. I have not as yet had an opportunity
to speak to Mr. Clark on this subject but intend to inform him that
the idea of leaving the employ to which I have bound myself never
entered my head, & if he asks me what I know about the subject, I
shall immediately inform him for I [crossed out: really] consider
that we have been subject [to] some real insults on account of an
imagin[ary tiff] of Mr. N.

We have now been 113 days conf[ined] on board ship together,
in this long time there has [been] as few quarrels I believe as would
hav[e] happe[ned] to any set of young men & we have . . . the
Captn. of the ship & officers. . . . to me a great . . . should be
broken at a time when the exercise of self command for a few more
days, would allow us to part all friends, but broken it is, & the
manner I shall endeavour to conduct myself in future [crossed out:
while] will be, that I may not give offence to either, & I hope I
shall find it practicable; it will be a happy day when we arrive at
our destination, & seperate, for although we do not actually quarrel, yet there has not been any solid friendship formed between any
of us, & I do not believe there would be if we were to remain
together for a much more longer space of time.

Thursday afternoon. [February] 20th 1812. S Lat. 20° 28'. W
Long. . . . 10'.

The boats returned with [the] water casks on the 7th about 4
oclock. . . . With a light breeze, we . . . the Island of Masafuero,
for . . . [prev]ented from making much . . . wind, but in Lat S.
30°, we took the SE. Trades, after two days of calm. They are
driving us on very fast, towards the Sandwich Isles. We have every
Sail set to advantage. Skysails, top-gallant & royal Steering Sails
fore & aft on both sides, & our ship once more begins to look like
the Beaver. We likewise experience very pleasant weather. This
added to our fair winds would make our time pass pleasantly
enough, if it were not for the unpleasant difference between
[crossed out: the] our gen[tlemen] & the Captn. This has a great
effect upon [all] our actions, but thank God, in all probabi[lity]
. . . days will take us hence to the Isles, [&] . . . days from thence

will land us on [the b]anks of the Columbia, & the only. . . . are inclined to . . . [conduct] themselves . . . , civility. This I have endeavoured to do, & shall continue.

On Sunday last in the calm, Some of the Sailors went [crossed out: in to] overboard to swim. Seeing they come out in safety, three of us [crossed out: sprang aft] followed their example & had but just reached the deck, when a man sung out Shark, & in five minutes, the Rascal was on deck. This narrow escape will I expect prevent any of our Young bloods from cooling themselves in the Sea again.

I have determined not to tou[ch] my journal again, untill my arrival at the [San]dwich Isles unless something extraordinary [occurs]. My time will be pretty well occu[pied] writing letters to my cronies in N.Y. for [I can] not [ex]pect after my arrival at Columbia [River I] shall have much time. . . .

Hawaiian Stopover

Thursday, 9th April 1812.[1] N Lat. 22° 5′. W Long. 158° 45′.
The Islands of Woahoo & Atooi in sight.[2]

Nothing remarkable occurred in our passage from the the Island of Massafuero to the Sandwich Islands. The weather was in general very pleasant, this with a smooth sea & favourable wind made our time pass off very pleasantly.

In S Lat. 29° 40′ we first too[k] the SE trade wind & it continued with [us un]till we reached the Lat of 6° S. where the . . . [tr]ade struck us. This carried us over the Equ[ator on] the 6th March in the Long. 120 . . . with a fine seven knot breeze [broug]ht us expeditiously to the Long[. of the San]dwich Isles. Our . . . to S Islands was 161 days. From NY to the Falkland Islands, the first land we made, it was 65 days, & from the F.I. to Massafuero, 45 days. 4 days we were detained at M. watering, from thence to the Sandwich Islands 47 days, making as before stated one hundred & sixty one days.

The misunderstanding between Mr. C[3] & the Captn. & officers which I mentioned some time ago, and which then I prophecied would one day break out in an open quarrel, has taken place. Cox, one of the clerks, who in my opinion is a young man destitute of good m[anner]s & who possesses a greater share of i[nsolen]ce than generally falls to the . . . [of] one man, was the occasion of the quarre[l. He is] very fond of playing upon a fife & had [injud]iciously disturbed the officers wh[o . . . the] day watch. They often complai[ned] . . . play on, this day . . . table, Mr. Cox began with his music while Mr. Rhodes the first officer & Mr. Dean the third were eating. Mr. R asked him to stop once or twice, but Cox still persisted, when Rhodes got angry & told Cox what he thought of him. Dean then said something to Cox & he replied, when Dean clinched him & gave him a drubbing. Mr. Clark interfered when Mr. Rhodes asked him if he had a mind to take up the quarrel & offered to meet him any where even at t[he] present time across the

---

[1] Although Seton's recounting of his adventures in the Hawaiian Islands usually takes the form of a daily journal, it was written on April 9 while the *Beaver* was sailing toward the Columbia River. Because of the narrative's circumstantial character, it must have been written from notes he had made of his experiences.

[2] Oahu and Kauai, islands in the Hawaiian group.

[3] John Clarke.

table & the nois[e bro]ught the Captn. down. When the dispute [was] stated to him & he agreed with Mr. Rh[odes] understanding that the dispute be[gan about] music, forbade all kind of . . . cabin. Mr. Clark said that p[lay]ing . . . was the only . . . determined to play when he pleased. The Captn. told him[4] not to attempt to play in the cabin again, for he was Master of the Ship & would have his orders obeyed by all on board. Mr. Clark told him then, that he hoped he would give him satisfaction for this. The Captn. replied, Yes, Sir, & thus this dispute ended. They are now as great friends as ever they were, but there is no music in the cabin.

In this dispute Clapp & myself were for some time under the displeasure of his royal Highness,[5] on acct. of our being neuter but this miff like all the others of our Colonel soon disappeared & at the Sight [of] . . . Land, all hands in the ship were in the gr[eatest] good humour & all former disputes & miff[s were] forgiven and forgot. This good effect . . . sight of the Island of Owhy[ee][6] . . . & I hope that all ships may . . . unanimity among their . . . a[mon]g us when the Land . . . view.

On Sunday afternoon March 22d 1812 we made the Island of Owhyhee & next morning at day light we were up with the Island of Mowee.[7] A favourable wind took up rapidly past this, & brought us up with Moratai,[8] betwixt this latter Island & Mowee we passed, & run down with a seven knot breeze close along the shore. Several canoes attempted to come along side but the ship was going too fast. In the afternoon at [6] oclock saw Woahoo,[9] directly ahead, & [distant] about 30 miles, stood in for it until 8 [oclock.] We hauled off shore, intending . . . light next morning to be at. . . . On Tuesday morning[10] we stood in . . . Land with a fine . . . 16 or 17 miles. . . . This calm was a great disappointment to most of our bloods in the cabin, for they were all rigged out in their Sunday clothes to go on shore.[11] Our Colonel[12] I believe felt it most, for he

---

[4] That is, Ross Cox.

[5] Probably Clarke.

[6] Hawaii, at that time, was usually spelled as Seton did.

[7] Maui.

[8] Molokai.

[9] Oahu.

[10] March 24, 1812.

[11] The *Beaver* was apparently becalmed off Oahu for a day.

[12] That is, Clarke.

intends to astonish the natives by the magnificence of his apparel, & was accordingly dressed out to the nines, but alas! he had not the satisfaction of being seen & admired by the natives this day, for the calm envious of the joy he anticipated, was resolved to disappoint him at least for one day. At 3 in the afternoon two canoes were seen standing [towar]ds us from Moratai, [crossed out: &] but to our g[reat dis]appointment they passed astern of u[s not] paying us the least attention. . . . the evening a light breeze sprung up [and we] stood toward the Harbour. . . . two hours & stood off & on. . . .

Wednesday[13] morning at day break stood towards the Island again, with a light breeze. At 9 two canoes came along side from which we purchased some water melons, [crossed out: for] with a Jack Knife, at 11 fired a gun for a Pilot, & at 12 repeated it, & then lay too. In abt. half an hour a chief by name Tiama came off to us in his large double canoe & brought some cocoa nuts. The ship was run in to [an] anchorage by his direction in Whyte[tee Ba]y[14] opposite the village of the same [name. A] great many canoes came off to us, [but as a cons]equence of a taboo[15] they could not [come on] board. This Taboo likewise pr[ohibits vis]its from the fair sex for it. . . . [Captn.] Sowle went . . . visit to his Majesty, Tamaahmaah,[16] & returned about six in the evening. To morrow his majesty with his wives & suit pay us a visit, & after that we will be free to trade with whom we please.

Clapp, Nicoll, Halsey & Cox took a freak in their heads to [crossed out: go on] spend the night on shore & at nine oclock accompanied Tiama to his house. On Thursday[17] Morning at day light, I went with Capt. Sowle for the first time on Shore, & there

---

[13] March 25, 1812.

[14] Waikiki.

[15] The word was pronounced kapu and the practice itself, that of forbidding the touching of a place, person, or thing, by the common people, was exercised by nobles and priests. A. Grove Day, *Hawaii and Its People*, rev. ed. (New York: Meredith, 1968), p. 10; hereafter, Day, *Hawaii*. See Ross, *Adventures*, p. 45, and below, p. 80, for contemporary—Ross's book was first printed in London in 1849—impressions of the practice by the Astorians.

[16] Kamehameha I (1758?–1819?) was an especially competent ruler who managed, by artful maneuvering and skillful leadership in battle, to unite the Islands under his rule. Day, *Hawaii*, pp. 18–90.

[17] March 26, 1812.

saw Clapp & his party. They had passed the night [most] comfortably with Tiama & had three or [four] wives, apiece.[18]

I soon found in . . . [s]light a degree female chastity . . . , for
I had not been a shore five m[in]utes, . . . I had a dozen invitations
from the w[omen,] & it was of no use to deny . . . the[y] [w]ould
absolutely draw . . . as they did not suit my taste exactly & as I not
taken my breakfast yet, I resisted them as long as I was able, but
was at last obliged to comply. Their manners at first so completely
disgusted me, that I almost resolved to have no more connections
with them, & I tolerably well kept my resolution.[19]

To one who has been always accustomed to view the modest looks
& pretty faces of American fem[ales], these nearly naked Indians
are comp[letely] disgusting, & they in a great measure ad[vance]
their ugliness by plastering the front [of their] Head with a kind
of white lime[20] . . . with the strong smell of cocoa [nut o]il with
which they anoint thems[elves] . . . a day or two . . . little familiar
to their looks & manners.

We returned on board & there found Tamaahmaah with his three
wives, his Prime minister Krēimōkōō,[21] & all his nobles. They
were likewise accompanied by Mr. Harebottle & Meneni[22] two
Europeans, the former an Englishman & the latter a Spaniard, who

---

[18] Cox had a different story. His party had been serenaded in an harmonious
and "amatory" manner by "a bevy of young females," after which they "enjoyed
the remainder of the night in undisturbed repose on soft beds of island cloth."
Columbia, p. 26.

[19] The missing portion of this entry allows full rein to the reader's imagination, but it seems likely that Seton, a very pious and conventional (by the strait-
laced standards of his corner of early nineteenth-century New York society)
young man, was shocked by the immodest loquaciousness of the island women
and that his compliance consisted of nothing more than awkward conversations
with the maidens. However, the editor cannot compel the reader's agreement
with this judgment.

[20] Gabriel Franchère, who had touched at the islands the previous year as a
passenger on board the *Tonquin*, described this: "Some, to heighten their charms,
dye their black hair (cut short for the purpose) with quick lime, forming round
the head a strip of pure white, which disfigures them monstrously." *Voyage*, p.
44.

[21] Kalanimoku.

[22] Harbottle and Don Francisco de Paula Marin, known in the islands as
Manini or Menini.

have resided on the Island for the last 12 or 14 years & have arrived
at great honours in Tama.'s dominions. All these done us the honour to breakfast & dine on board ship.

We received from Harebottle the melancholy acct. of the Tonquins (the ship that left New York for the Columbia the year before
our Ship) being cut off on the NW coast by the Ind[ians] & her
being blown up by the Captn. when [the dec]ks were filled with
Natives.[23] This acct. was [truly dis]tressing to us, for our success
depends in [great me]asure, upon the Gentlemen of the Tonqu[in,
for] they were pitched upon as the most competent [to er]ect the
first settlement & they ca[rried aboard the]ir ship the principal
means, by [which the set]tle[ment] was to succeed. Our . . . idea,
that we should find them there settled.

If this should not be the case & if Mr. Hunts party[24] should not
have arrived, we will be in a melancholy plight, indeed! In the first
place we have not a man in whom we could place any confidence in
a trying situation, to conduct our party. Mr. C[25], the only partner
in the establishment, with us, is certainly, if we judge from his
conduct on board ship, not calculated for such an undertaking. He
is too fleeting & inconstant in his disposition, & does not possess
sufficient au[thori]ty over the men. To acknowledge any other of
[the pre]sent party, as a head, will not I am sure [be resorted] to,
even if Mr. C. is content to give up [the] rig[ht].

In the next place our party only [consists] of twenty men, with
so few men . . . whom we can place . . . [in my op]inion be the
extreme . . . settlement, in such a case, I believe, it will be determined to return in the ship at any rate as far as the Sandwich Islands.

---

[23] This brief mention indicates clearly enough that Seton had heard a circumstantial and, it would seem, largely accurate account of the loss of the *Tonquin*, a
event that was every bit as serious for the prospects of Astor's enterprise as Seton
indicates.

[24] This was the overland party, led by Wilson Price Hunt, an American,
which had left St. Louis in October 1810, wintered about 500 miles up the
Missouri, and finally set out for Astoria in March 1811. It was an especially
difficult trip, and the party filtered in to Astoria in several groups in January–
February 1812. Ronda, *Astoria*, pp. 135–95.

[25] John Clarke.

This is the worst view of our situation. There is some probability that the Tonquins party may be safely landed, as Wiccinnish,[26] the place where the Ship was cut off is considerably to the northward of the Columbia. If so, & no accident should since have happened to them, our undertaking may yet succeed & one day it may repay us for the difficulties we have to undergo.[27]

Mr. Hunts party may have arrived also, & if we should have the satisfaction of finding a countryman [there] as the Head of the establishment, we [will b]e extremely fortunate. All the partners, [Mr. Hunt excepted,] are Scotchmen, & they on in gen[eral are mu]ch prejudiced against us <u>Yankees</u>. I [w]ould [not] have made this remark, had it [not been said] in confidence to Cox the Irish[man] . . . [th]at the American clerks w[ould] . . . all the Proprietors. I trust though that the Gentleman who uttered this sentiment will be mistaken, & that most of the proprietors will be enough of Gentlemen not to make any distinction between European or American clerks.

We will soon know now the particulars of our situation; a fortnight from this time, we expect to be landed on the Banks of the Columbia. Untill that time I will defer any more acct. of our situation & thoughts.

---

[26] This is the name, not of a place, but rather of a young and powerful Nootka Indian headman, who lived at Clayoquot Sound, on the west coast of Vancouver Island, about forty miles south of Nootka Sound. He, and his father of the same name (usually spelled Wickananish), were well known to European sailors and traders and, although usually friendly, had been known to take extreme umbrage at real or fancied insults or impositions by the Europeans. See Frederic W. Howay, "The Voyage of the *Hope*: 1790–1792," *The Washington Historical Quarterly*, 11, No. 1 (January 1920), 3, 23–24, 25–26, for skirmishes between the elder Wickananish and Captain Joseph Ingraham, the first American to trade in the area. Not long after Ingraham's difficulties, Captain Robert Gray, the discoverer of the Columbia River, had similar experiences with Wickananish; see John Boit's "A New Log of the Columbia," edited by Worthington C. Ford and Edmond S. Meany, ibid., 12, No. 1 (January 1921), 8, 20–28, 43. Irving has him as Wicananish in *Astoria*, p. 73. See above, p. 91–93, for the significance of this reference.

[27] Seton's journal was a primary source for Irving's account of the reception of the *Tonquin*'s fate by the men of the *Beaver*; see *Astoria*, p. 254.

At 3 in th[e af]ternoon Tama. with all his Gang went on [shore].[28] Immediately after his departure the Taboo [was ta]ken off, & females in abundance vis[ited the s]hip. Clapp, Nicoll, Halsey & Ehninger [deter]mined to remain on shore this night. I w[ould h]ave accompanied them, but was . . . [which] continued in . . . of the night, occasioned, I suppose by eating too much fruit after so long a voyage.[29] Next morng. [crossed out: Thursday] Friday 26th[30] after breakfast I went on shore with Mr. Clark intending to walk to Honaroora[31] the residence of the King, dist. abt. 5 miles from the place where the ship was anchored. We landed at Whytete opposite the dwelling of Tiama & after paying him a visit, where we were received with the greatest cordiality & treated with the best his hut afforded, we proceeded on our walk to the village. About a mile from Whytete we met Clapp & all his party attended with Mr. Cook an officer of a ship, which he left at this place about three months since. [We joi]ned their party & proceeded to Tiama's h[ut. T]here we resolved to dine on board & come on [shore aga]in in the afternoon. We accordingly p[er]sua[ded] Cook to accompany us & repaired on board. We . . . found that the Captn. dined on shore. . . . & the other officers received us & . . . the [great]est attention & treat[ed us] . . . wine, which we should not have enjoyed, had our saving Captn. been on board. After finishing 4 or five bottles at 3, we jumped in a canoe alongside & once more

---

[28] Understandably, Seton made no mention of an amusing, but probably embarassing (to him at any rate) incident during the King's visit to the *Beaver*. Cox gleefully recorded it: "Observing Mr. Seton writing, he [the King] approached him, and began to examine the various little nic-nacs with which the desk was furnished. Seton showed him a handsome penknife of curious workmanship, containing a pair of blades, *not* with an intention of bestowing it; with this he appeared particularly pleased, and putting it into one of the pockets of his capacious vest, said, '*Mytye, nue nue mytie*' (good, very good), and walked away. It was in vain for Seton to expostulate; his majesty did not understand English, and all entreaties to induce him to return the penknife were ineffectual." *Columbia*, p. 29.

[29] Seton seems to have been taken ill.

[30] Actually the date was March 27, 1812; for one week, Seton continued dating entries one day earlier than the correct date.

[31] Honolulu.

started for the shore & landed near our old friend Tiama's Hut. There it was determined that Nicoll & myself should go with Cook, & spend the night at Mr. Holme's,[32] at Honaroōra, where he (Cook) resided, & that Clapp & Halsey should pass the night at Tiama's. After staying at Whytete t[ill fi]ve we set out on our walk each one a[ttende]d by a servant to carry us over the p[onds of] which there are several between the [two place]s.

We arrived at Mr. H.'s abt. 7 ocloc[k in] the evening & were very cordially welco[med] . . . & although he had fin[ished hi]s [meal] he immediately [ordered an evening meal] prepared for us.

Cook gave us up his sleeping house, & we slept soundly on mats, covered with tappa,[33] accordg. to the custom of the country.

Next morng. Saturday 27,[34] we walked with Cook to see the village & his Majesty, the Great Tamaahmaah. We found him with his principal chiefs & surrounded by a guard of abt. 15 men with muskets, viewing a game of rolling stones, which they are very expert in & roll a great distance, as far again as any of us could do. He recd. us with attention & shook hands. All the young chiefs seemed to be delighted with us, & followed us wherever we went. We procee[ded] through the whole village followed by crowds [of] Inhabitants & were introduced to some of . . . chiefs. We then visited Tama.'s f[leet] co[nsisti]ng of one ship American built called the Bird, & several Schooners & T[enders] . . . which have been built on the Islan[d]. . . . The Tenders of . . . at 1/2 past 11 we returned to Mr. Holmes, much fatigued. In conversation with him I learned that he was an American by birth, & had left Boston as a Stewart of a vessel bound to the NW coast of America, that he went on the coast & on his return to the Sandwich Islands the vessel was cut off by the natives at Woahoo & that he has remained on the Island since—nearly 22 years. He has a wife & several children & is more in the good graces of the King than [any] white man on the Island & possesses [much] property. He has determined to end [his days there] in which I think he is perfectly ri[ght.]

Charles Cook the young man I have mention[ed is] a native of

---

[32] Oliver Holmes.
[33] A native cloth, made from tree bark.
[34] March 28, 1812.

New York & left there at the ag[e] of . . . without the consent of his [parents]. . . . I remained on. . . . He told me some acct. of what had happened to him & of his real name which is Nicholas Saltus.[35] After leaving NY. in the way he did, he immediately changed his name, & has been known by no other, during the five years he remained in Canton; he was second officer of a ship from Canton to the NW; after leaving the coast, he determined to remain some time on the Island, on acct. of some difficulty with the Captn. & has taken up his residence with Mr. Holmes, where he appears to live comfortably & contented.[36]

At 12' a messenger arrived to us from Clapp & H[37] at Whytete saying they would w[ait] dinner for us but after some consultation we [chose] to dine at Daddy Holme's & walk do[wn in la]te afternoon. We accordingly dispatched . . . this message. After dining with the old man [he pointed] out to me his wife & children . . . s[poke] to them. His daughter . . . [the] p[retti]est girl I saw on the [Island] . . . of age & her behaviour is very modest. George his son is likewise a very fine boy. I tried to persuade the old man to send him to America to learn the Language, but he cannot bear the idea of parting with him.

At 4 p.m. we started (Cook in company) for Whytete & arrived there a little before six. We found Clapp & Halsey waiting for us at Tiama's. Mr. Rhodes & Champenois (1st and 2nd officers) happened to be on shore in the jolly boat. I determined to sleep on [board,] while the remainder were to remain on [shore,] & breakfast on board in the morning; [after a] good swim in the surf, I went on [board.] Meneni & his wife with Harebottle [were] there & the ship full of girls.

Sunday Mo[rng.] 28th[38] Clapp & the rest with Cook came

---

[35] There may have been two, or only one, Saltus family in Manhattan about the time Nicholas left. In 1798, Solomon Saltus was listed as a merchant, living at 12 Stone Street; in 1797, there was a Saltus & Son, Ship Chandlers, at 65 Front Street. On the basis of their service to the maritime community, the latter is more likely to have been Nicholas' family. *City Directory.*

[36] Cox saw it differently; Cook, "of a highly respectable family, . . . did not appear to relish his situation." *Columbia*, p. 32.

[37] John C. Halsey.

[38] March 29, 1812.

[aboard and were] . . . welcomed by all the . . . did not in the least notice him, this is what we all expected of him & which we had apprised Cook off. We well knew that he could not get any thing from Cook & his disposition is such, that where he expects no [crossed out: retu] advantage, he shows no civility.[39]

At breakfast we learned that the ship was to be moved from her present anchorage to the village of Honaroora, for the convenience of getting on board the supplies which were bought of the King. We were all very glad to hear this, as it would be much nearer Mr. Holmes house, where we contemplated to spend much of our time, & of course mu[ch m]ore convenient for us. Mr. Cook mentioned to Cla[pp] that he was rather short of clothes & did [not know] how much longer he might remain on [the Islan]d, & that if we could spare any, h[e] wou[ld be] very thankful. We accordingly made u[p a t]olerable large bundle. I contributed . . . w[aistc]oats a pair of Quarter. . . . Wishing to get out of the confusion of getting the ship underway we resolved to land & walk to Honaroora & take dinner with Mr. Holmes. I put in my pocket a Handsome pr. of razors & some scissors, & beads, to distribute among Tiama's & Mr. Holmes children. We landed near our old friend Tiama's & after spending an hour or two with him set out for the last time to Honaroora & reached there about 12 oclock. After dinner I gave Mr. Holmes the razors, which pleased him much. [A n]ative came & told us, that the ship was anchored [oppos]ite the village. I resolved then to spend my n[ights aboa]rd ship & days on shore walking a[bout] and l[earn]ing something of the Islands. This night I [am] prevented from sleeping on board on acct. of . . . being absent & of no . . . ship; Clapp Halsey & Nicoll also staid on shore this night. After supping with the old man & talking with him & Cook for two or three hours, about Home, we all turned in, in Cook's Sleeping house & slept as before said on <u>mats</u> & <u>Tappa</u>. From this day till the day of our departure I spent my time mostly at Mr. Holmes. His canoes were always at my service whenever I wanted them & would regularly take me off in the evening & bring me on shore in the morning. One day by invita-

---

[39] Seton is probably referring to Clarke, definitely not one of his favorite people.

tation I dined at Mr. Davis's (a white man (European) who has resided some time on the Island) i[n com]pany with the Captn., Mr. Clark, George Ehning[er, . . . &] Meneni, & for the first time saw Roast [dog]. I have been so long taught to consider . . . animal as exempted from that fa[tal]ity t[o wh]ich the Pig & other domestic animals are liable . . . that I could not so far conquer my . . . to taste a piece of him, in fact the . . . against a Dish of . . . the table. Captn. S. & Mr. Clarke though found the Dog very good & equal they say to any veal or mutton.

It was from Mr. Davis, that we recd. two Letters, directed to Captn. Jon. Thorn, & to Mr. McKay.[40] Mr. Clark opened them & found one from Mr. Astor giving some instructions to Captn. Thorn of the Tonquin—the other from Capt. Ebbetts[41] of the Enterprise (owned by Mr. Astor) stating that as he had not met the Tonquin on the coast, he concluded that she would not be out that year & mentionin[g] the report that prevailed at the Islands resp[ecting] her fate & [crossed out: of] his opinion that it was [correct].

Mr. Holmes made me a present of a . . . 240 fathoms long & two mats. His w[ife al]so gave me two mats & a very fine pup Dog . . . English breed; the only presents I . . . in return, were to . . . & 1½ dozen cakes of shaving soap, a silk umbrella, one or two books & some other little things, that he mentioned would be useful. To his wife I gave two white shirts a Hnkf. & some thread & needles, & to his daughter a large silk Hnkf., scissors, beads, &c. &c & we all by supscription purchased a fowling piece & gave to the old man.

I likewise traded with Kreimokoo, or Billy Pitt the prime minister[42] a coarse Surtout coat for eleven mats & one hundred & twenty cocoa nuts. These were all the articles I traded for, except some fruit which at different times I purchased from the canoes along side, for jack Knife[s & Be]ads, &c &c.

The ships trade was mostly wit[h the] King. About sixty Hogs, three hundred co[coa nuts,] quantities of Tarra[43] & sweet Potatoes

---

[40] Jonathan Thorn, captain of the *Tonquin*, and Alexander McKay, an Astor partner who sailed with Thorn. Ronda, *Astoria*, pp. 95–96, 58.

[41] John Ebbets. Ibid., pp. 72–74.

[42] For William Pitt, the British statesman.

[43] Taro, a tropical plant, cultivated for its sweet, tuberous root.

[&] me[lon]s & sugarcane, were purchased for a qua[rter ca]sk of Teneriffe wine, a piece of . . . & twelve or fourteen bbls of Tar. . . . of . . . that was carried. . . .

I regularry spent every day on shore, dining at Mr. Holmes, & was always welcomed by him, indeed. I shall never forget his hospitality, & hope I one day may have it in my power to return it to him, or to some of his children.

Nothing material happened to the ship untill Saturday 4th April, when the wind sprung up from the westward, which made a lee shore for us, & before we knew that we drifted, we found the breakers, not two ships lenghts [as]tern. Going to warp her farther out, they f[ound o]ut that the Hawser was chafed off, [the sh]ip then only held by the small . . . [&] if that was to go, she must inevitably g[o to] pieces. Got down Royal Yd's & mast & to[p mast] & Lower Yards, & the Long[es]t . . . the wind by this . . . with a tremendous sea running, & the ship was a scene of the utmost confusion. Cook (who came on board before breakfast) & myself were on the quarter deck, the wh[ol]e day, while it was raining as hard as it could pour down. About two oclock they succeeded in carrying out in the long boat another Anchor ahead, & another Kedge & warped the Ship out from Seven fathoms to ten.

I never saw a man in so great a flurry as Captn. S. was this day. He was standing on the Bowsprit, the whole time, with his speaking tru[mpe]t, & issuing his commands in a screeching & [unin]telligible tone—rather discouraging [than enligh]tening the men; Poor Dean, our t[hird] of[ficer,] suffered on acct. of this storm, or rather [the] cut of the Humour the storm put our . . . Captn. in.

The Captn. was bell[owing at] Dean for a considerable time. . . . understand one word that was said, the Captn. damned him for a stupid puppy, before the whole crew & some of the residents of the Island. Dean told him he was not more stupid than he was, when the Captn. struck him over the head two or three times with his trumpet, & told him not to do duty as an officer any longer on board the ship.

Dean the next morning asked liberty to remain on shore, which was granted; as he & myself have the whole passage been [on] the most friendly terms, I interested myself [con]siderably in his wel-

fare, & spoke to Capt. . . . about his residence with him on the
[Island. It] was some time before I could get t[he o]ld [man] to
consent &c. but at last had the [satis]faction of procuring a home
for [Dea]n . . . W traders, touch . . . way to Canton;[44] which will
be about the months of October & November, when he is to proceed to Canton.

For this arrangement I had to give [a] draft on New York for
Seventy two dolls. in favour of Dean, who is to indorse it over to
Holmes. I advised Edward[45] that I had drawn on him & that Dean
would reimburse him. I also wrote my Father some acct. of our
passage, & the report of the Tonquins fate. These letters were left
in the care of Mr. Meneni to be forwarded in the first ship bound
to Canton.

I gave Cook a letter to My Father & Dean [a] letter to Ned, as
they requested to be introduced to [my] friends at home.

It was given out on board sh[ip to a]ll who intended to proceed
in the sh[ip should be] on board on Tuesday morning, as a[t the]
tim[e of] a first wind the ship would go to sea. [We we]re all
accordingly on board, . . . win[d & d]id not get out before
Wed[nesday]. . . . [Tama]ahmaah with his three wives & all his
Nobles dined on board of us on Wednesday the 8th for the last time
& as the Topsails were sheeting home, he bade us farewell.

I bid adieu to the young chiefs who were with him & who
seemed to take some pleasure in my company. Their names were
Kreikoopouree, Tahōōmōmānō, Manono, Koulepoolepoo, Kulou-
chow & Housep. I was likewise very great with the Heir of the
Throne, Tama's Son, a young man abt. 18, by name. . . .

The Islanders could not mak[e . . . my] name. Kingy was the
appellation [b]y w[hic]h I was known & the nearest they [cou]ld
come to Seton. . . . [46] The . . . these Islands as far as I . . . by
similar to what th[e]. . . . The Government is under a King, who
deputes chiefs over the different islands & these must be all ready

---

[44] From the context, it would seem that Seton described a plan for Dean to
take passage on a ship bound for Canton, from which point he could probably
secure a berth on a vessel bound for an east coast American port.

[45] Edward A. ("Ned") Seton.

[46] From what follows, Seton probably described and analyzed the islands' society and inhabitants in these missing lines.

to pay their supplies, when it pleases the King to demand them. Of
their Religion, the principal ceremony of which is the Taboo, I
could not learn much. I saw several images, & once approached
very near the Morai,[47] but was angrily told that it was tabooed.
This Taboo can be laid on any person or any thing at the will of the
King, & a great many of the chiefs have likewise a power of taboo-
ing, but there are four regular taboos, every month, at the new
moon, first quarter, full-moon & last quarter. These, only, as far
as I could understand prevented the chiefs & the women from going into any canoes. They were two of this last kind [wh]ile the
ship remained at anchor.

A man [and a wom]an cannot eat under the same roof, nor can
. . . one thing, which another has tasted. [There are a gre]at many
other curious customs which have been [menti]oned by voyagers,
who have been more able to descr[ibe t]hem, than I am, & who
have favoured . . . [wi]th their tr[ave]ls.

It was Wednesdsay 8[48] . . . [as] stated that with a fine breeze
from the NE we bade adieu to the Sandwich Islands. This breeze
though did not conduct us on very rapidly for it was not untill
Sunday 12th that we lost sight [crossed out: that we lost sight] of
Atooi.

On this day Thursday April 23rd we are in N Lat. 38° W Long
144° about half the distance between Woahoo & the Columbia.
Nothing remarkable has occurred since we left the Island. Most of
our days have been pleasant with light breezes, & great unanimity
seems to prevail among all hands, which makes our time pass off
. . . pleasantly. We often indulge in specula[tion conc]erning the
Tonquin & her party & a[bout our pro]bable future destiny, but
cannot come to any [d]etermination, untill we land on the
Colum[bia], which in all probability will not [be] more t[han].
. . . I shall before that time [note down] . . . [a]ny little circumstance that may occur in our future progress.

I forgot to mention before, that we made a considerable rein-
forcement to our little band at the Sandwich Islands. Mr. Wadsworth, an American by birth & Seaman by profession is engaged

---

[47] A place of public worship. Ross, *Adventures*, p. 44.
[48] April 8, 1812; this entry was written on April 23.

by Mr. C. for the purpose of taking charge of one of the Schooners which are to be built. He was an officer of an American vessel which touched at Owyhee, & on acct. of some disagreement with the Captn, remained on shore. He is the only one on board ship who has taken a girl with him.[49]

Mr. C. engaged ten of the natives to accompany us, & gave permission to each of the [cler]ks to take a boy. Clapp, Halsey & myself [are t]he only ones that profited by this good [humour] of our Colonels.[50]

One of the Queens had g[iven] De[an] a fine little Boy about 12 or 14; when he determined to remain on shore, he (Dean) gave him to [me] & told the Queen that I was his B[rother, whic]h satisfied [he]r.

The boy appears . . . [dis]position, & I trust will prove a valuable acquisition. It is my present intention if ever it should please Providence to permit my return, to take him home with me, if it is agreeable to him.[51]

Since our departure from the Islands, our Boatswain has been broke by the Captn., very much in my opinion, to the dissatisfaction of the Officers, who have often said in my presence that he was "all in all" the best Seaman on board ship. It certainly does not concern me to say or feel any thing in this business, but one cannot help have [one's f]eelings touched when he sees a civil & good [man] suffer, (where no redress is to be had) by the hu[mour] of another. Such in my opinion is the case of Mr. . . . the boatswain, & I heartily hope he may [reco]nsider [w]hen he returns the whole acct. of his wages.

T[oday] a very cold raw day with the wind. . . . We are out from [the Islands] . . . days.

Saturday May 2d 1812. N Lat. 43° 22'. W Long. 126° 17'. Since my last date of April 23d, the Wind has been constantly from the

---

[49] Cox related that Wadsworth had flatly declared he was not accustomed "to live in a state of single blessedness." *Columbia*, p. 45.

[50] Cox reported that twenty-six islanders were hired. Ibid. Irving rejected both Cox and Seton and accepted Franchère's total of "a dozen Sandwich Islanders." *Voyage*, p. 70.

[51] There is no further mention of this boy, either in Seton's journal or in the other chronicles of Astoria.

N. We stood [crossed out: towards the shore] close hauled to the Eastwd. & progressed very fast towards the continent & at 9 in the morning of Thursday 30th[52] Land was discovered right ahead, at 12 oclock by our observn. We ascertained it to be Cape Orford[53] in Lat N. 42.50' & Long. W. 124° 25'. At six in the Evening we were near enough to see the trees on th[e] shore & the snow on the top of the mount[ains.] The wind at this time blew a gale fro[m] . . . & reduced us to our close reefed topsails, . . . all day yesterday with a fresh bree[ze] from the same quarter (which is as dead ahead as it can [be]) & this morng. at 4 oclock wore . . . N & E. The weather had moderated a g[reat] . . . [in] hopes of a Southerly wind. [crossed out: the weather] It has been calm & foggy all the morning, but the wind has sprung up from its old quarter the N. Our Lat to day was 43° 19', three degrees to the Southward of Columbia River. It is mortifying indeed to be within so short a distance of your port & to experience the impossibility of reaching it with the present wind. Land is seen now under our Lee, & we are standing towards it.

The weather is not quite as cold as it was, which is the only appearance we have of change of Wind.

Sunday [morn]ing.[54] The wind has at last shifted [about] favourable for us, & we are making . . . our way, towards the Columbia, & no doub[t] will arrive there in a day or two at mos[t]. We have been for the most part [e]mployed [during our] passage from the Islands . . . [ca]lculations of our future destiny, & of forming some rules for our future behaviour.

Mr. C.[55] has for a day or two put on a more dignified behaviour than usual, & has not enlightened the clerks much by his improving conversation. I suppose he begins to feel now the importance of his situation & no doubt expects to be treated with more reverence, by us; but we are so perfectly acquainted with his excessive weakness of character, that any airs of self importance now put on, only makes him more a subject of ridicule.

---

[52] April 30, 1812.
[53] Now called Cape Blanco in southern Oregon.
[54] May 3, 1812.
[55] John Clarke.

Since I have made these remarks on the chara[cter] of this Gentleman, with whom I have cer[tainl]y had a good opportunity of being acquainte[d, I] w[ill] mention the amiable. parts of his chara[cter. Mr.] C. is certainly in every sense of the word, A Good Natured Man & is possessed of a ge[nerou]s disposition. He left Canada at the age . . . before it can be supposed he acquired . . . [56] say in fact he exposes his ignorance in almost every sentence he utters.

Whether a man of this character is preferable to a severe & firm man for undertaking the charge of this expedition—I am ignorant. But in our present situation, doubtful of meeting any associates at the river, a man of a firm & impartial mind would most undoubtedly in my opinion claim the preference. He would not perhaps possess as much of the love of the common men, but he would certain[ly] have more of their fear & respect.

Mr. C. ear[ns] himself enemies by showing a partiality . . . for one & sometimes for another. his convers[ation to tho]se, who happen to be in his good graces, is entirely about the bad qualities of the other clerks. This reaches their ears & makes them enemies at [once b]ut in short time, they can . . . or Anger.

I can safely say, this is the opinion of all of us now, that we neither wish for, nor care for his good or bad opinion [crossed out: of us]. What his report of our conduct on board ship will be, is not difficult to judge, & I dare affirm, it will be [crossed out: in a] favourable [crossed out: view]. But if I should be mistaken, I have by the goodness of my friends, strong letters to several of the Gentlemen.[57] These must make them take some notice of me, & I have so much confidence in myself to think, that if I get with a man capable of judging, that he will be pleased with my exertions.

Whether this confidence in myself is ill placed or not, time must dete[rmi]ne. I can for the present only say that it is [my de]termination to spare neither my person or my [strenuous] exertions in any service I am employed in.

---

[56] Seton probably referred to Clarke's limited formal education.

[57] Here Seton means letters of recommendation which had been written for him by his well-placed kinsmen from the New York mercantile community to various of the partners in Astor's enterprise. This family support may have helped him secure the higher salary noted above, p. 30n9.

Our Lat by obsn. was 43° 54' N & our distance from the River 195 m[iles. To]day at 12 oclock, the wind has again retu[rned to] the N. which may make our time on b[oard] . . . longer.

Monday 4th[58] [crossed out: Morg.] was a pleasant calm day. We stood on to the NE the whole day. Our Lat. at Meridian was 44° 36' & distance from Columbia 120 miles.

The Captn., Clapp & some others were employed making car‑tridges & other preparations for the Indians.

Tuesday the 5th was likewise a pleasant day our Lat was 45° 40' [crossed out: we stood] & distance from River 40 miles. We stood off shore the southward & westwd. till midnight, & this morning Wednesday at 10 oclock we judge ourselves dist. f[rom] the River about 30 miles. There is about a . . . knot breeze favourable for us & we most cer[tainly ough]t to reach our port in [the] course of the day. The cables are bent, & every preparation for Landing is made & there is no doubt now tha[t] . . . hours, we will view the spot wh[ere it is] more than probable a . . . lives must be spent.

On Wednesday Evening[59] at six oclock saw Columbia River, stood towards Cape Disappointment[60] & when within 4 miles, fired two Guns, to which there was no answer, & we saw no sign of any Inhabi‑tants except a smoke made as they all judged by some Indians. We stood off all night, all very much dejected at the non appearance of the Gentlemen of the Tonquin. At two Oclock the next day Thursday 7th we were [crossed out: about] near about in the same spot, that we were in the night before all anxiously looking out for some signal, but none appearing we fired a gun & sent the jolly boat with Mr. Rhodes, M[r. W]adsworth & six men, armed with muskets, pi[sto]ls & cutlasses to sound the channel & endeavo[ur] to [get] some information about the other Party. At [t]hree stood in & at 4 the boat came along side. On acct. of the tremendous seas . . . they were unable to sound, & had not seen [anyone] from whom any information could be f[orthcoming. We con]tinued to stand towards the shore, untill six oclock, when we were not more than three miles off. Two Guns were then fired & all eyes &

---

[58] This entry was written on Wednesday, May 6, 1812.

[59] This entry was written on Friday, May 8, 1812.

[60] A promontory marking the north shore of the Columbia River.

ears looking & listening for some reply, but in vain; after waiting half an hour the ship stood off shore again.

Mr. Clark came to a determination then to attempt the settlement with our present party, & signified the same to Capt. Sowle. It gives me pleasure to add that at this time there was not a single person, who seemed at the least disheartened at our prospect, but all expressed their willin[gne]ss to attempt it. For myself although I co[nfe]ss I would rather have been snug at [home]. I immediately told Mr. C. that if [he] reso[lved] to stay, I would also remain. He told me his plan & I accordingly agreed to it.

On this Morg. Friday 8th[61] at six we found ourselves a[way from] the Cape 6 miles. It was a mild . . . little sea running, the Bar . . . & accoutrements & the same expedition once more started. After they had left the ship, we stood again off shore. At 1/4 before ten Three guns were distinctly heard & they were the report of great guns. This cheered our spirits a little; but still they might be the muskets from the Boat. At 11 the boat came along side, & the first question they asked us was, whether we had heard six guns? & that they had heard three heavy & three smaller ones very distinctly; this confirmation of our hopes as may be supposed, made us feel happy, & orders were immediately given to answer with two guns, which was done.

The same cause that prevented the Boat from executing her errand yesterday, stopped her t[his] morg. & Mr. R[62] gave it his opinion that it wo[uld] at [thi]s time be smooth enough for a small [boa]t to venture & advised running the ship in immediately by chart, but this opinion did not suit the timidity of Captn. S. who prefers standing off [shore & s]ending in the boat once a day to attempt to . . . are now accordgly. standing towards the shore . . . & then I suppose will be within two or three miles & then stand off again. In this way I have no doubt we will proceed, untill an unlucky blow drives us off the coast, which I hope will make the old Man repent his over prudence.

We (the clerks) have employed ourselves since within sight of the river in getting our pistols & other arms & apparatus in readiness. Our speculations about our success, when all hopes were given up

---

[61] May 8, 1812.
[62] Rhodes.

of finding the gentlemen there, were numerous. We all thought though that for the first year we could maintain our post with safety, [&] all hoped that John Jacob Astor mig[ht loo]k upon our risque with a favourabl[e] eye.

Thank God, there is little doubt now of our finding the other party there. Whether or not we will get over the Bar in s[afety mus]t be regulated by him who has [guided] us through so ma[ny] . . . [dan]gers safely.

Saturday afternoon 9th.[63] Thank God, all is right. This morg. at 8 two boats were seen standing towards the ship. At 9 they came along side. Mr. McDougall[64] & six men were in the first, & the other was a canoe with Indians in. We learnt from Mr. McD. the particulars of the Tonquin's fate, which will be mentioned hereafter, & the welcome intelligence of the arrival of Mr. Hunt.

The first officer went in the boat to sound & upon a signal from him, stood towds. him with the ship & anchored safely at 1 oclock opposite to Cape Disappointment. The tide at present is so very strong, that it is not practicable to proceed to the Fort, [it being] about ten miles up the River. There is so much confusion that it is impossible to be particular. In a day or two I intend, Dei Gratia to be as copious as possible.[65]

The number of mi[les] . . . this passage are . . . 200[0].

---

[63] May 9, 1812.

[64] Duncan McDougall, one of the Astor partners who had come out on the Tonquin.

[65] Irving used details from Seton for his account of the arrival of the Beaver at the Columbia. Astoria, pp. 254–55. The author's description of Captain Sowle's caution and timidity probably owe a good bit to Seton. The mouth of the Columbia River, even with dependable power and modern navigation aids, is still a tricky channel; see Hobe Kytr, "The Lady is Changeable. Catch Her When She is Angry," Sea History, No. 61 (Spring 1992), 46.

JOHN JACOB ASTOR, BY GILBERT STUART. OIL, 29 × 24″. PRIVATE
COLLECTION. COURTESY OF THE FRICK ART REFERENCE LIBRARY.
NEGATIVE NUMBER 362.

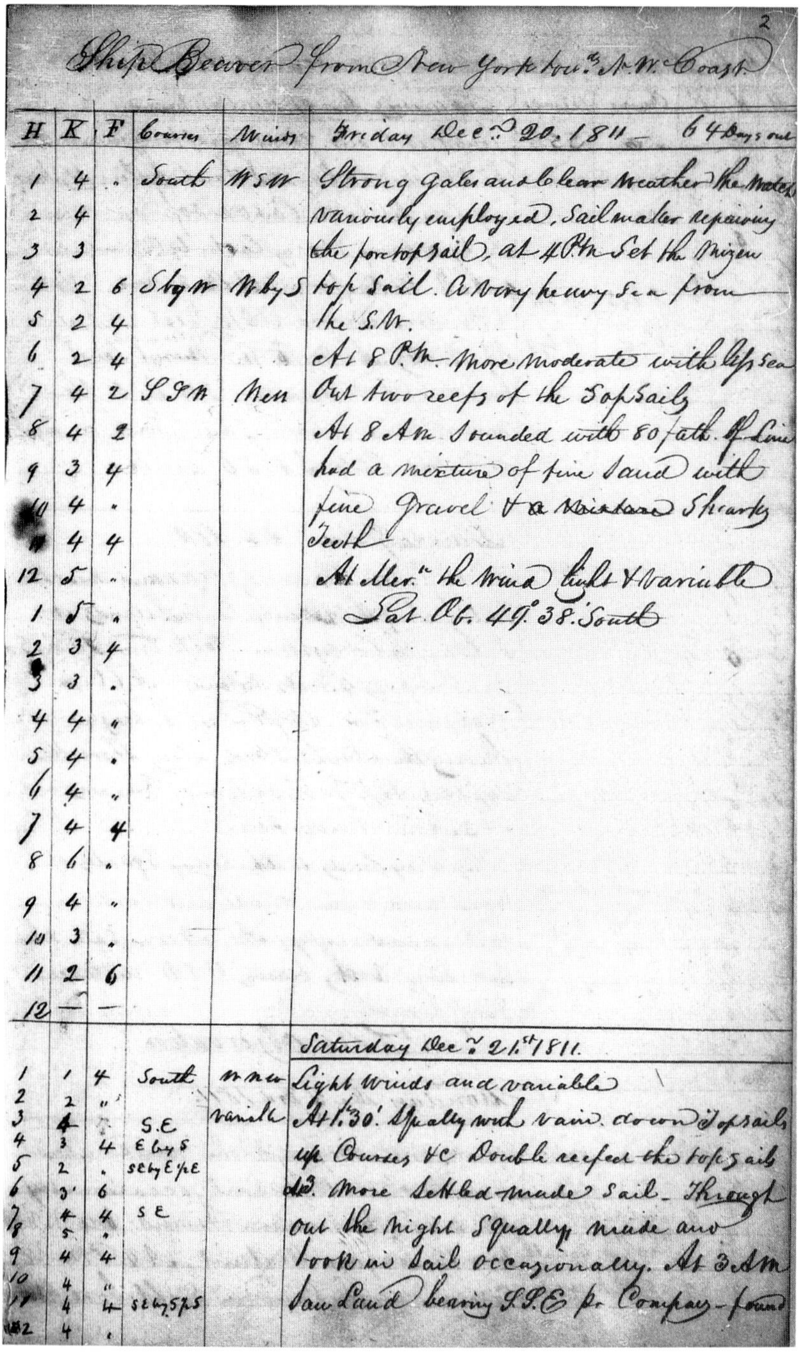

Page 1

Journal of a voyage to Columbia River on the North West coast of America made by Alfred Seton on board the Ship Beaver, Cornelius Sowle, master.

It is the intention of the Writer of the following pages to note down the little occurrences that happened to himself & his companions during the voyage alluded to above, & to state the object, pursuits of it, & the causes that induced him undertake it, with the hope that (if it shou[ld] please Providence to permit his return future day in the Bosom of his friends & [he may] peruse these line) I call to mind [the] sensations he then experienced — — The ob[ject] our voyage to so remote [a part] of the World is to a[cquire] trade with the natives. = my [   ] was formed [   ] To [   ]

OPENING PAGE OF SETON'S JOURNAL. COURTESY OF ROCKEFELLER ARCHIVES, POCANTICO HILLS, NEW YORK.

THE *BEAVER*, BY ISAAC POWER, 1840. WATERCOLOR ON PAPER, 18¼ × 25". PHOTOGRAPHY BY OZZIE SWEET. PRIVATE COLLECTION.

The Hawaiian scene and people, watercolors by a Russian visitor, Louis Choris, 1816. Courtesy of Honolulu Academy of Arts. Gift of Honolulu Art Society, 1944. L'Interieur d'une Maison d'un chef aux Iles Sandwich. Watercolor on paper, 10¾ × 7″. Tammeamea, Roi des Iles Sandwich (Kamehameha I). Watercolor on paper, 3½ × 5′. Port d'Honarourou, sur l'Ile de Vahou (Iles Sandwich). Watercolor and graphite on paper. 6⅛ × 17¾″.

ATTACK AND MASSACRE OF CREW OF SHIP TONQUIN BY THE SAVAGES OF THE NW. COAST

Maverick Lith. NY

DESTRUCTION OF THE *TONQUIN*, FROM EDWARD FANNING'S *VOYAGE TO THE SOUTH SEAS, THE PACIFIC OCEAN, AND THE NORTHWEST COAST*. NEW YORK, 1838.

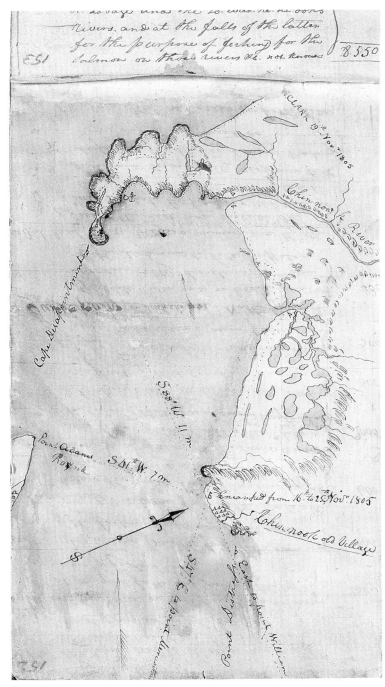

WILLIAM CLARK'S MAP OF THE MOUTH OF THE COLUMBIA, C. 1806.
COURTESY OF THE AMERICAN PHILOSOPHICAL SOCIETY LIBRARY,
PHILADELPHIA. NEG. NUMBER 913.

VIEW OF FORT ASTORIA, FROM *WEST SHORE MAGAZINE*, FEBRUARY 22, 1890. OREGON HIS-
TORICAL SOCIETY, #ORHI 691.

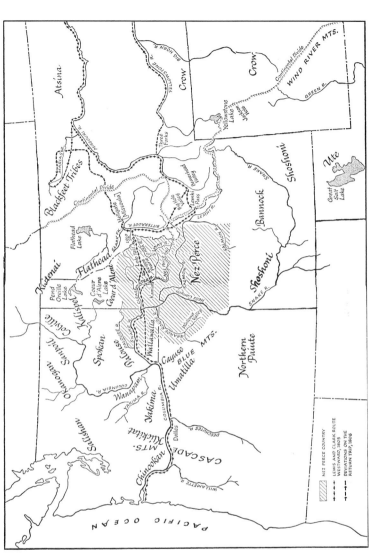

THE NORTHWEST AT THE TIME OF LEWIS AND CLARK, 1805–1806, FROM ALVIN M. JOSEPHY, JR., *THE NEZ PERCE INDIANS AND THE OPENING OF THE NORTHWEST*. NEW HAVEN: YALE UNIVERSITY PRESS, 1965. REPRINTED WITH PERMISSION OF ALVIN M. JOSEPHY, JR.

Count Alexander Baranov. Oregon Historical Society, #OrHi 35410.

View of Sitka, from George H. Langsdorff's *Voyage and Travels in Various Parts of the World, during the Years 1803, 1804, 1805, 1806, and 1807.* London: Colbern, 1813–1814.

WILSON PRICE HUNT, BY O. L. ERICKSON. PASTEL ON CANVAS.
COURTESY OF THE MISSOURI HISTORICAL SOCIETY. NEGATIVE
NUMBER POR-H-87B.

Astoria
9 May 1812 —
25 August 1813

Wollamut river in the interior of North West America (about 100 miles from Pacific Ocean) July 28th 1813.[1]

Fifteen months now have glided away since I first set foot in this miserable country, in which time I have passed through many different scenes. As Hope flatters me that one day or another I may again visit my Native home, and as a Journal of these occurrences may be then some amusement to me, I have resolved to spend an Hour or two daily to recall to my recollection the events of this time, in the order that they happened, commencing from my first debarkation from on board to [the] present time, & continuing it, until [my] arr[iv]al at New York if I am ever destined to reach that Happy Place.

To commence then where I ceased on the opposite [Page:] In the afternoon of May 9th, 1812 when . . . Wind little. Mr. McDougall, and myself [crossed out: embarked] left the ship in Mr. McD's boat,[2] on our way to the Fort (or as it is called Astoria, (from Mr. John Jacob Astor, the Principal person in this company) which is situated about fifteen miles up the river. We arrived there after dark, & were introduced to Mr. Hunt and Messrs. Franchere, Pillet, & Wallace,[3] clerks to the company.

---

[1] The Willamette River. On several previous occasions, Seton had abandoned daily entries in his journal in favor of retrospective ones covering extended periods of time. For these he obviously had some kind of notes; see, for example, April 9, 1812 (p. 79). Here he goes far beyond anything he had previously done of this sort, abandoning the journal for fifteen months, May 1812 to July 1813. He began writing on July 28th, but did not finish until August 25th. This was a consequential time in the history of Astoria and the Astorians, and one wishes he had kept a contemporaneous record. When he was absent from Astoria, trading in the interior, he preferred to leave his journal safely back at the fort, making rough notes on whatever scraps came to hand; see, for example, September 24, 1813 (p. 125). Still, when he did write it up, he kept his journal in a standard format and resisted the attempt to put in any obvious hindsight. There are no "had I but known" soliloquies here. And the accounts of most events are quite circumstantial, attesting both to rough notes of his own and to company records which would have been available to him as a clerk.

[2] Clarke, Ehninger, and Seton were the first to come ashore from the *Beaver*, according to Franchère, who gives the date as May 10. *Voyage*, p. 112.

[3] Wilson Price Hunt was the partner in charge at Astoria and the person who had led the overland party from St. Louis. Gabriel Franchère, Francis P. Pillet, and William Wallace, all had come out on the *Tonquin*. Irving, *Astoria* (Todd), p. 41n. Pillet is better known in the chronicles of the Northwest as B. C. Payette,

I delivered my letters to Mr. H. & was received by him in a polite manner. After reading them, he told me that in a few days he would have a particular conversation with me.

The next morning when I rose, I found the Fort was situated on a rising bank of the river in a thick wooded country of pines, Spruce, [He]mlocks &c., that it was a square of 80 or [90] feet [pic]keted in by pickets of 12 or 14 feet high on the opposite corners of which were two Bas[tio]ns of 2 stories high each of which had 3 or 4 swivel [guns]. A Dwelling house built of [squared logs formed one] side of the Fort, & the . . . [cor]ner opposite to it, formed another, the other two sides as I have said before were formed by Pickets.[4] The ground between the Fort & the river was cleared off & fenced round, near the centre of which was a platform on which were mounted 4 Six-pound Guns, & a Flag staff where the American Flag was displayed to the Savages around. On the other sides of the Factory the woods were still thick, but the Hands were daily employed in clearing it.

The river here is about 6 miles wide, on the opposite side of it to the Fort are two villages of Indians. Chinooks[5] [as] they call themselves, these have never as yet attempted to kill white men, but

---

who left his name on a number of locations in the present state of Idaho. He left behind miscellaneous records of his own and others' adventures in *The Oregon Country Under the Union Jack* . . . (Montreal: Payette Radio, 1961) and *The Oregon Country Under the Union Jack — Postscript Edition* (Montreal: Payette Radio, 1962), largely unedited and repetitive; the latter will hereafter be cited as Payette, *Postscript*.

[4] In the missing matter, Seton probably observed that a dwelling house formed another side of the fort.

[5] Chinooks were a tribe that lived on the north side of the mouth of the Columbia and along the coast into southern Washington. Parts of their language became the foundation for Chinook Jargon, a trading language used in the Northwest, and their tribal name was used for a warm Pacific wind, a climatic feature of the area. Duncan McDougall, one of the Astor partners, married the daughter of Comcomly, the area Chinook chief, in an effort to bring stability to Indian-white relations at Astoria; see below, p. 116. See also Robert H. Ruby, John A. Brown, *A Guide to the Indian Tribes of the Pacific Northwest* (Norman: University of Oklahoma Press, 1986), pp. 23–25 (hereafter, Ruby, Brown, *Guide*), and Ronda, *Astoria*, p. 295.

from some suspicious circumstances that happened in the course of last year, the party are much on their guard against them.[6] About ten miles down towards the sea on [the] same side of the river as the establishment [i]s is another village who call themselves Clatsops.[7] These Indians are likewise as suspicious as the Chinooks. They both trade considerable Fur with . . . on the sea coast t[o] the Southward & . . . the river here. Two nations of daring . . . the Southward who are . . . close friendship with the Clatsops & also trade some furs with the Fort. Those t[o] the Northward (Chehelis by name[8]) intermarry with the Chinooks & [crossed out: are] very much resemble them in appearance. These make an annual visit to the Columbia, & stay during the Salmon season, say from the beginning of July to the latter end of August. These latter are a daring villanous band, & have already cut off several vessels, who came in their harbours to trade, during their visit to this river. They at this place always keep a strict guard night & Day & allow only a certain number to enter within the pickets. Above the Fort on both sides of the river are numerous villages & tribes, some good, but mostly bad. They all furnish the Co. with more or less Fur.

The Face of the Country from the Fort is very rugged & wild, thickly covered with Hemlock & Spruce, whose dreary & savage appearance see[ms] well to suit with its naked Inhabitants.

[In the cou]rse of the conversation that passed . . . among us I learned the . . . the Fate of the Tonquin. She left this river on the first of June 1811 on her way to the northward. She stopped in one or two harbours close to the river, from one of these an Indian was persuaded to embark as a guide & Interpreter.[9]

---

[6] See Franchère, *Voyage*, p. 88, for this episode; the feared attack never came.

[7] Clatsops were a tribe that lived on the south shore of the Columbia River and along the coast south of that river. Lewis and Clark wintered among them in 1805–1806 at a post they called Fort Clatsop. Ruby, Brown, *Guide*, pp. 30–31; and James P. Ronda, *Lewis and Clark Among the Indians* (Lincoln: University of Nebraska Press, 1984), chap. 8, "The Clatsop Winter," passim.

[8] The Lower Chehalis were a tribe that lived along the coast of central Washington, around Gray's Harbor and Point Chehalis; see also "the Confederated Tribes of the Chehalis Reservation." Ruby, Brown, *Guide*, pp. 105–106.

[9] Washington Irving's account of the *Tonquin* disaster is on pages 72–78 of *Astoria*; see Ronda, *Astoria*, pp. 235–37, for a brief modern treatment. Wayne

This is the only person who has escaped to tell the melancholy tale, which he recounts nearly as follows.

The ship entered a Harbour to the Northward, called Wiccanninish,[10] where the Captn.[11] much against the advice of the Indian cast anchor; Mr. McKay[12] went on shore here to Smoke with the Indians, but took the precaution to detain several on board ship as hostages for his return, during his absence the Indians brought on board the[ir] skins to trade. Capt. Thorn could not agree with them about the price, in the course of talking abou[t] it, one of them so much enraged th[e] Captn. that he rubbed the skin in his face & turned him out of the ship. This unfortunately was a considerable chief, who with his people instan[tly] left the ship. When Mr. McK came on board [that] [eve]ning, the Indian told him what had [happened]. . . . the place immediately, he says he observed Mr. McK & the Captn. in conversation & that the latter appeared to be ridiculing Mr. McK for his fears. The next morning the Indians came on board in great numbers, apparently very friendly, bringing their skins to trade. It was then our Indian says, that he saw their plot was agreed upon & told Mr. McK.

So Mr. McK again spoke to the Captn. who at this time appears to have thought that there was some danger. The men were instantly ordered aloft to loose the Topsails & to man the windlass. The anchor was so near up that it could be seen from Deck, when the Indians, who during this time had been trading their skins at the Captns. own prices, viz a blanket & a Knife [ea]ch, suddenly made the signal of attack by [s]tabbing through the back Mr. Lewis[13]

R. Kime in "Seton's Journal: . . . Source for Irving's *Tonquin* . . . Account," demonstrates Irving's reliance on Seton as a major source for his history. He also assesses the reliability of the other Astorians' treatments.

[10] Clayoquot Sound, on the west coast of Vancouver Island. As noted above, Seton had learned of the *Tonquin* disaster while in Hawaii, where he was told that the site was "Wiccinnish." This is actually the name of the Indian chief of the area, Wicananish, a man with a reputation for a short temper, possibly inherited from his father, who had the same name and the same reputation. Seton's record of Wicananish's connection with the *Tonquin* incident is one of the earliest and most reliable pieces of evidence that the site of the explosion was Clayoquot Sound, and not Nootka Sound; see p. 72n26.

[11] Jonathan Thorn.

[12] Alexander McKay, one of the company partners.

[13] James Lewis, a clerk.

who was leaning over a bale of Blankets trading with them. At the same instant, Mr. McKay who was sitting on the [taff]erel rail was stabbed & thrown [over]board [back]wards into a canoe, where the [women]. . . .[14] Capt. Thorn who was . . . was attacked, who so bravely defended himself with only his pocket Knife, that he killed four Indians, among whom was the chief, the ringleader of the disturbance. At this time, when he had nearly reached the Cabin door he was stabbed from behind, & fell dead upon the spot; the sailors were most of them killed as they descended from the yards. Some few of them reached the Cabin, where they fired upon the Indians & prevented them coming down. They then got up some Gun powder between decks, set a match[15] to it, & also a slow one to the magasine. Immediately before the first took fire, they hauled the boat which was towing astern, to the cabin windows, embarked & set sail. The upper deck blew off & mangled & tore a great many Indians. The Principal body of the [na]tives supposing now that the ship was in their power, gathered around it in crowds of canoes, endeavouring to extinguish the fire, by throwing water upon it with their paddles, when with [a] horrible crash the magasine took, & [threw] the canoes, & Indians, in the air.

190 of them . . . vengeance for the loss of. . . . The boats crew was killed by the third nation to the Southward of the Wiccinninish, on its way to the Columbia.

The Indian who tells this story was in the mizen chains at the commencement of the fray, & staid there untill the upper deck was blown off when he was thrown into the water, & swam ashore. Amidst the confusion he was taken for one of their tribe & by this means escaped through the woods to his own village, where he was induced by the promises of Mr. McDougall to come here & give us the account.[16]

---

[14] Franchère writes that McKay was killed by Indian women who were alongside in a canoe; Seton probably had that grisly detail in the missing line. *Voyage*, p. 126.

[15] A "fire match" or fuse.

[16] It should be emphasized that all the various versions of the *Tonquin* disaster which have come down to us rely on this one survivor's account. He is identified as George Ramsay, the son of a shipwrecked British sailor and a Chehalis woman, who went along as a guide and interpreter. He is frequently referred to as La-

It is as well to observe in this place that Capt. Thorn left this
river, without any of the Officers he had shipped in New York. Two
of them viz Mr. Fox & Ai[ki]ns[17] the 1st & 3d wer[e] drowned
in sounding the ch[an]nel of Columbia river, & the 2d Mr.
Mumford[18] preferred staying here untill another ship would come
out to going on the c[oast] in the Tonquin. This last Gentleman
. . . he has engaged as . . . Beaver.

I also learnt some particulars of Mr. Hunts voyage across the
Continent.[19] They embarked on Horseback at the Ree village on
the Missourri about 1300 miles from St. Louis, & came on without
any accidents over the Rocky Mountains, untill they fell on the
Head waters of the Columbia. Here all, tired with their long voyage on Horse back, cried out for canoes, & as the river[20] appeared
fine, they let their horses go, & set about building canoes, which
they accomplished after some labour. They came down with out any
obstructions several days, when they came to cut rocks, rapids &
falls, so bad that it was impossible to advance. Here then without
any provision, they were obliged to make cachés (hiding places) for
their goods & to divide the party, into three under Mr. Hunt, Mr.
McKenzie, & Mr. Croo[ks], who were to take different routs.[21]

Mr. McK's party arrived here in January last safe. For fourteen
days after leaving Mr. Hunt they . . . beaver skins; this with the
violent exercise . . . soon have made them give . . . they fell in with
a band of Horses, of which they eat a good many. This recruit
strengthened them a great deal. About 500 miles from this they
bought Canoes from the Indians & arrived here the middle of January.

Mr. Hunt's party arrived in February. They struck over the

---

masee because the Indians apparently had difficulty pronouncing the letter r. See
Franchère, *Voyage*, p. 124*n*1.

[17] Ebenezer D. Fox, Job Aikin.

[18] John M. Mumford.

[19] Irving took almost 200 pages to narrate the adventures and trials of the
overland Astorians. For a modern and more concise account, see Ronda, *Astoria*,
chaps. 6, 7, passim.

[20] Henry's Fork of the Snake River, near St. Anthony, Idaho.

[21] Donald McKenzie and Ramsay Crooks. At this point, the party was on the
Snake River, near Burley, in southern Idaho.

mountains to the left Hand of the Columbia each man with his load
on his back, up to his knees in snow, & eating not enough to support Nature. In this manner they arrived at the Scietogas,[22] a large
band of Indians inland about 300 miles from the sea, from whom
they procured Horses & a guide to the main Columbia, where they
got canoes for their horses, & reached this as before said.

Mr. Crooks whose party is small had not yet arrived.

Two or three days after this time the Party from the [inter]ior of
the Country some of whom had . . . to trade, & some to explore.
. . . The following Gentlemen . . . D. McKensie,[23] R. Stuart,
Ramsay Crooks, R. McClellan, proprietors of the Co. & Messrs.
Reed, Farnham, & Matthews, clerks.[24] Mr. David Stuart had been
absent since the first landing at Columbia River. He had established
a post for trading about 600 miles up the river, where there were
some beaver.[25] Mr. R. Stuart & Mr. McClellan had gone up in the
spring about two months before our arrival, with a supply of goods
for them.[26] They had unfortunately though been robbed by the Indians about 200 miles from here at a portage (carrying place) of the
river, where Mr. McC. had killed one Indian & badly wounded
another. The circumstances were as follows:[27]

---

[22] Sciatogas, a Cayuse tribe. Ruby, Brown, *Guide*, pp. 13–15.

[23] This latter party had left Astoria on March 30th; it consisted of three sub-
groups: one to supply David Stuart's post (see below), another to recover Hunt's
cache left along the Snake River, and a third to deliver dispatches to Astor by the
overland route. Seton went on to describe some of their subsequent adventures,
and Irving used him for some of the details in his chapter 41 of *Astoria*. The
major group returned to Astoria on May 11, 1812, just after the *Beaver*'s arrival.
See Ronda, *Astoria*, pp. 238–40.

[24] Donald McKenzie, Robert Stuart, Robert McClellan, John Reed, Russell
Farnham, and William Matthews.

[25] David Stuart (Robert Stuart's uncle) and a small party had left Astoria in
July 1811; his post was at the confluence of the Okanogan and the Columbia,
near present-day Brewster, Washington. Ronda, *Astoria*, p. 232.

[26] McClellan had quit the company, and he intended to return east with the
party which was carrying dispatches to Astor. Ibid., pp. 238–39.

[27] Seton's account, which depends entirely on hearsay, compresses a series of
exciting events too much for them to be appreciated fully; see Irving, *Astoria*,
pp. 247–50, for a more adequate treatment. See also Robert Stuart's "Travelling
Memoranda," in *The Discovery of the Oregon Trail: Robert Stuart's Narrative of
His Overland Trip Eastward from Astoria in 1812–13*, ed. Philip Ashton Rollins
(New York: Eberstadt, 1935), pp. 55–59.

The party under the command of Mr. Robt. Stuart consisting of 2 canoes & 14 men left this in March for the purpose above mentioned. They went on without any accident untill they reached the Falls of the river (200 miles from this) where they were obliged to carry goods, canoes, &c. They met here a strong camp of Indians. They allowed them to assist in carrying the goods upon their Horses. These rascals seeing so few men took the liberty to go off with . . . Horses loaded, & became also very impudent & inra[ged] . . . the whites. On that day they finished the . . . next morning they . . . [&] Mr. Farnham were at the far end the portage. The men were carrying their loads on their backs, nearly there, while Mr. McC. & Mr. Reed only remained at this end, with the canoes. Twenty or thirty Indians who were present began to be troublesome & endeavoured to break the canoes. This Mr. McC. & Mr. R. endeavoured to prevent [crossed out: them]. One rascal more impudent than the rest sprung at Mr. McC. endeavouring to cover his head with his robe, that he might stab him. Mr. McC. in jumping backwards jumped over a canoe, the Indian following him remained in it, when Mr. Mc.C. had only room to lift his rifle & shoot him through the heart. Mr. Reed who had a lock cover tied on his lock,[28] was knocked down with a war club, & his rifle & pistols taken away. [As] soon as Mr. McC. had killed the Indian he saw Mr. Reed was down & an Indian standing over [crossed out: t] him with his war club raised. He drew a pocket pistol & shot him.[29] When the other Indians saw two of their principal persons down, they run off. Mr. McC. with [an] empty gun, raised the war whoop & pur[sued them] untill they were far enough to allow . . . here a party of them . . . scene of action for the canoes and Mr. Reed. They carried them to the other end as quick as possible, & embarked. A large party of Indians followed & overtook them about ten miles further up the river. Here Mr. R. S. lashed his two canoes together & prepared to give them battle. The Indians sayed they would be satisfied if Mr. Reed was given up to them. This could not be thought of; they at last consented to make

---

[28] The flintlock on his gun.

[29] Irving credits Ben Jones, a hunter, with firing the shot that saved Reed. *Astoria*, p. 248.

peace if a certain Quantity of Goods were given them, which con-
sindering the weakness of his party, Mr. R. S. gave them.[30]
They arrived without further accident at Mr. David Stuart's
post, where they remained two or three days & set out again for
their return to the Fort, Mr. S. leaving inland two Clerks & some
men to [crossed out: guar] trade. Below the Forks of the Columbia
(300 miles from this)[31] they fell in with Mr. Crooks & John Day,
a Hunter both entirely naked. They had been robbed of every thing
they possessed a few days before by the Natives.

Of the three parties[32] that started at the head of this river, Mr.
Crook's had seen the most difficult times. It consisted of 4 Frenchmen, 1 American Hunter, & himself. His men reduced by the
excessive fatigue of crossing the mountains in two or three feet snow
& want of food were obliged to remain behind. Mr. C[rooks &]
John Day, the hunter, came on & fortunately fell . . . a good band
of Indians,[33] who received them kindly & killed a Horse for them
to eat, & gave them directions to find the Columbia, but told them
at the same time that its Inhabitants were a rascally band & would
in all probability murder & rob them. They proceeded and found
the river & had advanced down it one hundred miles to within 20
miles of the place where Mr. McC.[34] had killed the Indian. At this
place the Indians came to them in a friendly manner & brought
them to eat. Whilst they were eating, they sprung upon their guns,
& began immediately to strip them & soon left them with as little
clothing as they themselves had on. Mr. C. asked hard for a fire
steel,[35] but the Indians denied him any thing & told him instantly
to depart or they would kill him. They set off in this melancholy
plight on their way back to find the good Indians they had before
met with, & advanced 70 or 80 miles along the riv[er] when most

---

[30] Lost in all of this was the tin box containing the dispatches for Astor; deprived of this, Reed decided to return to Astoria.

[31] The confluence of the Snake and Columbia rivers.

[32] By this is meant the overland Astorians under Hunt, after they divided into
three parties near the end of their travels.

[33] Walla Wallas, known for their friendly relations with the whites and their
animosity toward tribes on the Columbia. Ruby, Brown, *Guide*, pp. 258–60.

[34] Robert McClellan.

[35] That is, Ramsay Crooks asked for a flint and steel.

luckily for them, on the very morning they were going to leave the river to go inland, Mr. Stuart's canoes hove in sight.[36]

Mr. McKenzies party had been up exploring a river [crossed out: about] that emptied [into] the Columbia about 80 miles from this. He aga[in] . . . 500 miles up it & speaks . . . of animals. As I am present up this very river, at some future time I shall give a more particular acct. of it.[37]

It is time now to say something about the report of Mr. Clark, concerning our different talents, dispositions, & conduct on board ship. At some time since while on board the Beaver, I prophecied that he [crossed out: will] would give a favourable account of us. I owe it to myself here to say that I was not mistaken; but there were many different grades of which Mr. Nicoll held the first, then Mr. Clapp. Messrs. Halsey, Cox & myself were nearly equal in our Colonel's opinion. Unfortunately for him, the Captns opinion was asked of our conduct on board. Three he praised viz Mr. Clapp, Halsey & myself, & the other two Mr. Nicoll & Cox were not spoken off by him in too favourable terms. A day or two after this the Captns opinion was confirmed by the conduct of Mr. N, who being discouraged by the hardness that the country presented, demande[d i]n rather a rude manner, leave to go in the ship.[38] After some days, [the] Gentlemen informed him, provided he would work his passage as a Common sailor he might go. This he accepted.

Mr. Hunt some day[s af]ter this called me aside, where I had a l[engthy] . . . with him. The subject substance of it was . . . that he had received strong letters of recommendation, in my favour,[39] that he would be happy to interest himself in my promot[i]on in this country, and that it would depend entirely upon my own conduct to merit this promotion. Also that as the head of this business

---

[36] Irving used some of Seton's words in narrating the adventure of Crooks and Day. *Astoria*, pp. 250–52.

[37] Seton's "particular acct." of the Willamette appears in the entry for August 26, 1813.

[38] The *Beaver*.

[39] These were the letters of recommendation which Seton had brought with him from New York; on July 28, 1813, he had written of delivering his letters to Hunt on his arrival at Astoria; see above, p. 90.

it behoved him to maintain a strict impartiality in his outward behaviour, & as it was generally known I had brought letters to him,
I must not be surprised at any outward mark of severity; that for
first year I would go inland under Mr. McKenzie, after that if the
business went as expected, he would find a situation for me. He
likewise mentioned to me the fault that Captn. Sowle & Mr. Clarke
found with me on board ship, which was my haughtiness of disposition. He explained to me that I ought to use my utmost endeavours
to rid myself of this vice in this country, or that it would acquire
me the dislike of the men &c. & that I would be placed [in] situations where address[40] must be used to get through.

He then pointed out the particular business of a Clerk which
was — to overlook & command the men, to [trad]e with the Indians, take charge of . . . , keep a particular acct. of every. . . . Also
as French was almost the . . . would do well to apply himself.[41]

Mr. N's[42] conduct was also mentioned. Mr. Hunt expressed his
disapprobation at it, & said that it did not look well in a Young
Man to be deterred by the difficuties of the country, from fullfilling
his engagement — & that if Mr. N had asked in a <u>decent</u> manner
for leave of return, that he could have returned in the <u>same</u> manner
he come out, viz — As a Gentleman in the cabin. But as he chose to
follow a different line of conduct, he has reaped the fruits of it.[43]

From this time untill the 1st. July[44] I was employed in writing
for the Co. My leisure moments were dedicated to my friends. As
there was an express going across the Continent, with information
to Mr. Astor, I obtained permission to write one letter by it. Owing
to the goodness of Mr. R Stuart, the Conductor of the express, I
was enabled to write to my different friends. He informed me pri-

---

[40] At this time, the word was often used to mean "tact," a quality Seton could
well afford to cultivate.

[41] Hunt probably pointed out to Seton that French was the lingua franca of
the fur trade and he would do well to learn it, advice he seems to have followed;
see below, pp. 108, 116, 126, 131, 135, 136–37, 141, 147.

[42] Charles Nicoll.

[43] On September 11, 1813, Seton confirmed that Nicoll was aboard the *Beaver*
when she left the Columbia on August 4, "from which he engaged as clerk on
board another ship." See below, p. 125.

[44] That is, July 1, 1812.

vately that he would take charge of [as] many letters as I chose to write. He took from me 5, viz 1 to my Father, 1 to Miss Sarah Hoffman, 1 to Jos. O. Hoffman, Esqr., 1 to Mr. Martin Hoffman, [&] 1 to Edwd. A. Seton.[45] I would have written more [bu]t my time absolutely would not permit.

Before my departure for the interior I paid . . . [vi]sit to the ship, where I was kindly received & treated with the greatest attention. Captn. S.[46] made me two or three little presents, of articles useful in this country, & wished me every success in my undertaking. I cannot leave this Gentleman or his Officers without paying a small tribute due to the treatment I received from them. While under their orders on board ship, it was generally kind & obliging, as much so as circumstances would permit. It will ever leave an impression on my mind.

On Monday Morning 29th June 1812, we left the Fort for the interior, in 10 canoes & 2 boats, viz [crossed out: the] Mr. David Stuart had 2 canoes loaded with articles suited to the Indians of his department,[47] Mr. Clark 1 boat & 5 canoes, going to oppose the NW Co.[48] who had establis[hed] the country on this side of the mountains, & Mr. McKenzie 1 boat & 2 canoes, bound to the Fork of the River[49] on which Lewis & Clark descend[ed] after crossing the Rocky Mountai[ns]. Our canoes were each manned with 3 canadia[ns] . . . Indians,[50] & instead of paddles customa[ry] . . . countries, we had oars.

---

[45] Sarah Hoffman was Seton's cousin and the current light of his life. Josiah Ogden Hoffman (1767–1837), a New York lawyer and political figure, and Martin Hoffman (1763–1828), a merchant of the city, were his mother's brothers, and may have given him some of the letters he gave Hunt. Edward A. Seton, previously identified, was Alfred's uncle also, but almost his age and seems to have been a special friend. Hoffman, *Hoffman Genealogy*, 12.

[46] Captain Cornelius Sowle.

[47] The post at the mouth of the Okanogan.

[48] Since 1807, David Thompson and other members of the North West Company, working out of Montreal, had been moving into present-day northwestern Montana, northern Idaho, and northeastern Washington, but they had not yet come down into the lower Columbia. It was Astor's intention that the Pacific Fur Company should block them from doing so; see Ronda, *Astoria*, pp. 21–24.

[49] Seton probably meant the confluence of the Clearwater and the Snake.

[50] Here Seton refers to the Hawaiians brought out by the *Beaver* and the *Tonquin*.

The first night we encamped around Tongue Point ten or twelve miles above the Fort. Captn. Sowle, Mr. Hunt & Mr. McDougall accompanied us thus far & passed the night with us. At day light next morning we bade them adieu, & continued our voyage up the Columbia & sun set again encamped. In this manner we travelled for seven days, untill we came to the rapids of the river where it was necessary to carry canoes, goods, &c.; this portage was about 2 miles & owing to delays by accident we were three or four days in passing it. Three days march above this we came to the Falls of the river, where there are two portages about 3 miles in lengths. It was at this place where Mr. R Stuart was robbed by the Indians. We passed them without any difficulty by keeping them at a distance & by a strict watch. A few days after this we fell in with the rascals who had robbed Mr. Crooks. We took them prisoners & kept them so untill they restored the guns & other property they had deprived them of.

By the 1st of August we . . . Wol[la] Wolla[51] river (300 miles from the sea). . . . canoe & took horses for his voyage across the continent.[52] We encamped with him two days prior to his departure. I who had been very unwell for the last fortnight, could not see him depart without regret. The little I had seen of this country had already made me most heartily sick of it, which, when circumstances are considered, need not much be wondered at. Brought up in a situation among friends where I enjoyed all the necessaries & most of the luxuries of life, I found myself suddenly transported to a wild Indian country, where every privation was to be endured & every Hardship unending one. From being accustomed to the society of friends & schoolfellows, I was transported among a set of mortals ignorant of their language, ways or manners, where unaccustomed as I was to act from myself I was obliged to make my way through them. When I mention a few of the hardships incident to the country & voyaging, it will easily be perceived how [hard] I found the change.

---

[51] The Walla Walla.

[52] Seton is referring to Robert Stuart, who set off with five men to take dispatches to Astor; his party reached St. Louis in April 1813. See Ronda, *Astoria*, pp. 240, 268–69.

In the . . . the dimness of the stars . . . of day, the general cry of Rise & embark arouses one from his bed, (if a couple of blankets can be so called) he embarks in his canoe & is there exposed to the weather, let it be what it may untill night. At the time I am now speaking of, it was excessively hot. I had never felt it so much so, not even under the Tropics.

After laying in canoe all day with the rays of the sun pouring down upon me, at night [crossed out: when] the first sand beach we come to, we encamp, that is we bring our blankets on shore & under the cano[py] of the [crossed out: Heavens] skies we lay down, our only food during the day Horse or Dog meat. I had heard of persons reduced by Hunger being obliged to eat their Horses or Dogs, but had never believed it would be a constant article of food untill my experience in this wretched country convinced me it was our only dependance, for from this time untill the middle of Jany. 1813, the constant & principal food of our party was Horseflesh.

To continue [our voyage,] Mr. Stuart embarked on Horseback . . . [on his] voyage across the country . . . led on to the Forks of the Columbia & there seperated. Mr. D Stuart, with his brigade went up the left hand Fork,[53] Mr. Clarke remained to trade Horses [crossed out: fit] to go to the NW posts, & our brigade took [crossed out: up] the right hand Fork. We parted in this manner for the year.

We went on for 15 or 16 days untill we came to the Forks of the Fork we were on. We there traded Horses & Mr. McKenzie dispatched Mr. Reed[54] & 4 men to look for the cachés the grand party[55] were obliged to make on their voyage across the continent. We kept up the left Hand fork, or the river that Lewis & Clark descended & in three or four days came to the Head of navigable

---

[53] As Seton notes, when the party reached the junction of the Snake and Columbia rivers, David Stuart took his party up the Columbia to the post at the Okanogan River; Clarke and his people went overland to compete with the North West Company among the Spokan, Coeur d'Alène, Flathead, Kutenai, and other interior tribes. Seton traveled with McKenzie up the Snake River, heading for the Clearwater and the Nez Perce. See Irving, *Astoria*, pp. 260–61.

[54] John Reed.

[55] Wilson Price Hunt and the overland Astorians.

water on this side of the Mountains & the place where L & C had built their c[an]oes.[56] We encamped in their encampment. Here Mr. McK with 4 men went up the river two days march to determine if it had more the appearance of a beaver country above, leaving me with . . . charge of the goods, &c. It . . . to reach this from the sea . . . be made with light canoes in half the time, by our rude calculation we make it Six hundred miles, the current very strong & the last three hundred miles interspersed with frequent rapids.

The face of the Country from the Sea to the Falls of the Columbia is thick woods of Hemlock, Spruce, Pine &c. From there to the spot where we are (about 400 miles) the country is plain, not a tree to be seen, a barren sandy desert producing a little wormwood, & in some places a few miserable tufts of grass—scarcely affording sustenance to the numerous herds of Horses that are every where to be seen, not the least appearance of [crossed out: a] beaver.[57]

The Indians all along the river numerous & powerful & very independent. From the falls to the Sea they are more stationary than above. They live in large lodges on the banks of the river & depending upon its produce for their support. Above the falls they also fish the salmon but do not always procure sufficient for their winter store. The deficiency they make up with H[unting gibi]er.[58]

---

[56] This is now part of the Nez Perce National Historic Park and is called Canoe Camp; it is opposite the mouth of the north fork of the Clearwater, near Ahaska, Idaho. Lewis and Clark camped there from September 26 to October 7, 1805, while they built canoes for the balance of their journey to the Pacific. See A. W. Thompson, "New Light on Donald McKenzie's Post on the Clearwater, 1812–1813," *Idaho Yesterdays*, 18, No. 3 (Fall 1974), 25.

[57] Wormwood is sagebrush. Seton did not get a very comprehensive view of the country from the vantage point of a canoe on the river and even contradicts himself somewhat. If the country was that miserable, what supported the "numerous herds of Horses" he saw? There was ample pasturage for the natives' herds and ample timber along the draws and streams that fed the rivers, as well as pine on the higher elevations. But it does not seem to have been good beaver country.

[58] Seton was very accurate here. Too many tribes to list lived along the river and ate not only the fish from it, but also wild herbs, roots, vegetables, and berries. Also, some Nez Perce went into western Montana to hunt buffalo. See Alvin M. Josephy, Jr., *The Nez Perce and the Opening of the Northwest* (New Haven: Yale University Press, 1965) pp. 18–19; hereafter, Josephy, *Nez Perce*.

When Mr. McKenzie returned . . . it necessary to remove further down . . . quarters, on account of provisions.

The country he had been through afforded no [crossed out: more] sign of Beaver, to which all our enquiries were directed, & as it was now found that we must lay aside hopes of getting beaver from this quarter, he thought it best to remove down to the Forks which is in the center of a numerous nation of Indians, from whom by chance we might now & then get a skin, & who abound in Horses which we now perceive must be our only Food.[59]

Accordingly we removed down and chose upon a spot about 5 miles above the Forks, on a Prairie where in the beginning of Septr. we commenced building with drift wood, as there was not a tree to be seen. In three weeks we had finished our buildings, which consisted of a store, a house for the men & one for Mr. McK & myself. The method of building was as follows. Logs were piled up about six feet high, fitted to each other in the ends. A ridge pole [was raised] about 4 feet above the square & the . . . these planks forming the [roof]. . . . [spa]ces filled up with mud—the chimneys in the center of the house built of mud.

Although this building might appear uncouth in the eyes of a man accustomed to view the works of mechanics, yet it fully answered our purpose & served as a shelter from winds & weather.[60]

The river that we are built upon is called by the Natives Shahaptin—from the nation[61] who live at the heads of it, at the scite of whose village Mr. McK. was. The river in which this empties itself is called Kamoenum, this latter name *Gass* in his journal gives correct,[62] he also calls it Lewis River from Captn. Lewis. The nation

---

[59] Seton described his (and McKenzie's) activities among the Nez Perce much more fully in two articles published in the *American Monthly Magazine*, May, July, 1835, signed only with the initial, "A." They are reprinted here as Appendix A. Fred Perrine identified the author as Seton and edited the articles in 1935. Alfred Seton, "Life on the Oregon," with introduction and notes by Fred S. Perrine, *Oregon Historical Quarterly*, 36, No. 2 (June 1935), 187–204.

[60] This was on the Clearwater, about five miles above where it empties into the Snake, near Hatwai Creek (present-day Lewiston, Idaho); Seton's is the first mention and the only detailed description of the post. See Thompson, *Idaho Yesterdays*, 26.

[61] The Nez Perce.

[62] Patrick Gass's journal, published in 1807, was the only one available when Seton was writing. He refers to the Snake as the Ki-mo-ee-nem. Ibid., p. 26.

that inhabit the Shahaptin river, are at present gone to war against the Blackfeet & to hunt the Buffaloe & will not return before the next spring.

The other nation that live upon the Kamoenum are called Tushep[ais]. This is a very powerful & warlike nation divided into many tribes under different chiefs, possessing almost innumerable Horses. With this latter tribe it was that we wintered, and we found them . . . troublesome set, little valuing or respec[ting] . . . . every opportunity in their power to steal & to give us trouble.[63]

Of their manners & customs I will not pretend to say much, leaving it to a more willing and able pen then mine, a few of the most striking of them I wall only observe. Contrary to the custom of most Indians, Female chastity is here regarded in a very particular manner, & the woman who breaks through its bounds is regarded in as disgraceful a light, as they are in most civilized countries. The dress of the Women is here, a leather petticoat from the neck to the ankles, which as completely veils their charms as the closest dress in our own country, & when handsomely ornamented with beads, shells, &c. is far from being an ungraceful habit. The common dress of the men is leggins of [d]ressed Deer skin & Buffaloe robes. In the beginning of the summer they are generally employed in war or hunting the Deer. They go to war against the Tuelicums or Snakes who inhabit fur[ther] . . . [the r]iver & are seperated from the[m] . . . ridge of mountains. Their arms (before white men [crossed out: were] introduced into the country, guns) were bow & arrows, the arrows pointed with a sharp flint stone in the shape of a diamond ◆. Most of their bows made of a Hard kind of wood & covered with a rattle snake skin (which abound in this country). There are some of them made of Horn which are much valued among them.[64] Among this nation a few of the [crossed out: Indians] Chiefs are only supplied with guns, but with the Shahaptins who war against the Blackfeet, they are common.

---

[63] Irving called them Tushepaws and copied Seton exactly in describing them as "a powerful and warlike nation, divided into many tribes, under different chiefs. . . ." *Astoria*, p. 316. They were actually part of the Nez Perce, and Sergeant Gass had found them "the most friendly, honest, and ingenuous" of all natives he had met; see Josephy, *Nez Perce*, p. 14.

[64] This is confirmed in Josephy, *Nez Perce*, p. 19.

The chiefs appear to possess their power from the number of Horses they have, & only exercise it in time of War. Like the Indians on the other side of the mountains they take the scalp of their enemy killed in battle, & according to the number of scalps in possession, so much is the Possessor respected.

When a chief dies they bury with him his principal articles of dress, arms, &c. & commonly stick a pole over his grave on the top of which is placed the most valuable article in their possession, there to remain untill it rots. They likewise . . . a number of horses to the manes of the decea[sed]. . . . [Of t]heir [re]ligion & objects of their worship I never could learn much, as they appear very shy of communicating any thing on that subject.

When we first went among these Indians a Horse could be procured for 40 or 50 loads ammunition, the price in a few months rose to blankets axes &c.

About the middle of October Mr. Reed arrived from his voyage to the Cachés. He was accompanied by 4 Frenchmen whom Mr. Crooks left in the mountains last year & who had made their way to the Snake nation, with whom they had passed the winter. Most of the caches had been found & destroyed by the Indians.

As the Indians had been telling us for some time past that white men were building houses two days journey off, Mr. McK sent me with four men in the latter end of this month[65] to ascertain who they were. Accordingly we started each one on Horseback with his blanket under him & two meals of dried salmon attached to his saddle, with an Indian for our guide. After [ridin]g hard all day, at night when I aske[d the gui]de what time the next day we . . . he informed me that I would have to ride three days in the same manner, before I would reach the spot. As we had only one meal of provision more, this was rather discouraging news.

We did not arrive at Mr. Clarke's who was the person alluded to by the Indians untill the third day from this, during which time we had nothing to eat, riding excessively hard all day, & at night when we camped rolling ourselves up in our blanket as close to the fire as we dared to approach — it was rather unpleasant travelling.

Mr. C. received me very kindly & treated me to the best his

---

[65] October 1812.

house afforded, which was but Horse. The NW Co. has had an establishmt. for trade here some years, & did not much like the idea of our opposing them.[66] They get their goods from the opposite side of the mountains, [crossed out: where] at the bottom of which they have a post, & they commonly reach this about the middle of November. It is a much better Beaver country than where we are, Mr. C. having already 14 or 15 packs.

I reached Home[67] again in the beginning of Novem[ber]. . . . [Mr.] Reed had started off with 4 men to live. . . . As affairs looked gloomy in our quarter—no Beaver, nor any to be expected, Horses rising so fast that we are in doubt whether our goods will hold out to spring[68]—Mr. McK. thought it best to go and consult Mr. Clarke himself. Accordingly he started, leaving me at the House in charge. During his absence several of our men whom we had sent in pursuit of their living[69] returned after having suffered extremely from the cold & hunger. Fearing that this might be the case with all, I dispatched an express immediately to Mr. McK. that he might make his arrangements accordingly. He returned a few days after 25th Novr. 1812. While at Mr. Clarkes the NW goods & traders had come in under the charge of Mr. McTavish.[70] This gentleman had been as far down as Lake Winnipeg where an an express had been sent him from the grand Portage[71] containing a declaration of War between the United States and G Britain. He showed James Maddisons proclomation dated June 19th 1812 to that effect. As thi[s news] must [crossed out: have] regulate in some mann[er the rel]ations of this Company it . . . [Mr. Mc]K. & Mr. Clarke that it should reach the Sea as soon as possible, also

---

[66] Clarke had planted himself at the confluence of the Spokane and Little Spokane rivers, near the North West Company's Spokane House, a few miles southeast of the site of modern Spokane. See Ronda, *Astoria*, p. 241.

[67] Seton had been away from New York a little too long; the "home" to which he referred was the camp on the Clearwater, not even Astoria.

[68] It had not taken the Indians long to pick up white business practices; they were charging ever higher trade goods prices for their horses.

[69] That is, trapping and hunting.

[70] John George McTavish.

[71] This was the North West Company post at the western end of Lake Superior, also known as Fort William, where the "wintering partners" worked.

as the N Westers had mentioned [crossed out: a report] that a ship would be at the mouth of the river in the Spring for them.⁷² It was concluded upon, that Mr. McKenzie should proceed to the sea with his party after he had sent his goods to Mr. Clarke. I was accordingly dispatched a second time with three men & thirteen horses loaded with merchandise (the beginning of December) but was not destined to reach that place. I fortunately took provision for ten days. At the first days march from the House it began to snow, we pushed on, untill it fell so thick that it compelled us to stop. At this encamppment, on the top of a mountain we were unable to stir backwards or forwards for thirteen days. It may easily be conceived in how unpleasant a situation we were. I was the [crossed out: the] only person of the party that had two blankets, with which we made a lodge to prevent the snow from coming in upon us, and all stowed together inside as close as we were able. On the 12th day it rained, when Mr. McK sent off to see if we had passed the mountain, which finding the impractibility at this season of the year, we loaded our [goods] & endeavoured to go back but found the Horses so wea[k from lack] of [past]ure that we were unable to proceed [on horseback] . . . and on a nipping morning set off to walk thirty miles in two feet snow. We reached the house an hour before sun set & dispatched fresh horses the next morning for the goods, which all reached the house in tolerable good order.

Seeing the impractibility of getting the property to Mr. Clarkes without detaining us too long time, we concluded to send our Horses there light & to cácher our goods. The Horses were accordingly sent by Mr. Clarkes men, who happened to be with us at the time. The 1st January⁷³ was the time fixed upon for starting to the sea. An express was sent off to Mr. Reed enjoining him to be at the house the 25th December. Some hunters whom we had in the mountains, hunting beaver, come in. The lakes & rivers had taken

---

⁷² This was the North West Company's *Isaac Todd*, twenty guns, reported to be sailing from London with letters of marque, permitting it to take Astoria as enemy property. Understandably, the Astorians were very concerned about it. Ronda, *Astoria*, p. 264. Irving drew upon this part of Seton's journal for his account of the effects of this news on the Pacific Company men. *Astoria*, pp. 342–44.

⁷³ That is, January 1, 1813.

with ice & they had been obliged to kill and eat their Horses. One of their party remained about 5 days march off with traps and a gun belonging to the [crossed out: party] Company and his companions said was not much inclined to a voyage to the sea. As this was a free man, I was sent to persuade him to accompany us. If he . . . not to take away his gun and traps. . . . on horseback with two . . . with his squaw with a strong band of Indians. After some little persuasion I prevailed upon him to accompany us.[74] The Indians that he was with, were a band of the Tushepas who in every respect ressembled their neighbours of the same nation.[75] The same rascally worthless behaviour, endeavouring to take our horses away from us, which when they found we would not put up with, they tried how far they could provoke us, which they so completely did that we knocked down one or two in the midst of the village. This made some talk among them, which observing, I went to the chief and told him the consequence if his men behaved again in a similar manner. He immediately got up & addressed them in our favour, when they became more quiet. I gave him then some tobacco & took my leave.

For three last days of this trip I had only one beaver tail for my share of the provision & walking two thirds of the time as we passed over mountains & precipices where I did not choose to risk my neck on horseback.

I reached the house 25th December and found all our party together. We must[ere]d counting every body 20 men 1 boy & 1 squaw. From [that] time till the 1st Jany. we were employed baling sep[erate] . . . putting them in cáche, and in the night of the last of December we dug holes inside of our houses under the floor & there put the goods, covered them up, and floored it the same as before. We remained here the next day & passed our New Year as jollily as was in our power. We had a famous horse pye & a couple of quarts of real Boston particular with which we regaled ourselves pas mal[76] as the Frenchmen say. In the evening we removed our

---

[74] The identity of this hunter is not known.

[75] By this, Seton meant the natives with whom he had wintered at the Clearwater post.

[76] "Not badly."

blankets about two hundred yards off, & after letting the dirt from the roof of the house fall upon the Floor, we set fire to the buildings in the hopes by these means the Indians would not discover our goods.

Early next morning which was cold & raw we embarked on board our canoes, on our voyage to the sea, the water being low the current was excessively strong & the rapids very dangerous. We passed all of them though without any accident [crossed out: difficulty] & reached the falls of the Columbia on the 7th day. We made [the] portage in very little time each man with his [pack]age on his back, his gun in his h[and,] . . . under the canoe.

Between the falls & the rapids of the Columbia we were wind bound five days, in the night of one of which, some Indians come into our camp and stole Mr. Reed's rifle and one of the men's gun, this was as daring an act of Indians as ever I heard of. It was a bright moon light night & if by any accident, a man had been [crossed out: a] awake, the Indian would have lost his life, but he succeeded in his roguery & our pursuit of him was in vain.

I cannot but mention the real hardship of this voyage, which was from cold. One can easily suppose how uncomfortable it must have been setting in a canoe from day light to sun set in the month of January in the high lat. we are in, where every drop of water from the paddles was ice in a moment & when at night we would put ashore to sleep, barely sufficient wood to cook our Kettle. I can say that from the first hour after embarking in the morning I had very little feeling in my hands or feet. Notwithstanding this cold & the hard work, our voyageurs would sing from morning to n[igh]t. We reached the Fort on the 17th Jany. to [the] great surprize off all hands within.[77]

Our . . . disappointment greater in finding that Mr. Hunt was absent from the place. He had embarked on board [crossed out: on] the Beaver in August last on her voyage along the coast to settle some affairs with the Russians, intending to be back here in the fall. Since that time . . . no news of any kind has reached the place concerning the Beaver, or her crew & we cannot but fear that she

[77] Both Franchère, *Voyage*, p. 117, and Ross, *Adventures*, p. 236, reported that McKenzie's party arrived on January 15, 1813.

has either experienced the same fate as the Tonquin, or suffered by shipwreck, which of these Fates she has met with, God knows, it is melancholy enough.[78] One cannot help here observing how unfortunate this company have been, loss of lives, and loss of property have generally been the consequences of its principal undertakings. This is the second vessel with its crew that has in all probability fallen a victim to the savage ferocity of the natives of this cursed country; and if we may be allowed to judge from experience, how very uncertain is our return from it. Whatever our destiny may be, it becomes us to act now with fortitude, trusting to that Providence who [orders] affairs here below, for the best.

Contrary to our expectation . . . both for Provision & goods, & as the account of a war did not allow us to hope for a vessel[79] in the Spring, all trade with the Natives was immediately stopped, & parties sent out different ways to look for their living. Among the rest Mr. Reed & myself were despatched on the first of Febuary in two canoes & 14 men to the river Wollamut, (a large river which puts in on the South side of the Columbia about 85 miles from the sea) we were supplied with traps for beaver & guns and ammunition. Up this river there was a party already for the same purpose, who had left the Fort in the fall under the charge of Messrs. Wallace & Halsey.[80]

---

[78] When Seton was writing this, in July–August 1813, in a cabin far up the Willamette, no news of the *Beaver* had yet come to him. It should be remembered that gaining a favorable trading arrangement with the Russians at Sitka was a vital ingredient in Astor's plans for the Pacific Fur Company. Accordingly, Hunt had taken the *Beaver* there in August 1812, intending to return in the fall. However, after it had been filled with skins, the vessel was badly damaged in a storm, and Hunt chose to sail to Hawaii; the voyage would be easier, and the vessel could be more readily repaired there. Once it had been repaired, Hunt ordered Captain Sowle to take the skins to Canton where they should find a good market. Hunt remained, waiting for the arrival of a supply ship from Astor. When the ship did not arrive, but news of the war did, in June 1813, Hunt cast about for a way of returning to the settlement. He finally arrived there in a chartered ship on August 20th. See Seton's entry below for September 11, 1813. Ronda, *Astoria*, pp. 242, 283–84.

[79] Seton means the yearly supply ship from New York which Astor, had his plan ever gone into full operation, was to send to the Northwest.

[80] Clerks William Wallace and John Halsey.

When I mention that from the month of October to the month of May, there is one continual sheet of rain in this country below the falls of the Columbia (which let those explain who are versed in such matters) & that we started upon this voyage with nothing to shelter us from the weather [crossed out: from] but our blankets, our situation may be supposed. In short the twentieth day after suffering from hunger, from fatigue & from weather, (4 nights of which by the neglect & shameful conduct of Mr. Reed myself & 2 others were . . . from the canoes, & suffered from every thing) we met . . . W & Halsey. They were situated in a part of the country, where game was tolerably plenty, had built themselves a small house to shelter them from the weather, & they had sent their party in different directions to trap beaver & get their living. We remained with them untill the middle of March, at which time our orders were to return to the Fort, which we accordingly obeyed & arrived a few days after.[81]

No change had taken place during our absence, no news of the Beaver or Mr. Hunt.

Mr. McDougall & Mr. McKenzie had come to a resolution, which circumstances rendered absolutely necessary, provided no ship came in the spring—to abandon the country immediately.[82] They wrote Messrs. Clarke & Stewart[83] above to that purpose, & Mr. McKenzie's party were to start on the first of April, to carry these despatches, & also a fresh supply of axes, knives, &c., which with the goods in our cáche at Shahaptin River were hoped would be sufficient to purchase a large stock of Horses.[84] We started accordingly the first April with two canoes & 20 men in the same

---

[81] According to Franchère, this was on March 20, 1813. *Voyage*, p. 118.

[82] Seton was putting this in before he forgot it, as this key decision had been reached in January, according to the other accounts, when McKenzie returned to Astoria. Franchère's is the fullest description: "We held . . . a sort of council of war, to which the clerks of the factory were invited *pro forma*, as they had no voice in the deliberations. Having maturely weighed our situation . . . we concluded to abandon the establishment in the ensuing spring, or, at latest, in the beginning of the summer." *Voyage*, p. 117. Seton presumably attended this council. See also Ronda, *Astoria*, pp. 264–65.

[83] David Stuart.

[84] Needed to carry the men and supplies on the projected evacuation overland.

manner that [we c]ame down. Above the [falls of] the Columbia w[e] met with Mr. McTavish and 2 canoes of NW. Co. on their way to the sea. We encamped with them for the night, & next morning each took our respective ways.[85]

On the 21st April we reached our wintering grounds & had there the extreme mortification of finding that our cachés had been lifted by the Indians & all our property stolen.[86] Mr. Reed with one man was immediately dispatched to Mr. Clark with the letters from Mr. McDougall & also the account of our loss.

The remainder of us 18 in number, were continually employed from this time untill the 1st June in endeavouring to get back our goods from the natives, in which service we were several times in dangerous and trying situations. Once we arrived at a large village of the Tushepas in which we understood was a considerable quantity of goods. As we put ashore we observed the men placed on the bank, with their guns in their hands & bullets in their mouths, & one of our [crossed out: the] men observing a sign among themselves as if they intended to shoot Mr. Mc.K, who with myself was advancing towards them [crossed out: selves], he instantly ordered the men to jump on shore with their g[uns] which they immediately did & going up to the Indians, demanded of them our property, of which they denied the p[ossession]. . . . [McKenzie] tol[d th]em that if they wished to fight, we were prepared for them, and that we would not stir from their village untill he got his property. Leaving me then to watch the Indians he went into every lodge himself, taking our property wherever it could be found, after which embarking it on board our canoes, we fired 4 or 5 guns to show in their own manner that we were not afraid & went & encamped about 2 miles off.[87]

---

[85] John George McTavish, with twenty men, was on the way to the mouth of the Columbia, to wait for the arrival of the North West Company ship, the *Isaac Todd*.

[86] In his 1835 essay, Seton claimed that they had expected to find the goods stolen; see Appendix A, p. 192.

[87] Alexander Ross described this action as "at the time considered the boldest step ever taken by the whites on Columbian ground." *Adventures*, p. 240. Seton's subsequent account confirms this. See Appendix A, pp. 194–95 and Seton's "Life on the Oregon" (Perrine, ed.), 201.

Another time a great war chief whom we distinguish by the name of Le Grand Coquin,[88] came to our camp under the pretence of being a great friend to us, & to better cover his bad intentions, he brought us considerable some trifling articles, promising to return next day with a greater quantity. Next day he did return, accompanied by his band of 60 men all armed with guns. He fortunately found with us a band of Scietogas,[89] whom he addressed in our very camp to join with him against us, & among other arguments, he made use of (which I understood perfectly myself[90]) that we were 18 men, that our [crossed out: camps] guns w[ere few], that we were situated in . . . without any cover and that they could soon rush upon us & destroy us. The old chief that was there answered in our favour, & positively denied having any thing to do with it. Le grand Coquin & his band went off with out taking any notice of us. He was no sooner gone than we fixed our bayonets on our guns & loading them with buckshot, explained to the Indians, that we were come among them to trade, not to fight, that they had at first stole our property, and that now we would recover by any means, where we could see it. They allowed the justness of this & after smoking with us, took their leave. As circumstances looked rather suspicious we removed our camp about 20 miles down the river on the opposite side where we remained untill the 1st June, continually upon our guard night and day.[91] As the Indians would not trade their Horses with us we were under the necessity of killing them, for provision. This displeased the Indians very much for we sometimes killed a favorite animal, but necessity has no law.

We started on 1st June on our way again to the Fort. . . . days

---

[88] This was a Nez Perce, or Tushepaw, chief, to whose village Seton had gone the previous December to search for a hunter; see above, p. 109.

[89] See above, note 22.

[90] This is one of the few occasions on which Seton refers directly to some of the woods lore and language which he had picked up and was daily using.

[91] Seton gave much more circumstantial accounts of both of these encounters in the 1835 *American Monthly Magazine* articles. He did not mention at all in the journal a third encounter (treated at length in 1835) in which he, McKenzie, and the company cook faced down a lodge-full of angry natives; see Appendix A, pp. 185–87. Irving followed closely Seton's 1835 treatment of this tense episode when he included it in *Astoria*, pp. 318–19.

march down the current, at a small river called by us Riviere au Pavion,[92] we met with Mr. Farnham[93] whom Mr. Clark had sent to get his canoes & boat in readiness by the time he would be there, which would be in two or three days. We kept on & encamped on the Wollawolla river below the Forks of the Columbia, where in a few days we were joined by both Messrs. Clarke & Stuart. These Gentlemen had both been in tolerable Beaver countries especially Mr. S. who brought down 70 packs & Mr. C. 40.

At the riviere au Pavion, since we passed there, Mr. C. had caused to be hung an Indian. The first night he arrived there his silver goblet & some other things were stolen from his tent. He made a great search for them the next day in vain. In the night expecting another visit, he set a watch, & caught an Indian in the fact, whom he made return the property he had stolen, & then much against the will of his party, he hung him. The Indians present begged for his life desiring he might be whipped or any thing done to him but taking away his life. Mr. Clarke was inexorable, [thou]gh at that very time [he] was obliged to [order] 2 men to take his Horses back to the house. The fate of Mr. McClellan who was one of these has not been yet heard of here. If he has escaped with his life, it is expected he will owe it to the swiftness of his horse.[94] This action[95] was very much blamed by the Company, & will no doubt in the end be productive of bad consequences, if we consider only the policy of the thing; but when humanity is considered, it is a dreadful crime & no doubt one of these days it will weigh heavy on the conscience of the actor.[96]

We reached the Fort 13th June, & there had our fears of the non arrival of a ship realized. Mr. McTavish with his party were encamped there, & were also disappointed in their vessel. Mr. McD[97]

---

[92] The Palouse River, which flows into the Snake, upriver from Ayer, Washington.

[93] Russell Farnham.

[94] This was probably Donald McLennan who did reach Clarke's Spokane River post safely.

[95] That is, the hanging of the Indian.

[96] Irving wrote that Stuart and McKenzie "strongly censured" Clarke's action, "as inhuman, unnecessary, and likely to provoke hostilities," which, for the next year, it did. *Astoria*, p. 322.

[97] That is, Duncan McDougall.

had before our arrival publickly given out that we would leave the sea on 1st July on our voyage across the continent. His disappointment was very great when he found that no arrangements had been entered into regarding Horses, & of course that our voyage must be deferred another year, arrangements for which purpose were immediately entered into. The small stock of goods were mostly laid aside [to buy] horses next spring, & an agreement was made with Mr. McTavish on the part of the NW Co. to prevent opposition . . . as nearly immaterial, where the different parties wintered, as each one would only have to procure a living for themselves.[98] Mr. McKenzie was appointed to the Wollamut & Messrs. Clarke & Stuart to their old posts above. On the 1st July Mr. Wallace & myself with some hunters & men were dispatched to Wollamut to kill & dry meat for a winter stock at the Fort. In this River tame Deer & Elk abound & hopes are entertained that a considerable quantity of meat may be procured. We commenced hunting 5th July & by the 4th August a canoe load of 33 Bales was got together, with which & 4 men I started to the Fort. Every thing there went on well owing to Mr. McDougall's marriage with Comcomoly's (Chinook chief) daughter.[99] On the 10th I started from the Fort again with 9 men with me & arrived here a few days afterwards. Since that time till this present, the 25th August 1813, I have employed myself in writing the foregoing pages.

I have thus . . . a short account of the various [ways] I spent the last 16 months of my life. I intend in future for my own satisfaction, to be more diffuse, to state my thoughts, & prospects of getting clear of the country to which at present all my views are bent.

I need not enter into an excuse for the bad spelling, frequent repetitions, & bad orthography of the foregoing lines. I trust that the person who reads them, will be a sufficient friend to me, to enter into my situation at the time of writing, which is exactly as follows; sitting under a tree, my wooden box for my escritoire, &

---

[98] McKenzie, McDougall, Stuart, and Clarke had agreed on June 25, 1813, to propose dividing the trade with the North West Company people for the coming winter. Ronda, *Astoria*, p. 281.

[99] McDougall regarded his marriage to Comcomly's daughter "as a high state alliance, and great stroke of policy," according to Irving, *Astoria*, p. 328.

being obliged at the same time to overlook a parcel of babbling frenchmen who are employed cutting up meat close to me, who interrupt me a thousand times a day for something or another. Added to this my being so much unaccustomed to Books of any kind for so long a time past, & universally babbling bad French from morning to night.

If therefore Mr. D M Hoffman, or you Mr. Ogden H or you my friend Olly, or you my [d]ear Edward, or you Mr. S. W. S. or in short any of my polished friends[100] . . . You should lay your fingers by any chance upon it . . . excuse it. I think that the writer of it is better fitted to face the storms of Nature, than to . . . at her Works.

---

[100] As previously identified, David Murray Hoffman and Ogden Hoffman were Seton's first cousins; Edward A. Seton and Samuel W. Seton ("S. W. S."), his uncles. Olly is not otherwise known.

Astoria
26 August 1813—
26 March 1814

Thursday 26th August 1813. Of the river Wollamut, on which I at present am, little is known. Mr. McKenzie was the first person of our party who explored & penetrated about 500 miles up it. Mr. Wallace this last spring went a few days march above this, in the mountains as far as was practicable to get a canoe along.[1] It no doubt rises in these mountains, which are a branch of the rocky Mountains that turns towards the sea coast after dividing the Snakes from the Tushepas on the Columbia.[2] From the forks of the Columbia the windings of this ridge are plainly to be seen, which tend towards the sea coast. It is from this [crossed out: that] I judge, that this must be the ridge from which this river takes its scource.

It winds very much & after running to the N. & Westward about 600 miles it falls into the Columbia [crossed out: about] 80 or 85 miles from the sea — the Lat. of its scource may be in abt. 40°N.

30 miles from its mouth the navigation is interrupted by Falls of about 30 feet, over which it is necessary to carry every thing. Above these the River abounds in beaver, & its banks with [crossed out: with] Elk, Deer & Bear; the latter of which are extremely ferocious & will almost universally attack a man.[3] The Face of the country is mountainous, interspersed though with beautiful [forests] . . . where oak, maple, ash, pine and cedar abound. Along the river are cotton wood bottoms, in which we chiefly find the elk, and in the hills and prairies the deer.[4] There are several small streams that put in on both sides of the river — 40 miles from the Falls there is one called by us Yellow river, that puts in from the westward, up which there are a band of Indians who call themselves Yumhéla, of these we know very little.[5]

---

[1] William Wallace was one of the Canadian clerks who came out to Astoria in the *Tonquin*. Irving, *Astoria* (Todd), p. 41*n*.

[2] Seton is correct about one thing; the Willamette rises in the Cascades, north of Crater Lake. However, that chain is not connected to the Rockies, although some other ranges, the Blues, for example, stretch across parts of eastern and central Oregon. Also, further down this page, he made the Willamette to be about twice as long as it actually is. Its source is about 43°40′N.

[3] Grizzly bears, at that time abundant throughout the West.

[4] Irving's description of the Willamette and the area it drains appears to depend heavily on Seton. *Astoria*, p. 316.

[5] These were Kalapuyan-speaking Yamel, usually corrupted to Yam Hill Indians; the Yellow River is now called the Yamhill. Ruby, Brown, *Guide*, pp. 274–75.

Up the main river there is a nation called Calipuyaws, which as far as we can judge are very numerous. They have not many articles of white men among them, are clothed in Deer skin robes, which, with their bows & arrows form all their riches; these are a miserable wandering set, always in small parties of 3 or 4, living upon roots & now & then an animal.[6]

If in the course of events, a settlement should be undertaken in this country; this river is (in my opinion) the most eligible place — as the land is good and spots large enough for farms, all ready cleared, are common, added to this the conveniency of it to the sea, from which the navigation for large vessels is good as far as the Falls. The Indians are peaceable & animals abound.[7] I know of no other place where. . . .

Sunday 29th.[8] A Beautiful clear day, with a serene sky, and gentle breeze. Such a day forcibly recalls to my recollection times of yore, when I used to mount my Horse in company with Edward or some other friend & gaily gallop to either my Uncle Ogden's & Uncle Martins or to my Aunt Farquhars . . . when there I used to be welcomed by the smiles of friendship & love, & pass my Sunday as happy as happy could be.[9]

What a contrast to the present time! In the wild woods in a savage country in a savage dress, [crossed out: surrounded] accompanied

---

[6] The Kalapuyas probably numbered about 3,000 around the present site of Eugene, along the McKenzie, and around the forks of the Willamette; they did not merit Seton's superficial judgment, as they gathered a satisfactory subsistence by taking advantage of natural, seasonal crops, and resources. They were part of the same tribe as the Yamel, mentioned above. Ibid., pp. 274–75.

[7] Seton could not have been more prophetic, and accurate. The Willamette became the first area in Oregon to be settled by Americans.

[8] August 29, 1813.

[9] Edward A. Seton has already been identified as Alfred's uncle (although very close in age) and good friend. Josiah Ogden Hoffman and Martin Hoffman were his mother's brothers. Aunt Farquhar was his grandmother's sister, Elizabeth Curzon Farquhar. At that time she lived outside the city proper on Stuyvesant Lane, a little east of present-day Washington Square. When Alfred was a teenager, his family lived successively on Greenwich Street, Pearl Street, and Cedar Street. Melville, *Seton*, p. 109; Pleasants, *Curzon Family*, pp. 46–47; Longworth's *City Directory*.

by Mortals but one degree above the brute creation, whose whims & fancies it is necessary to consult to lead any thing of a quiet life; where friendship & love are names never heard of, in short where one lives more like a Brute than a Christian, wandering about from place to place in search of a miserable existence.

In this manner do my days drag heavily on without profit to myself or to my employers;[10] the day will be happy when I leave for ever this country. Our Bourgeois have determined to leave the sea 1st April next on their way across the continent.[11] I cannot say how anxiously that time is looked for, how each day is counted as it brings us so much nearer the time.

Saturday — September 11th 1813 — River Wollamut.

Since my last date, some unexpected events have taken place. In the latter end of August, some Indians from the Big river[12] passed our Encampment & informed us that Mr. Hunt & a ship were at the Fort. We paid little attention to it, thinking that like most Indian reports it was only told to procure the narrator some tobacco &c. [crossed out: this] It was however repeated to us so often by different Indians, that I began to give some credit to it, and although contrary to the orders of Our Bourgeois I started off with three men in a small canoe to ascertain the truth. This was on Monday 6th.[13] We made the portage of the Falls that day & travelling nearly all night we met Mr. McKenzie the next day on a voyage up to trade salmon. From him I had the satisfaction of hearing of the safety of Mr. Hunt, who arrived in the mouth of the River on 26th August in the ship Albatross Captn. Smith from Sandwich Islands, where Mr. Hunt had passed the last year.[14] The Ship Beaver had

---

[10] The men with Seton were gathering food for Astoria.

[11] That is, not until 1814. For the best chance of good weather, an overland party would have to leave in spring or early summer. If they had been able to obtain sufficient horses, the partners probably would have left in the spring of 1813. Ronda, *Astoria*, p. 281.

[12] That is, the Columbia.

[13] September 6, 1813.

[14] Hunt actually arrived on August 20, according to Pacific Fur Company records; the commander of the vessel was William Smith. Irving, *Astoria* (Todd), pp. 463*n*, 472*n*.

made a good voyage, disposed of her cargo to the Russians, &
received Seal skins in payment, which she had arrived with in Canton to a good marke[t]. This business took so [much] time that it
was too late for the Ship to stop at the river & Mr. H. was accordingly left at the Islands. The news of the war had reached there by
a vessel from Canton, & was confirmed by the arrival of the Schooner Tamaamaah Captn. Porter from Boston who left America as
late as Feby. 1813.[15]

The Ship Albatross was hired by Mr. Hunt to land him at the
river which she accordingly did [crossed out: the]. On his understanding the situation of affairs, it was thought best for him to
proceed immediately to the Islands to purchase a vessel which was
there for sale, to embark the Owyhee Indians[16] & Beaver in her.
He after remaining only six days at Astoria went off again for this
purpose in the Ship. He took Mr. Clapp with him. Mr. McKenzie
is to start up to the Rocky Mountains to Mr. Clarkes & Mr.
Stuart's posts to get the Beaver & the Owyhee Indians. He sent me
back again to our [crossed out: the] Camp up Wollamut, which I
reached yesterday, with orders for all hands immediately to leave
the river & descend to the Fort. As the men are wanting to go with
him, this day we are making preparations & are to start to morrow.[17]

I understood from him, that had I been at the F[or]t, I would
have gone with Mr. Hunt. My unlucky planet was surely in full
[crossed out: inf] lustre when I missed this opportunity; yet it is
weakness to complain. Instead of passing my winter with him in a
mild climate, I am now in the beginning of winter to make a voyage

---

[15] The *Tamaahmaah* was an armed brig, chartered by Boston merchants to
protect their ships; it had letters of marque, permitting it to take enemy vessels.
The spelling was contemporary for King Kamehameha I. Ronda, *Astoria*, pp.
252, 292.

[16] The agreement with King Kamehameha for his peoples' employment re-
quired that the Company return them to the Islands when their time was com-
pleted. Franchère, *Voyage*, p. 70. See George Verne Blue, "A Hudson's Bay
Company Contract for Hawaiian Labor," *Oregon Historical Society*, 25, No. 1
(March 1924), 72–75, for a contract probably similar to the one the Pacific Fur
Company signed.

[17] That is, that Seton and the others on the Willamette were needed to go with
McKenzie to the posts of Clarke and Stuart.

to the Rocky Mountains, where with out any great foresight I can easily perceive that our situation will not be the most comfortable.

Of the Five Clerks that came out together in the Beaver — Halsey & myself are the only two that now remain. Nicoll as I have before said left the River in the Beaver, from which he engaged as clerk on board another ship. Cox engaged last spring to the NW Co.[18] & left Astoria in company with Mr. McTavish, & Clapp is now gone & is at liberty if he receives any offer that suits him to accept of it. Thus Halsey & myself are the only two that now remain, & in justice to my friend let me say that a better fellow never breathed. I have universally found him obliging in every dealing with him & I believe I can assert, that there is a sincere friendship between us.

Mr. McK also informed that Mr. Hunt had left a letter for me at the Fort, with some little presents that would be useful in this country. The content of this letter will be noticed at some fut[ure ti]me.

My hand and arm are so lazy from the work of the four last days that I can scarcely hold my pen & feel stupid, lazy, & weak. I have got now to make preparations for our voyage to morrow; when I arrive at the Fort I intend to notice events more particularrly.

Thursday[19] 24th Septr. 1813 Astoria.

I reached this place 10 or 12 days ago, & there received the letter of Mr. Hunts, in which there is nothing particular, only wishing me to go with Mr. McKenzie to the upper country, for which voyage I am accordingly making preparations. He intends starting in a few days with 12 men, as we have almost certain accounts here that there has been a party of our men cut off by the Natives above, & as we have to pass through them I am doubtful of some accident happening. In such a case as I leave my journal here, my friends will see how my time has been employed.

There is nothing doing here worth mentioning, every p[repa]ration tends to leaving the country, as Mr. Hunt will be

---

[18] The Astoria partners had decided the concern had more clerks than were required and had, on June 25, given Cox leave to sign on with their rivals. Irving, *Astoria* (Todd), p. 455n.

[19] Actually, Friday.

here in all Febuary next with a vessel. We have papers here from
the US. as late as Feby 1813, by which I see that War with all his
miseries is carried on there. Ye Gods! Can I express how anxiously
I look forward to the time when I shall receive some accounts from
home, it is now two years since I have seen or heard from my
friends. Whenever my thoughts wander on this subject I stifle them
as soon as possible, & endeavour to consider myself an isolated
being, without a Father, without Sisters, without a friend to attach
me to this world.

I did intend while here to notice some of the manners & customs
of the Indians about the place, but as I am continually occupied in
something or another, I have put it off, untill I come down again
in Feby when Dieu Merci[20] I shall have the happiness of seeing Mr.
Hunt.

Sunday October 10th 1813 — Astoria.

Here I am again after a weeks absence, miracula nunquam ces-
sabunt.[21] On Saturday 2d October we started off in two canoes and
12 men, on a voyage as we then supposed of five months. About
100 miles above this we were much surprised to meet a large brigade of 10 canoes of white men with the British colours flying. Mr.
McTavish of the NW Co. with 9 canoes was on his way to the sea
there to meet 2 ships, one of which the above Co. had sent out, &
the other a frigate to "destroy every thing American on the NW
Coast of America."[22] Mr. John Clarke of our Company was in the
10th canoe. As business of importance relative to our unfortunate
concern had brought Mr. Clarke from above, it was necessary that
Mr. McKenzie the leader of our brigade should also return. We
accordingly t[urned] about, & encamped that night with the Gens
du nord. Mr. McTavish with two canoes & Mr. McKenzie and
Mr. Clarke in one started off in the night time, leaving the remainder of the party behind.[23] 7 canoes of the NW have not as yet ar-

---

[20] "God willing."

[21] "Will wonders never cease."

[22] They were the North West Company's armed ship *Isaac Todd* and the Royal
Navy frigate *Phoebe*; see below, pp. 140–43, for more details.

[23] This was actually an attempt by McKenzie and Clarke to get away from the
North Westers and to warn the Pacific people at Astoria of the coming of both
the large force of Canadians and the two ships of the rival company. John G.

rived. We left them encamped about 70 miles above this place, waiting to hear of the arrangements entered into between the leaders of the respective parties. The British party consist of 2 Bourgeois, viz Messrs McTavish & Stuart & 7 clerks, viz Messrs McMullen, Bethune, Henry, Jos. McGillvery, McDonald, Montour & Cox & about 40 common men.[24] Their object in coming down is to establish the country, and to drive us out of it. This will not be very difficult to effect, as our business has already been given up these six months, and every arrangement since that time has tended to our leaving the country; they make their demands though with a high hand & certainly conduct themselves . . . in a haughty mann[er] at their camp at . . . distance [from] our Fort. They display 2 British colours, while on our side this is the first Sunday that our flag has not been displayed; it is indeed unfortunate that Mr. Hunt is absent. If present I am confident that our dignity would be kept up, until we were compelled to strike.[25] It does not become me to say much on this subject, as perhaps before long myself with the other Americans here will be prisoners of war or at rate will be obliged to pass through their territories to reach our homes. They are in daily expectation of their vessels. Accounts of their sailing from London 18 March last, are in their hands, & an extract of a Letter to that purpose from A. Shaw agent of the NW. Co. I have seen, where it mentions that their Frigate is "to destroy every thing American on the NW coast."[26]

McTavish was too alert for them, however, and accompanied them. Irving, *Astoria*, p. 342. *Gens du Nord*, literally, "Men of the North," is probably a reference to the North Westers.

[24] These men are fully identified in Irving, *Astoria* (Todd), and in Franchère; unless otherwise noted, the reference is to Irving: John Stuart, James McMullen (McMillan?), Angus Bethune (p. 481*n*), William Henry (Franchère, *Voyage*, p. 166*n*), Finan McDonald (p. 95*n*), and Nicholas Montour (p. 436*n*). Cox is Ross Cox, late of the Pacific Fur Company.

[25] Irving may have relied on Seton for his description of the anger of the American clerks at what Seton took to be the craven or perhaps treacherous attitude of the Pacific Fur Company partners then present at Astoria, most of whom were British subjects. *Astoria*, pp. 342–43.

[26] Seton is referring to a copy of Angus Shaw's letter which McDougall, McKenzie, and Clarke made on October 9; they, along with clerks Seton, Hal-

The arrangements have not as yet been settled. I have been though informed that the British will take possession of our territories, immediately, that the packs & goods will be sold them & that [any] of our people [might] enter into their service, & that the remainder with the Proprietors of our Company will have a passage through the NW posts to Canada, where they will receive passports to enable them to reach their respective homes; thus after all our labour, all our hardships, we return to our native homes in a far worse condition than we left them. When I reflect upon my once situation there, & my own preverseness, which in spite of the advice of my Father, I entered into this expedition, I almost think that I am rightly paid in suffering mortifications & disappointment as a punishment for not listening to the voice of a Parent. Reflections now are too late, our Company has failed in their object, & are at present weighed down by the want of support, & a superior force in their presence, who will no doubt act in a manner to show us, that what they agree to for our relief is only done through charity.

If though we were determined to keep our Fort, we could do it in spite of their Frigate & in spite of their men, for the [Frigate] cannot necessarily . . .[27] boats they could send, we could easily destroy them. But our <u>Chiefs</u> think the miseries of war are far enough extended already. We do not therefore hoist our flag, & no doubt in a few days we will see the British standard <u>adorn</u> our Staff—this is conformable to prudence & conformable to interest. We might indeed keep our situation untill supplies would arrive, but then that would offend the great NW Co., and God knows that the Great NW Co. are not to be offended with impunity. 20 men

---

sey, Franchère, and Wallace, signed the copy. In January 1818, Seton and Halsey deposed in New York City on the accuracy of a "true copy" of the Shaw letter "which Duncan McDougal had recorded in a book of the Pacific Fur Company for the purpose of Justifying him in transferring the property of said Company at Astoria to the North West Company. . . ." Their deposition, along with the bill of sale and inventory for Astoria, is included in *Message from the President of the United States . . . Relating to an Establishment Made at the Mouth of Columbia River*. Ronda, *Astoria*, p. 287.

[27] In the missing line, Seton probably questioned whether the British frigate could get over the troublesome bar at the mouth of the Columbia.

therefore under the guns of the Fort display the British colours while 60 men in a good fort surrounded with guns are fearful of offending these potent men, these men so celebrated in the annals of history, every individual of which is a hero equal to the greatest hero of antiquity. In short, these men so great so very, very, very great, that my feeble imagination cannot encompass epithets great enough to express. . . .[28]

River Wollamut, November 19th, 1813

Once more in this <u>paradise</u> again—in the River Wollamut, with a North West party, wandering about in the commencement of Winter without a shelter over our heads to protect us from the weather.

Since my last date the Pacific Fur Co.'s death warrant has been signed. Now that & all its possessions in this Country, belong to the NW Company, who have purchased them at a fair price.[29] Mr. McTavish remains at the Sea, at the Fort formerly called <u>Astoria</u>. Most of the men lately employed in our Concern have engaged to him. I know of no excep[tions] but Halsey & myself, who being Americans, & knowing well from good information the conduct of that Compy. never made application to engage. I would willingly push my fortune in Indian Countries if I saw any motive that would

---

[28] Irving certainly relied on Seton, especially the passage here, in writing that the "young men in the fort, natives of the United States . . . had been stung to the quick . . . by the vaunting airs assumed by the Northwesters. In this mood of mind, they would willingly have nailed their colors to the staff, and defied the frigate. She could not come within many miles of the fort, they observed, and any boats she might send could be destroyed by their cannon." *Astoria*, pp. 342–43.

[29] Seton witnessed the sale agreement, dated October 16, 1813. He later changed his mind as to the fairness of the price; see his entry for March 26, 1814, below, p. 149. For details of the sale, see Thompson C. Elliott, ed., "Sale of Astoria, 1813," *Oregon Historical Quarterly*, 33, No. 1 (March 1932), 43–50. Irving claimed (*Astoria*, p. 344) that the price paid was only about one-third the actual value of the furs and merchandise. His opinion on this was certainly shaped by Astor's judgment on "the supposed fraudulent above mentioned arrangement," as the latter described it to Secretary of State James Monroe on August 17, 1815. Porter, *Astor*, I, 585. See Ronda, *Astoria*, pp. 288–91, 298–301, for the most recent judgment.

authorize me to expect a reward suitable to the sacrifice. The NW Co. does not offer that recompense. After serving them 7 years in the Capacity of an Apprentice Clerk, I would get 100 £ & all . . . or $400 p annum with a further expectancy of being admitted to a share. There are so many Young Men who have already served them that time, & whose services are not rewarded & who in fact never expect to receive from them more than their salary (400$), already in the country, that I could not think of spending my days in a Savage Country for the prospects held out to me.

I therefore at present find myself in a Strange Country out of employ (For I was discharged from the late Pacific Fur Co. the 1st of this month[30]) and not exactly knowing when I shall leave it.

I cannot but think my situation hard. I embarked in this enterprise with ideas that good Conduct would secure my Fortune, & I have endeavoured to keep [crossed out: my] sight of my Interest in all transactions I have been in. At the end of two years I find all my prospects faded, my time lost, bad habits of indolence acquired by the manner of living, & what little I once knew almost eradicated from my mind; these evils I am sensible of myself, & no doubt they are many others visible [to] the eyes of my Enemies.

[My] views therefore as I embark to a civilized world, & although I am conscious that at first the habits of industry after so long a Sloth will be hard to acquire yet as I feel the conviction of their necessity I have confidence enough in myself to know I shall stick to them — & notwithstanding the time spent here has not been rewarded by the object that induced me to come, it still has not been entirely thrown away.

In N York I was acquiring habits of expence, which my Father's affairs did not justify, & which I believe would insensibly have got the better of me & perhaps at this time if I had there remained I would have found myself overwhelmed with debts, in bad Company, & with little hopes of raising myself to a respectable situation of life. When I [return I shall at least be free] from some of these evils, & I sincerely hope my own knowledge will keep me from the remainder added to these.

I feel that this Country has learned me more practical lessons in

---

[30] That is, November 1813.

the ways of Mankind than I would have acquired at home. For in our little society here I see the same selfishness govern every individual, as it does in the grande monde[31] and as we here meet all as strangers, with no one a friend to counsel him or direct his conduct, we each acquire a certain manner of acting from ourselves, & of course our experience in the Ways of Mankind, is greater that those who on every little occurrence have the advice & counsel of an more experienced head.

Wollamut, Saturday, 4th December 1813.

Lonesome & unemployed, I have set down to add a page or two to my journal, although nothing either very strange or unaccountable have I to relate.

About the 28th of November Mr. Wallace arrived at our Encampmt. from the Sea, with the news that two Canoes had arrived there from Fort William—containing two proprietors & a clerk of the North West Co., viz Messrs. Henry, Alexr. Stewart, & Keith.[32] They left that place the 10th July, & bring accounts from the Civilized World as late as the 20th June, which contain nothing interresting to me.

The War still continues & it appears with no great advantage on either side, although every circumstance we hear here, is through the voice of . . . of the action.[33] that have distinguished this war cannot be hoped for in this remote quarter—il importe peu.[34] In all probability it will not now be a long time before I approach nearer the scenes of action, as we expect to leave this by the middle

---

[31] That is, the "outside world," the "world at large."

[32] Alexander Henry, Alexander Stewart, and clerk James Keith got to Astoria on November 15, 1813. Franchère, *Voyage*, p. 131.

[33] At this point, three sheets have been deliberately cut out from the bound copybook Seton is using. He began this entry by remarking that he had "nothing either very strange or unaccountable" to write about, but he was certainly referring to events on the Columbia or Willamette, for, at the bottom of the page, he began to write about the course of the War of 1812, or as much as he knew of it. Perhaps he went on for the next six pages, both commenting on the war and speculating about its eventual outcome, and then thought better of it. He was now dependent on the British and Canadians of the North West Company and, believing prudence to be the better part of valor, destroyed the pages.

[34] "It matters little."

of March on our voyage across the continent. In the arrangements between the two Companies, a passage through the NW posts for those that wished to leave the Country was stipulated, & Halseys & my name were particularry mentioned. He in the mean time is kept by Mr. McDougall at the Fort, & I am sent off here, with Mr. Wm. Henry,[35] a clerk of the NW Co., merely as a looker on. Although this life is irksome & disagreeable to me still I prefer it a thousand times to living in the same house with Mr. Duncan McDougall, who is a compound of all the mean & petty passions that generally disgrace the lowest of animals, by allmost . . . [he has] had the principal hand in, I could make it clearly appear, that I do not assert a thing without proofs to confirm it. A man that would be capable of having a spy upon all the private actions & conversations of his fellow copartners & clerks, & implicitely confide in a boy who has proved to be a Liar & a Scoundrel (for such is Vero, Mr. McD's spy[36]) in any report he chose to make against a clerk, is certainly a very mean fellow!

A man that would so far condescend to [crossed out: endeavour] slander his absent partner & superior to one in a inferior capacity & under the orders of both, & so plainly as not to cover his maliciousness — is certainly guilty of not only great malice but of great foolishness, for how can he himself expect to be respected if he teaches one that is inferior to himself not to respect his Superior! To myself has he spoken against Mr. Hunt, & to Mr. Clapp has he shown his envy & malice a hundred different ways, against this g[entle]man.[37]

A Man who, in so remote a corner as this (where except the little supplies we get from vessels are obliged to live upon Fish) placed at the head of the depot where these supplies are kept, would be guilty of hiding away a certain quantity, so that it might be kept from his partners, & at the same time accept a share in the remainder, is certainly guilty of great injustice & selfishness!

This to the knowledge of every body that has been employed at

---

[35] William Henry was a cousin of the North West Company partner, Alexander Henry; Franchère, *Voyage*, p. 143n.

[36] This boy, not otherwise identified, may have been one of the Hawaiians.

[37] That is, Wilson Price Hunt.

the Fort, has frequently been done—& it was no later than the other
day when an Inventory was taken before the property was delivered
to the NW Co., that 30 galls. of Molasses and 9 of Gin were thus
discovered, which had so long been cáched that the honorable gentleman had entirely forgot them.[38]

I could bring forward many more mean & unjustified actions
which he has done. Witness his treatment of Mr. Clapp, his great
presents from the Company's pocket to Comcomoly—the Chinook
chief—which let h[im a]ccount for to those who has a right to
demand it.[39] The language . . . the Indians that he was a great chief
& we were all his slaves, only that some such as the clerks were
from their knowledge of writing his confidential ones.

I could fill a quire of paper if I chose to collect [crossed out: to
collect] every ungentlemanly action that has disgraced him since
being concerned in this company, & if in time to come any person
who has been employed in this concern, should by any accident
happen upon the foregoing lines, if he will lay his hand upon his
heart & speak the truth, I will defy him to contradict a syllable I
have uttered; I will only add that if this country had abounded in
beaver as much as any Country ever did, & if Duncan McDougall
had a principal hand in it, or if it was under his direction, I would
venture to say it never would have succeeded. I therefore consider
Mr. John Jacob Astor as very fortunate in getting rid of the business
with so little loss; & much more so in havg. Mr. D. McKenzie in
this country.[40]

Fort Calipuyaw—30 miles above the Falls of the Wollamut.
Wednesday 8th December.[41]

The party under Mr. Henry,[42] of which I am a member, reached

---

[38] Hunt found other discrepancies in McDougall's accounts when he returned
to Astoria in February 1814; see below, March 26, 1814, and Irving, *Astoria*,
p. 350.

[39] Comcomly was now, of course, McDougall's father-in-law; see above, p.
116.

[40] McDougall's role in the sale of Astoria has long been argued. Seton's is the
most critical of any of the Astorians. See Porter, *Astor*, I, 227–29 and Ronda,
Astoria, pp. 288–91, 298–301 for more sympathetic modern interpretations.

[41] December 8, 1813.

[42] William Henry.

this place, where Buildings are to be erected, on Monday, the 29th Novr. It consists of 29 men, Mr. H's woman & child, composed of divers nations, & languages—there are 6 Sandwich Islanders, 4 Iroquois, 1 Missawyi, 1 Nipesang, 16 Canadians, & 1 American (myself).

The Buildings were commenced on Wednesday 1st December. The Party are in the mean time encamped, some under Lodges and some in Tents, where from the rain that always pours down in torrents at this time, we are not most comfortably situated. Now at this present time of writing, I am setting in my tent, & using my Cassette, for a writing desk. Mr. Henry is trading some roots with the Calipuyaws along side of me, for Beads, who not thinking the quantity s[ufficien]t, are loudly asking for [more.] Ye Gods when am I to get rid of this disagreeable way of life—where

"My days lag tardily on leaden wings,
"And night no comfort, no refreshment brings.[43]

If I am ever destined to see my Friends and Country once more; Grant ye All Directing Powers, that I may have steadiness & sense enough, not to leave it for every wild & undigested enterprize that offers, and that I may keep the remembrance of this in my mind as a beacon to warn me of the rocks & shoals the common fruits of crude undertakings!

December 14[44] Tuesday.

Overcome by ennui & Idleness, tired of reading, & listening to the damned nonsense of my [crossed out: associate] Comrades, I seise my pen to vent my spleen upon this Faithful [record] of all this . . . and folly.

20th December Monday 1813.

I was interrupted in my rage by Mr. Henry, last Tuesday, with a demand, if I would go a hunting, which we accordingly did, & had the luck of killing some Gibier,[45] with which this place abounds especially Geese & Duck, the former of the Kind the Ca-

---

[43] Unidentified.
[44] December 14, 1813.
[45] "Game," especially waterfowl.

nadians call des Outards, & the latter Les Canards de France or
Tame Ducks. There are also some Swans, but they are so difficult
to approche that it is not often we have the fortune to get one, but
with geese & ducks, Beaver, Deer & Elk, we make out in the eating
way almost as well as an Indian Country can furnish.

Yesterday a Trapper of Beaver reached this place from above in
this river.[46] They were seven together, & since the beginning of
November they had taken about 7 pack of Beaver. The reason of
h[urry]ing down was on acct. of the Indians, who [had] behaved
to them. . . . & on one occasion when only three were together,
they had discharged their arrows upon them, but fortunately with
no damage to the Whites. Instead of resenting this, by laying the
Indians dead at their feet, they immediately pushed off in their
canoe, which when the Natives saw, they justly concluded the White
Men were afraid of them, & took their measures so, as to oblige
them to run about, en descendant as the Frenchmen say.[47]

One of them left this place this morning for the Ci devant[48]
Astoria, to ask more men. By him we had the Opportunity of writ-
ing & I demanded the news of Franchere & Halsey. I am very
much in hopes they will up an Acct. of a Ship's arrival, also of Mr.
Hunts, in which latter case in all probability, I should immediately
go to the sea. As I was never informed of my dismissal from this
Company, I desired Halsey to ask [Mr.] McD. from me, whether
I was to consider myself as yet under the orders of the late PF Co.,
informing him at the same time, from the two circumstances of
McD's not speaking to me on the subject, & of his sending me up
here to winter, that I considered myself still under the effects of my
Engagement untill I was notified by authority, that I was a free
Man.[49]

---

[46] That is, the Willamette.

[47] Literally, "while going down"; if there is an idiomatic meaning to the
phrase, it has escaped my research.

[48] That is, former, the post having been renamed Fort George by its new
owners.

[49] Here Seton is contradicting his previous statement (see above, p. 130) that
he had been discharged from the Pacific Fur Company as of November 1, 1813.
Perhaps he is simply venting his ill-humor and boredom on McDougall, whose
many shortcomings he has already described; see above, pp. 132–33.

We are still out of Doors yet in rainy stormy weather, & God knows when we shall get under a roof. I only say it requires a stout heart & a good pair of breeches to be so continually out in all kinds of weather.

Wednesday. 29th December, 1813.

On Christmas Eve we removed in the house which is built of Logs, squared on two side, & the crevices inside & out are filled up with mud. It is d[ivided] in two chambers, one of 20 feet by 18, the other 16 by 18, in each of which there is a mud chimney; & three windows covered with deer skins. In the smallest of these, Mr. Wallace & myself reside, Mr. Henry & his wife occupy the other. Thus am I situated at last for the Winter, which may a la Time quick roll away, & give us sweetly smiling Spring, with all its beauties, which will be ten times more Beautiful to me, as I shall then take my departure from this Country of Idleness & Folly.

The Third Christmas is now passed away since I left My Country & Friends. My first was on board the Beaver, the remembrance of which is as fresh as if it were Yesterday. It was a Boisterous stormy day, with an excessive high sea, & we were all confined to the little cabin, where there was neither Harmony or Concord. Last Christmas I was near the Rocky Mountains on the Shahaptin [River][50] with Mr. McKenzie, & to make a grand regal,[51] we had a pye of Horseflesh for our dinner. We were at that time busy in hiding our property, preparatory to going to the Sea, which we did, & which the Indians found. This present I passed in hunting Gibier up to my middle in water. It was a very rainy, stormy day, & passed away as dismal & as gloomy as our other days do.

In fact I cannot express how Ennuyant[52] (as our Frenchmen call it) it is at this place, how melancholy & slowly the Time lags on. Lying down on our backs with a pipe in our mouths listening to the rain as it pours upon the roof, consumes our days and nights. When we talk upon any subject we get entangled in endless disputes, each one fond of his own opinion, & each one tenacious of

---

[50] The Clearwater.
[51] That is, a "feast."
[52] That is, "vexing" or "annoying."

it, & although we are but three here, we can not always [live] in peace. I have read somewhere, "that when a dispute grows warm he is the wisest, who first gives up."[53] But I think it would provoke the patience of even cet honnete homme la[54] to be [in th]is Society, where some things contradictory [to] common sense are every hour advanced.

For myself I make it a rule not to be too tenacious when the dispute is a trifling, but when any thing touching either the late business I was in, or My Countrymen are brought forward in the course of conversation, not to recede one inch, for although I am an American & lately of the PF Co., still I think I am as good a Man as a Englishman or a North Wester. I must say though, that these conversations are not now much introduced, & I have met with more consideration on their part, than I expected.

I am the only American of the whole party here. Mr. Henry & Mr. Wal[lace] are both Canadians of English Parents, the former is a cousin [of] Henry's of Albany who are related to our family by marriage,[55] & of course knows the rank they hold in society in NY. He treats me with some attention, & as yet I have cause to be satisfied with the generality of his [conduct].

Saturday Morning Jany. 1st 1814.

What various reflections, does this day give rise to? The commencement of another year? or another year perhaps of misery & trouble! Perhaps the year that will lead me to my grave, the common receptacle of all. How does it then become me, since Time slips away so fast, & imperceptable, to endeavour by a just & steady conduct, to be prepared to meet my Fate, whenever it shall please the Ruler of all Events, to call me from this life—& if a longer space is allowed me here, to study to acquire the good will of Men & the approbation of my conscience & my God. When I reflect [crossed out: how] to what little purpose the last year has been

---

[53] Unidentified, although it is reminiscent of Benjamin Franklin's "Poor Richard" aphorisms.

[54] That is, the "most upright of men."

[55] Alfred's father's aunts, Isabella and Charlotte Seton, had both married into the Henry family of Albany; they were daughters of Andrew Seton, William's brother. Seton, *Old Family*, p. 287.

[spent], & of what little consequence my being has been to Society, I have much to grieve at, & much to alter my ways, to gain the approbation of my conscience, & to square my accounts on the commencement of another Year, if I ever live to see that day. But here in these wilds, depending upon the chase for my sustenance, & where the name of the Almighty is never mentioned, except for the purposes of blasphemy, I hope I may meet with some little allowance. A good poet & a pious man, Wm. Cowper, if I remember aright, in describing the various situations of man thus speaks of those, whose Fate have placed them in a situation similar to mine—

> The chase for sustenance, precarious trust,
> His hard condition with severe constraint
> Binds all his faculties, forbids all growth
> Of wisdom, proves a school in which he learns
> Sly circumvention, unrelenting hate,
> Mean self attachment, & scarce au[ght be]side.
> Thus fare the shiv'ring natives of the North,
> And thus the rangers of the Western World,
> Where it advances far into the deep,
> Towards th' Antartic.[56]

I sincerely hope that I am not altogether as bad as these lines say, but I have witnessed those, whose long residence in the Savage world have made them exactly what the Poet pourtrays, mean selfishness, low cunning, & hate without cause, form their distinguishing characteristics; [crossed out: of their character,] I am unable to say whether, they find the same evils in mine, of selfishness, the most prevalent vice, I will only say, that I endeavour to act with a proper regard to myself without forgetting the rights of others. Oh, if Man could only act as his conscience prompted him! how [happy] would we be. Peace & harmony would regulate his actions in this life, & the reward of good men in the other! But strong

---

[56] William Cowper, *The Task* (1785), Book I, "The Sofa," in Brian Spiller, ed., *Cowper: Verse and Letters* (Cambridge: Harvard University Press, 1968), p. 412. Seton's transcription has only minor errors and may have been made from one of several books of poetry in the small library shipped to Astoria aboard the *Beaver*. See Porter, *Astor*, I, 500–501, for a list of titles.

temptation throws out her lures, & unthinking M[an, in] spite of good resolutions, seizes them &. . . .

Divided from you my Dear Friends, by a long continent, yet on such a day as this, Fancy brings one in your presence, & I embrace you with a heart of joy & pleasure. I am happy to see you still well, & hope you may enjoy many returns of this day. To you My Honoroued Father, I hope the blessings of Content & the rewards of Industry & Honesty may attend you always, & that the sigh caused by the ill conduct of your children, may never again affect your heart. You my Dear Sisters I kiss with the affection of a Brother, & sincerely hope your voyage through life may be attended by no boisterous gales or unpleasant weather, that prudence & virtue may be the compasses by which you direct all your actions, & that at last we may meet in that haven, "from whose bourn no traveller returns"![57] To my other Respected & loved Friends & Relativ[es I hope] . . . enjoy the rewards that their respective characters deserve, viz those of a good Husband & kind Father, of a tender & affectionate wife, & mother, of an obedient & dutiful son, & of a virtuous & prudent daughter! These are the characters which I have the honor to number among my relatives & friends, & these are the characters which I hope the next New Year will permit me to embrace more feelingly than the present.

To descend from the visions of imagination which conduct me where I would wish to be, I must now state how this day is spent [crossed out: is] here.

Before day light your men awaken you by a discharge of Fire Arms, & with the cry of bon anneé,[58] which, when Rum is to be had, is the signal that they expect it. You receive them [i]nto your house, & treat them with the best it affords; they then get their regál of Flour & Rum, & pass the day as merrily as these two articles can make them, which [is] as happy as they are capable of being, as the B[elly o]f a Canadian is his God.

In the evening, if they are not too much overcome by the liquor, all hands dance four handed reels or play some rough game, in

[57] *Hamlet*, III.i.32–33.
[58] "Happy New Year!"

which alertness & strength are necessary. As we have no rum at this place, the day will pass without much noise or trouble.

I [crossed out: was] am here interrupted by the arrival of some Indians from below who bring us accounts of 2 ships being at the Fort, & explain their story in so clear a manner, as leaves us no room to doubt it. This makes so much talk & stir among us, gives rise to so many surmises & opinions of what they are, or who for, that it is impossible for me to continue. They also mention a report of the two ships having an engagement, in which one had [te]n men killed & of the other standing out to s[ea].

All is anxiety here for letters from the sea, which in all probability will be received in the course of next week. In the mean time our days drag on ten times more heavily, on [account] of the desire & expectation this imperfect account puts us into. That there are ships & some extraordinary accident has happened, at the Fort, I have little doubt of, but what it is, or who they are, we as yet know nothing.

Tuesday 4th Jany.[59] Reports about the ships at the entrance of the river, thicken upon us every day. On Monday Evening an Intelligent Savage from the Falls,[60] gave us the following account, that the ship outside of the Bar had chased in the river the small vessel, firing upon it the whole time, that the small vessel was in such haste that she run through the Break[ers] without choosing the channel, when she was anchored, that a canoe from the Fort going to board her was fired upon (by the [small vess]el) & had 9 common men killed & one chief.

I cannot express the anxiety of all here. Some suppose that the small vessel is an American, chased in by a British vessel & tha[t a Cano]e with British colours, & without Know not knowing the circumstance, & anxious to learn the news, was attempting to go alongside, when the vessel seeing all British around, & not knowing their Intentions or numbers, fired & killed the forementioned number.

I can not give credit to the report, for I cannot think any vessel

---

[59] January 4, 1814.
[60] The falls of the Willamette.

would be fool enough to fire upon a small canoe of ten men, &
unarmed, but as improbable as it is, it causes universal anxiety
among the common men. Some of them have Brothers at the Fort,
you hear them rave & swear—they say Si Les Bostonés ont tué mon
Frére, ma consciénce de Bon Dieu, J'entuerai d'autre.[61] Another
answers him, moi et vous, & as I am the only [Bos]toné (Yankee)
here, one would suppose that my situation in respect to them would
be extremely unpleasant, but I do not know how it is or whence it
comes, but these men seem to have some respect for me. [The]
other day as they were talking in this strain, Mr. Henry asked of
them, which of the Yankees they would kill. They replied, oh Sacri
Dieu, le premier qui vient.[62] But says Mr. H.—La tete blanche
(my name) est le seul Bostoné ici,—Lui nous ne le tairons pas.[63]

I mention this little anecdote, as a memento of a mans name
among the Common Men, whom I have found remarkably civil &
polite, & if I have ever a chance to reward him, not to let it pass—
it is Majéou.

Mr. Henry and Mr. Wallace with all the men have gone to bring
in Eleven Elk which the Hunters killed yesterday, & I am here
very lonesome & not knowing how to employ myself. I feel so very
anxious for the news, that I cannot confine myself to the house but
am con[stantly] to the water side, looking out for a canoe—although as yet in vain.

Sunday Morning Jany. 9th[64]

[O]ur Expectations & doubts are at length [justi]fied. On
Thursday Evening the Trapper who left us on the 20th ult.[65] for
the Fort, returned to this place, by whom we all had letters—the
purport of which are, that on 30th November they saw a sail off the
Entrance of the River, & as it appear[ed] to come in without making any difficulty, they thought it was some American vessel from

---

[61] "If the Yankees have killed my brother, as God is my witness, I will kill
another," seconded by "me and you."

[62] "The first one who comes along."

[63] "White head [Seton] is the only Yankee here; him we will not silence"—
presumably because Seton was considered one of the group.

[64] January 9, 1814.

[65] This date is December 20, 1813; the trapper returned on January 6.

off the coast with Mr. Hunt on board. With this idea Mr. Mc-
Dougall & Halsey embarked in a Canoe to go & see him, while
Mr. McTavish with all the NW Co. packs started up the River to
secure them.[66] Mr. McD. and H. had not proceeded far in the
Canoe, before they perceived a boat from the vessel, for which they
immediately made, and wh[en within] hail were thus accosted—
"Who are you, & where from." Mr. McD. hesitated,[67] when the
demand was repeated—to which Mr. McD. answered—"From the
Fort up the [river"] & asked of them what ship it [was]. "It is
H.B.M. Sloop of War Raccoon, will you please to step on board
this boat." Mr. McD accordingly went, but seeing the canoe went
faster, the Officer, (2d Lieut.) embarked in it, & they proceeded
to the ship, where they were recd. politely by the Capt. Wm. Black
Esqr. & Mr. John McDonald a proprietor of the NW Co. This
vessel in company with the Phabe frigate & Cherub, sloop of war,
were ordered to accompany the NW Co. ship the Isaac Todd from
Rio Janeiro to this place. They parted with the latter vessel off Cape
Horn, & the P[habe] & Cherub off Lima who went in pursuit of
the US. Frigate Essex, which by their intelligence was cruising in
these seas.[68] These Gentleman were sadly disappointed at hearing
that all the property was disposed of to the NW Co. A few [days]
before coming in the Officers would not have taken a thousand
pounds for their share of the expected prize.[69] The Captn. visited

---

[66] That is, to put North West Company property beyond the reach of the new
arrivals, assumed to be American. Irving noted astringently: "It is singular that
this prompt mode of conveyancing valuable, but easily transportable effects beyond the reach of a hostile ship should not have suggested itself while the property
belonged to Mr. Astor." Irving, *Astoria*, p. 346.

[67] McDougall and Halsey were going to pass themselves off as Englishmen or
Americans, as the occasion demanded. Franchère, *Voyage*, p. 131.

[68] The *Essex*, under Captain David Porter, had been taking vessels from the
British whaling fleet. She was finally caught and defeated off Valparaiso, Chile,
on March 28, 1814. See below, pp. 175–76, for Seton's knowledge of this event.

[69] Irving used this detail in his version of the *Raccoon*'s arrival. Irving, *Astoria*, p. 348. However, he may have been in error, for Captain Black stated that
he had "no expectation of prize money [for Astoria], nor disappointment in any
respect. The force was sent to fulfill a duty to the North-West Company. It was
no government measure. They were as it were under my direction as a Partner
of that Company and acted accordingly." Barry M. Gough, "The 1813 [British]
Expedition to Astoria," *The Beaver*, Outfit 304.2 (Autumn 1973), 50.

the Fort & took possession of the com[pany] in the name of his Britannic Majesty & and in breaking a bottle of Madeira over the Gate of the Fort, called it Fort George. Thus ci-devant Astoria which a few Americans & Canadians knocked up to secure them from the Savages is now a fort of his Majesty.

The Raccoon left Mr. McDonald & about 80 pieces of trading articles here & at the date of my letter from the Fort (29th Decem. 1813) she was laying in Bakers Bay[70] expecting a fair wind for the Sandwich Islands. All is anxiety for the Isaac Todd. They parted with her in a terrible gale of wind off Cape Horn. Much doubt is entertained of her safe arrival.[71]

Five weeks before the Raccoon made the coast she met with a terrible accident on board. As they were ex[ercis]ing their great guns, a spark of fire communicated to about 50 lb. powder in cartridges which blew up & killed 8 men & wounded 19. Among the latter were Mr. McDonald & the 1st Lieutenant.

This [is the] story which the Indians embelli[shed] much, making two ships out of one, & changing an accident into an Engagement.

Mr. McDougall informs me that I will know by the next canoe, the answers to my enquiries, about my coming down, & if my account is ballanced. Mr. Wallace left this place this morning with a load of meat to Fort George, by whom I wrote to Halsey, Franchere & Mr. Clarke in answer to their letters; we expect him on the 20th.

Monday, Jany. 17th 1814.

We are all here at this time in a [state] of considerable agitation, owing to the news, which I am now going to note down.[72]

Yesterday three Indians on horseback, [arr]ived . . . in the entrance of this river[73] they brought [a] note from Mr. McDonald &

---

[70] On the north shore of the Columbia, in back of Cape Disappointment. The *Raccoon* sailed on December 31. Irving, *Astoria* (Todd), p. 492*n*.

[71] After various adventures, including helping the *Raccoon*, which damaged itself badly getting over the bar on its way out of the Columbia, the *Isaac Todd* reached Astoria in April 1814, after a voyage of more than a year. Franchère, *Voyage*, p. 148.

[72] Seton learned this "news" in bits and pieces and was not able to put down any details until January 26; see below, pp. 145–47.

[73] That is, at the mouth of the Willamette.

Mr. Alex Henry to Mr. W Henry of this place, informing him
that on 3rd Jany. two canoes with 30 pieces & 15 men started upon
a voy[age u]p the river with a supply for the upper posts, that in
the first portage of the rapids of the Columbia, they had some disturbance with the Indians in which Mr. Stuart[74] the Conductor of
the party was wounded & the party was obliged to turn about in so
much haste, that they left one canoe, all the baggage & 1 man,
behind. In consequence of which, 6 canoes & 60 men well armed
& appointed had been dispatched to recover the property by fair
mean[s] or foul, & telling us at the same to be very mu[ch on] our
guard, for if the last party proceeded to [the rapid]s, that there was
a great fear the Indians would revenge it. It was this last party who
stopping at the entrance of the river dispatched the Indian[s to us.]
One may easily suppose we are anxious to hear [of the] operations.
We are in the mean time endeavouring to put ourselves in a state of
defence by cutting pickets, with which we mean to enclose the
Buildings. This work goes on very slowly as we have only 7 working men & . . . whole . . . [cou]nting every body — 17. I will only
observe that the place where this accident happened is not two days
march from this place.

After we had dispatched the three Indians with letters from Mr.
H[enry] to his <u>Bourgeois</u> stating our situation &c. one of our
Hunters who had been on the opposite side of the River, came in.
About 4 Miles from this, while hunting he perceived ten Indians
on horseback dressed in their war dresses & painted, making towards him full speed & raising the war whoop. He immediately
gained a small [thicke]t of 5 or 6 large pine trees, & waited for
[them to come] up, as all hopes of getting off were done away with.
When they arrived opposite to him, he stepped behind a tree with
his Rifle [raised, ma]king signs to them to keep off. Fortunately
[there] was an old Man in the Company who advanced, & making
a long harangue, the purport of which was, that they had been three
nights without eating, & that Elk [& De]er were no more, the
reason . . . the White Men hunting with guns which scared them
away, & that they were determined to kill every white man they
met. The Hunter told them, there were many more white men close

---

[74] Alexander Stuart.

bye who would revenge themselves, & that if they would go off &
let him alone, that he would not hunt there any more. They had a
long consultation among themselves, in which it appears the old
man was his friend, for he debarked from his horse & staid by [the
Hu]nter untill the others were out of sig[ht, aft]er which he told
him to go & not come any more, he accordingly made the best of
his way here.[75]

The hunters & Common Men are all m[urmur]in[g] . . . &
asking to desert this place & go to [the] Fort, but as nothing of this
kind can be done without orders, we must patiently await the result,
endeavouring to keep together as much as possible, & in as good a
state of defence. . . .

Wednesday 19th 1814.[76] As yet we have no more accounts of what
has passed between the whites & the Indians, although anxiously
attending it. The business must now be settled, & if it should happen that their party should not recover the goods & should loose
two or three men by the Indians, the consequences would be se-
verely felt. There would be nothing less in my opinion than a general coalition among the Savages to destroy us or make us evacuate
the country. Those Scoundrels that brought us [the news] the other
day, although reckoned as . . . Friends of the Whites, boasted with
no little vani[ty] that there were as many white men kill[ed] as
Indians. Although this account is not true, . . . accounts of the death
of the . . . & Mr. Stuart the other is only wounded with an arro[w]
which entered his left arm & peirced a little way in his body.

Wednesday 26th Jany, 1814. On Sunday last, Mr. Alex. Henry a
proprietor of the NW Co. with Mr. Matthews, a clerk of our late
Company arrived at this place from the Rapids of Columbia River,
& started again this Morning on their return to Fort George. They
formed a part of the war party of the Whites to recover their goods
from the [In]dians.[77] They succeeded in getting back about 11

---

[75] This hunter was a Nipissing Cree Indian, known as the Grand Nepisengue.
Alexander Henry, Jr.'s Astoria Journal, in Payette, *Postscript*, p. 57.

[76] January 19, 1814.

[77] Seton seems to have relied on William Matthews and Henry for the following account.

[packs of] trading articles, without going to extremities. The remainder of the property, when all hopes of recovering it was lost, was given to the relations of. . . .

The following is a tolerable correct [account of the] commencement of this business. Two Canoes as before said with 17 men in all & 60 pieces including 30 of provision, left Fort George [i]n [t]he beginning of Jany. & travelled nigh[t] & day. [Pass]ing some villages below the portag[e] the Chief of one of them, Canook by name, observing the canoes heavily loaded, & with so few men instantly began to stir up the Indians to rob them. They formed their plan & followed them to the portage. As there were two Chiefs Messrs. Alex. Stuart and Mr. Keith[78] five Indians to kill them each at the same time were appointed, when it was supposed the men would save themselves by flight, & the goods be pillaged with impunity. As the Whites contrary to the usual custom, made the portage upon the South [bank of] the River, the Indians were obliged to [cross,] which they did in considerable numbers. Five with [Can]ook at their head approached Mr. Keith & five others with another chief as supposed, [Mr.] S[tuart,] the remainder in the mean time go[ing a]mong [the ba]ggage. When within 15 or 16 paces of Mr. S, who perceived some thing was in agitation & made them a motion to keep back & at the same time as the Indians say, snapped his gun at them, which when they saw the fire[79] [shot an arrow] into him which hit him in the shoulder & instantly afterwards, a second one, which wounded him [in] the side. The Indian had turned his back to go off, when a Man (by the name of Mackay[80]) standing alongside of Mr. S. shot him dead upon the spot. Another Indian that was standing bye at the same time got a Ball in his stomach, another in his head (fired by Mr. S.) & another in his shoulder which did not entirely kill him. The man that had shot him in the stomach ran up to him, cut t[he cord] that tied his war club to his wrist & cr[ushed his] head in. The five that were

---

[78] James Keith.

[79] That is, Stuart's gun, dampened by the rain, misfired, with the primer only "flashing." Franchère, *Voyage*, p. 138.

[80] Thomas Mackay, a son of Alexander. He had come out as a clerk on the *Tonquin*. Irving, *Astoria* (Todd), p. 41n.

approaching Mr. Keith [were] within a few steps of him, when the
. . . fired, he instantly aimed at the one ne[arest to] h[im,] who
told him not to fire, which [he] did not, & they ran off.

The goods & one of the canoes were at this time the other end of
the portage. Each man except an old Hunter from the other side of
the mountains, brought back . . . but instead of putting them in
the [can]oe threw them in the river, & unfortunately into an eddy
where the Indians the next day picked them up. They all embarked
then it appears in confusion except Mr. Keith, who asked three or
four of them to go back with him & bring the old Hunter. This
they positively refused. Mr. K. started alone, got over half the portage, where there were so many hiding places for Indians, that he
did not think it prudent to advance any further. He came again to
the canoe & asked them if it was possible they were going to leave
the old man to his fate. They [answer]ed him with these words—
Monsr. Keith vo[ulez vous] arguer, ou voulez vous rester a térre.[81]
Mr. K. cu[rsed them] then for a band of Cowards & to [save] his
own life was obliged to go in the water . . . canoe. The Indians say
they have not kil[led the hunter], but that he took the woods, where
in all probability [he] is already dead with hunger.[82]

Mr. Stuart would have been killed upon the spot, had it not been
for a pipe in his Capot pocket, which the arrow broke in pieces.
Som[e a]pprehensions are yet entertained of his [life].

Sunday, 7th February, 1814. Fort George at the Entrance of Columbia River.

Since my last date, from the river Wollamut, I received orders
from Mr. Duncan McDougall to come to this place, where I arrived on the last day of January, as he wished me to assist Mr.
Halsey in writing. My time is therefore busily occupied.

I am happy in saying that Mr. Stuart is now considered o[ut of]
danger, although at one time his situation was [considered] extremely precarious, but by applying pol[tic]es, the wound was
cleansed. It is the opinion of all [here] that [he] was shot with a

---

[81] "Mr. Keith, [do you want to argue]; or do you want us to die here?"

[82] The hunter, a second Nipissing Cree, eventually got to Astoria safely. Alexander Henry, Jr.'s Astoria Journal, in Payette, *Postscript*, pp. 60–61.

poisoned arrow, & the . . . not proving fatal is that it did not penetrat[e . . . ow]ing to his pipe which considerably stopped [its] force, & [the] poison being happily drawn out of his system by the poltices.[83]

The NW Gentlemen have determined to desert [the fort] & build another about 65 miles above on the [Columbia] at the lower Entrance of the [Woll]am[ut]. 30 or 40 men, with two of the proprietors have already gone up to commence these opperations. There are many reasons that render the latter place preferable to the present, as the spot is cleared, provision is more plenty, & in time of war, nothing can injure them. They have therefore payed 3 or 4000 Dollars for Fort George as the Frenchmen say, sans dessein.[84] Their ship the Isaac Todd is not arrived, & they begin to be anxious about her. There are some fears that the US Frigate Essex has fallen [in with] her. We are looking for Mr. Hunt every. . . . One advantage I have in being at this p[lace is that] whatever news turns up, I hear it immed[iately.]

The plan of building the Fort [at the mouth] of the Wollamut, has been give[n up o]win[g to] want of a commanding situation, & they have h[ow]ever fixed upon Tongue Point, as the place most suited for their purpose, & Mr. Matthews, formerly of our Company began his opperations for them, in the latter end of Febry.[85]

March 11th 1814.[86]

Saturday March 26th, 1814. On Board Brig Pedler of Boston — laying at anchor in Bakers Bay, Columbia River.[87]

---

[83] The Nez Perce sometimes used dried rattlesnake venom on their arrow heads; the poultices may have been as effective as Seton believed them to have been, but the drying of the venom also weakened its potency considerably. Josephy, *Nez Perce*, p. 19.

[84] That is, "to no purpose."

[85] This entry was probably written late in February 1814. The new fort Seton mentions was not actually built until 1824–1825, when it was situated on the north bank of the Columbia, opposite the mouth of the Willamette. By this time, the North West Company had been merged into the Hudson Bay Company, which called their new post Fort Vancouver. Rich, *History of the Hudson's Bay Company*, II, 448.

[86] Seton did not continue this entry beyond the date.

[87] Previously located; see above, p. 143*n*90.

Monday Evening Feby. 28th we were agreeably surprised at the sight of a vessel standing in the River, which proved to be Mr. Hunt in the above mentioned Brig. He bought her in the Sand[wi]ch Islands, for the purpose of taking a[board] Furs & other property, but the [crossed out: our] arrangem[ents with] the NW Co. had already disposed of them. [Mr.] H. [had] therefore only to look into the . . . them with the NW Co., which was . . . [and] required no little patience and management. For Mr. Dun. McDougall the agent for Mr. Astor, had been a secret proprietor of the NW Co. since December last,[88] and in that [time] without the knowledge of any of the Gentle[men] . . . of the PF Co., had acted still as Mr. [Astor's] agent, and with Mr. McTavish had priced the all the inventories of Mr. Astors property in this country. It was not then much to be wondered at, when this transaction was brought to light, that the per centage on some articles, differed most materrially from the agreement—in fact I believe Mr. Hunt considers that the property sold would be worth in this country, valued by an impartial man—Twenty thousand Dollars more than what it has now been sold for.[89]

The Amt. of p[roperty] sold was Fifty Eight Thousand Dollars, [which a]fter great difficulty Mr. H. procured . . . Draft on McTavish, McG. & Co.[90] for; in th[ese] dea[lings and] transactions with the North W[esters,] most of which I was an eye witness, . . . in that their conduct in every res[pect] . . . [not] like men of the World or men that regarded their characters too scrupulously.

Mr. Halsey & myself have embarked on board the Brig with Mr. Hunt an[d] . . . we are at present waiting for a . . . wind to go to sea. I wrote to My Father via Mr. Clarke, who with the

---

[88] McDougall became a North West Company partner on December 23, 1813. Irving, *Astoria*, p. 350.

[89] Irving, certainly reflecting Astor's opinion, later wrote that Hunt "now [i.e., March 1814] considered the whole conduct of M'Dougal hollow and collusive." *Astoria*, p. 350. In August 1815, Astor described McDougall's actions as " 'fraudulent.' " John Jacob Astor to James Monroe, August 17, 1815, in Porter, *Astor*, I, 585.

[90] McTavish, McGillivrays & Company, North West Company agents in Montreal; the transaction is described in Porter, *Astor*, I, 234–35.

remainder of our Gentlemen will sett off in about ten days on their voyage across the Continent.[91]

This is the voyage I have been looking forward to, with so much pleasure. At some future day I shall mention the circumstances that induced me to follow Mr. Hunt. At present I do not know where we are bound, nor with certainty what is to be. . . . On board of this Brig as Sailing [Master is] Mr. S. Northrop, formerly Command[er of the S]hip Lark belonging to Mr. J. J. Astor. This [vessel left] New York in March 1813, bound to [the Columbia] River, and was unfortunately cast [ashore ne]ar [the] Sandwich Islands, where vessel & cargo [were ent]irely lost; if she had had the good fortune to have reached this place, so great a sacrifice of Mr. A's property would in all probability not have happened, as Mr. O[gde]n, a Gentlemen in Mr. A's confidence w[as] on board.[92]

Owing to this melancholy circumstance, I was deprived of the pleasure of hearing from home, & Mr. Ogden who could have given me some information respecting my Friends I did not see, as he went from the Sandwich Islands to Canton. Not therefore having heard from Home for two & a half years, & of course entirely ignorant of the situation of my Father & Friends, I concluded it best to accompany Mr. Hunt. I took this resolution much more willingly from the Character of Mr. Hunt, being a man who is capable of instruc[ting and] bringing up a Young Man, & who . . . will if anything favourable turns up, us[e his best] endeavours, to forward his protégé.[93]

I am therefore at present on bo[ard the Pedler] of Boston, wait-

---

[91] This party left Astoria in early April 1814 and, traveling through Canada, reached Montreal in September. Franchère was a member of the party and described it in *Voyage*, pp. 145–88.

[92] Astor knew nothing of the situation at Astoria, but he did know of the *Isaac Todd*, so he dispatched the *Lark*, under Captain Samuel Northrop, to reinforce the outpost. She sailed from New York on March 6, 1813, with Seton's cousin, Nicholas G. Ogden, as supercargo. The *Lark* was wrecked in a gale off the island of Maui in August. Irving, *Astoria*, pp. 309, 339–41.

[93] Alexander Ross wrote that both he and Seton received $500 bonuses for their "zeal and merit." *Adventures*, pp. 296–97. Seton may have gone with Hunt hoping somehow to bring something profitable out of his past two years' labors, a motive Hunt may have shared.

ing for peace to [arrive. She] is of about 230 Tons, Copper[ed, in] every [respect] a first rate vessel.

I leave the Country & most of those I have met here, without regret, so much meanness, Selfishness, & Hypocricy [crossed out: are seldom met] among an equal number, are seldom [met] wit[h.]

Alaska, California,
and the Return Home

Brig Pedler at Sea Monday Night April 18th 1814 North Latitude 55° 40', West Longitude 134° 45'.[1]

With a favourable Breeze from the NW we passed the Bar of Columbia River on Saturday afternoon the 3d[2] of April and bent our course to the Northward, being bound to Sheetka[3] a Russian Establishment of long standing on the NW Coast. It is situated in Norfolk Sound L[at. 57° 2' Long. W. 135° 50' and is the Common ren[dezvous of] the Americans trading on the coast. Ow[ing to the] winds & light airs, we are not far[ther to the north] than noted above; but as the [W]ind [now] . . . favours us, we are in hopes of soon [arriv]ing in [the] expected Harbour. There are some expectations of meeting a vessel of Mr. Astor's, there from N York; if this fortunately should [be t]he case it will in all probability prove a lucky . . . for the old Gentleman,[4] & will be the means of accellerating our departure homeward; if no news is received from home, I do not believe that Mr. Hunt has determined what to do with the Brig. Perhaps get a freight from the Russians to and fro: the Seal Islands[5]—or procure Kodiak Indians to hunt the Sea Otters. Either of these would scarcely pay the crew, & would moreover prove a disagreeable & tedious way of life.

Navigation at present occupies my whole attention. By the desire of Mr. Hunt, Mr. Halsey & myself both keep the ships [nav.] and stand our watches, like the others on boa[rd. Were it] not for this last circumstance I shoul[d devote] my leisure time to the French Lang[uage. I will] endeavour after arriving in Port, [to make] arrangements for this purpose.

I find my situation [on boar]d as a[greea]ble as could be expected. Mr. [Hu]nt, Capt. Northrop, Mr. Gardner—2d officer—

---

[1] Off Prince of Wales Island, in Alaska's southern panhandle.

[2] Seton was mistaken as to either the date or the day of the week; April 3 fell on a Sunday in 1814.

[3] Sitka, or New Archangel, the field headquarters of the Russian American Fur Company, on Baranof Island. See Ronda, *Astoria*, chap. 3, for the background to the Russian presence there.

[4] Presumably Astor.

[5] The Pribilof Islands, in the Bering Sea.

Mr. Farnum,[6] a Clerk from the River acting as third officer, with Mr. Halsey and myself are the inmates of the Cabin.

Sunday May 1st 1814, at anchor in Norfolk Sound.[7]
We reached this place on Friday 22d Ult. and found at anchor here the Russian Ship Baring formerly the Atahualpa of Boston, Captn. Bennet. The Fort was saluted with nine Guns which compliment was returned, and Mr. Hunt with [Mr.] Halsey and Capt. Bennet went to pay [their respects] to Mr. Berrenoff,[8] the Gentleman ap[pointed by t]he Russian Company to have the . . . with the title of Governor. . . . [Mr.] Hunt introduced me to him, [a]nd . . . I have seen him frequently. The [old] Gentle[man is] somewhat particular in his way, and very fond of hot punch, with which he never fails of seasoning[9] whoever goes to [see] him, untill one or the other is under the table. [He is] likewise a great Disciplinarian, [a]nd keeps his men under great subjection. 7 men are upon guard night and day.

The Fort is built on a point of High Rocks, which it entirely occupies, and is impregnable to Indian efforts, unaided by artillery. The Company at this place receive the Principal Part of their supplies from the American Trading vessels on the coast. Friday 29th April the Baring sailed bound to Ochotz[10] in Siberia, with a valuable cargo of Furs and Peltries.

From the 7th to the 11th[11] a continual and violent sno[wstorm,]

---

[6] Russell Farnham, who came out on the *Tonquin*. Irving, *Astoria* (Todd), p. 41n.

[7] While Irving did not include the voyage of the *Pedler* in *Astoria*, he did use Seton's account of his stay in Sitka in 1814 as background for his treatment of Hunt's trip there in the *Beaver* in the fall of 1812 (chap. 57), especially in his character sketch of the Russian governor.

[8] Alexander Andreyvich Baranov (1746–1819); Warren L. Cook, *Flood Tide of Empire: Spain and the Pacific Northwest, 1543–1819* (New Haven: Yale University Press, 1973), p. 498; hereafter cited as Cook, *Flood Tide*.

[9] "Seasoning" was the term used to describe the acclimatization of Europeans or Africans to the American climate; it was an apt term here, for Baranov apparently did not trade or did so only with great reluctance with those who did not drink with him.

[10] Okhotsk.

[11] Seton means from the 7th to the 11th of May; this undated entry was apparently written about May 20, 1814.

on one of these days, the Governor had [a prosnic] (drunken frolic) on shore. When Mr. [Halsey] and myself were there, we did [not return abo]ard untill 3 o Clock in the Mor[ning.]

[Friday] Morning the 13th were agreeably . . . [the] sight of a sail in the off[ing]. . . . [Mr. Hunt &] myself boarded her, when she [proved] to be the Forrester of London, Capt. Pig[ot,] last from the coast of California. A Young Gentleman of the name Ebbets is on board.[12] Since her arrival [the time has] passed away much more agreeably. The old Governor has had several prosnics in one of which a serious fray happened, in which all Hands got gloriously drunk, but most fortunately ended only in bloody noses & bruised faces.

We are still in uncertainty where we are bound or, what Mr. Hunt intends to do with the Brig. Most Happy would I be if he would sell her and g[et] the skins on board the English Brig to Canton.

[The natives] of the vicinity are very troubles[ome to the Ru]ssians.[13] The other day from a Fishing Par[ty they took] 5 persons prisoners, and the Go[vernor and men] of the two Brigs to go to . . . on the other side of the Sound [about 30 miles? dis]tance, where there is a large village, to endeavour to [reco]ver them. Preparations [are] accordingly making.

---

[12] The *Forester* had been chartered by Astor when he became concerned that the *Lark* might be intercepted by a British vessel. He sent an agent to England who managed to charter the *Forester* "under British colours" and secure permission for the vessel to sail to the Pacific, part of the way in a British convoy. Its captain, William Pigot, separated from the convoy as soon as he could and sailed for Astoria. See "Memorandum for the Honorable William Jones, Secretary of the Navy," April 19, 1813, in Dorothy Wildes Bridgwater, "John Jacob Aster [*sic*] Relative to His Settlement on Columbia River," *Yale University Library Gazette*, 24, No. 2 (October 1949), 57; Ronda, *Astoria*, pp. 254, 267, 268, 276. As Seton notes below, Captain Pigot encountered the *Raccoon* at San Francisco, learned of Astoria's sale, and went on to Sitka. Mr. Ebbets's first name was Richard.

[13] This probably refers to the hostile Tlingit Indians, whom the Russians called Kolosh and treated very badly. Peaceful Aleuts and Kodiaks, the latter actually Inuit, made up the balance of the island's native population; these had been pacified by the Russians and brought there to hunt sea otter. John R. Swainton, *The Indian Tribes of North America* (Washington, D.C.: Smithsonian Institution, 1952), pp. 530–33, 540–43.

The Forrester gives us an account of the safe arrival of the North [West Company's] ship Isaac Todd on the coast of California, where she had passed the last winter. Also of the Racoon being there on the 22d April when the Forrester sailed, repairing the damages which she got, by unfortunately striking on the Bar of Columbia River in going out.

Monday 23d May.[14] Nothing is yet concluded upon for the employ of the Brig to my knowledge. Time hangs heavy upon my hands. Several unpleasant circumstances have taken place, which lets me more in the character of those I am obliged to pass . . . all of my time with; the more experience . . . that a mean selfishness governs . . . of men. Here I am though! [and] will be for some time. Whether a . . . and a wise man would . . . things easy, but I unfortunate[ly lack such] wisdom in my constitution, that [when I] am displeased I seldom fail to show [it.] And as it would require the patience of a greater [m]an than *I* am, to see every thing that I see with a calm mind; I make [my]self much more unhappy than a . . . .

May 26th.[15] Arrived here from the Sandwich Islands the Ship Isabella, Captn. Davis, an old visitor of this place.[16] During his stay, untill the latter end of June, there was much merry making.

Monday June 5th, celebrated the nativity of George 3d on board the English Brig Forrester. In the present state of the two countries, this circumstance would appear unpardonable to the professed patriots of my country; but let them consider that in this remot[e and] uncivilised corner, we hail with cordi[ality any stra]nger, without considering whether he be [an Englishman], Frenchman, German, Russ[ian,]. . . . In short we meet as citizens of the [world, with]out minutely enquiring the past . . . [of] each.

Captn. D. sold his [vessel to the Gover]nor and left us about the [29th J]une, . . . to make the best of his way home, & [ob]li[gingly] took charge of a letter from me to my [Father.]

---

[14] 1814.

[15] This summary entry was written sometime late in July 1814.

[16] William Heath Davis; Porter, *Astor*, I, 436, 448.

This [Gent]leman conferred several favors upon me, & Mr. Gale a young gentleman of his cabin conduced much to alleviate the ennui of this dismal hole.

In the beginning of July, Governor Barenoff with Captn. Pigot and Hunt, Messr. Halsey and myself in the pinnaces of the Brigs, accompanied by six Boydarchy's or Kodiak canoes,[17] and a gun boat of the Company, started upon a jaunt of pleasure to some warm springs about 25 miles SE from this. A Russian, and two or three Kodiaks reside there for the purpose of keeping the baths in order, of which there are two fr[om the hot] springs. The water is strongly imp[regnated with] sulphur, a crust of which of the [thickness of an] inch, covers the stones where the . . . under the Rocks. An . . . minutes, and a bright Dollar in . . . [complet]ely Blacked.[18] A [number] of [baths] of dif[ferent] temperatures might be . . . [t]hese springs. The Russians have conten[ted th]emselves with two, the temperature of [each] nearly equal, (not having a thermometer) we c[an]not determine their [crossed out: precise] degrees of heat, in any other manner, than [by] . . . sensation. By remaining still in the Bath, I with a little Inconvenience bear the Heat, but upon leaving it always felt a feebleness and faintness which preventing me for a minute or two from making any exertion. The Governor used to bath six and seven times a day and always appeared refreshed. He says it has great medicinal qualities and always invigorates whoever uses it. It had a contrary effect upon me. I yet have a severe cold caught by putting my head under the water.

I[t has] one virtue though, which those who are [required to] k[ee]p the Governors Company, duly ap[preciate] —that of diffusing the vapors wh[ich the continual] sacrifice to Bacchus is apt to [encourage. I] saw a certain Gentleman get [three times] drunk and three times sobered by this [means], and yet mirabile dictu[19] went . . . nearly. . . . Lest this should impeach the morali[ty of the Gen]tleman alluded to, I will bear witness tha[t he] c[o]uld not

---

[17] Light two-man skin kayaks, usually rendered as *bidarkas*.

[18] Seton is probably referring to the tarnishing effect of the sulphur in the springs.

[19] That is, "wonderful to relate."

without [crossed out: forfeiting the character] in[jur]ing the sale of his cargo escape making merry with the [fac]totum of New Archangel.[20]

We remained three days, and then went to a small establishment of the Russians, three or four miles to the Eastward of the springs, consisting of several buildings picketed in & defended by a square bastion where three or four swivels are mounted. 20 or 30 men Russians and Kodiaks may be about the number that are stationed here. The Fort is situated at an outlet of a considerable Lake, where it joins the Salt water. A wear[21] across this is so constructed, that it catches almost every salmon that endeavours to enter the Fresh water by this route, and one may say in[numerable ar]e the quantities they catch.[22] The F[alls of the Colum]bia is the only fishing spot, that [I know], which excels this, where the River is f[rom a width of] three or four miles compressed . . . two or three hundred yards. . . . Those stationed at this p[la]ce . . . fish for the winters consumption at . . . quarters. We returned next day [to the] vessels.

July 4th. Owing to our [shortage o]f almost all kind of stores were not enabled [to] celebrate the day otherwise than by firing the states salute at . . . all hands a holy day.

July 20th. After three months detention the Govr. among other

---

[20] Captain Pigot of the *Forester* might be the unnamed individual whose morality should not be impugned. The caution was hardly needed for Baranov's *prosnics* were infamous up and down the coast. In 1811 Captain Ebbets of the *Enterprise* had noted to Astor that they were "no small tax on a person's health that does business with him." John Ebbets to John Jacob Astor, Jan. 11, 1811, Porter, *Astor*, I, 451. Since part of the *Beaver's* mission to the Northwest had been to establish a preferential trading arrangement with Baranov, its cargo had included more than 3,000 gallons of various alchoholic beverages. Ibid., I, 478. Much later, Seton gave a more circumstantial account of a *prosnic* in the New York *Mirror*, September 9, 1837, over the signature, "A." It is given here as Appendix B. The author was identified by John Francis McDermott, who edited the account as "Hospitality at the Punch Bowl: An Astorian's Recollections of an Evening with Count Baranoff," *Pacific Northwest Quarterly*, 48, No. 2 (April 1957), 55–58. In it, Seton describes a downright gluttonous banquet, wild dancing, and a drunken game of billiards which ended in Baranov's collapse, "*lumpus* on the floor." This may be the *prosnic* to which Seton refers to above, pp. 157.

[21] Weir.

[22] This may be a reference to the Indian River, still known for its salmon catches.

offers for the employ of the Brig, proposed carrying a cargo to his establishment on the coast of California,[23] which was accepted by Mr. Hunt, and every preparation is now making for this purpose.

Mr. H. thought it necessary for either Mr. Halsey or Myself to remain at this place, in case of a vessel from the US. arriving with a cargo;[24] he left it to ourselves to determine [who] should remain. Mr. Halsey concluded to [stay], mentioning that I would prefer going in . . . account of practising & improving in [navigation]. This arrangement has been adopted by [Hunt &] the Govr. offers suitable accomoda[tions for Halsey to] stay.

I purchased a Sextant fro[m Mr. G]ale [of] the Isabella, for $70, and with a . . . & attenion, I am in hopes to be a tolerable . . . Lunar[i]an, Capt. Pigot has lent me . . . Longitude; which with Bowditch's Navigation,[25] will be all that is [necessar]y.

August 4th, Thursday.[26] On Sunday last we left Sheetka with a favourable wind which has brought us rapidly thus far, N. Lat. 46° W. Long. 134° 20'.[27]

Although the Governor offered very indifferent accomodations, the necessity of some person remaining to take charge of the papers &c. & to attend to the business of another vessel, provided one should come, induced Mr. Halsey to remain. Mr. Hunt fitted him in stores amply, & in every thing the place or vessels in the harbour afforded. Our abscence is only expected to be th[ree months]. I am in hopes he will make out . . . tolerably pleasant. We left [the Forester, Capt.] Pigot ready for sea, destination . . . . [28]

---

[23] The Russians had two posts north of San Francisco, Bodega and Fort Ross. Cook, *Flood Tide*, pp. 501–502.

[24] Hunt may have been thinking of the *Enterprise* which was then held in New York by a British blockade. Ronda, *Astoria*, pp. 273–76.

[25] Nathaniel Bowditch, *The New American Navigator* . . . First ed. Newburyport, Mass: printed by E. M. Blunt for Brown & Stansbury, New York, 1802. It was subsequently printed in many editions. Lunarian may have been a joking reference to Seton's future proficiency in lunar navigation.

[26] August 4, 1814.

[27] Approximately off the mouth of the Columbia River.

[28] The *Forester* sailed to, among other North Pacific ports, Kamchatka in Siberia. There clerk Russell Farnham set out overland, carrying dispatches and a

The Governor gives Mr. [Hunt] . . . [seal s]kins, 75c ea. for taking [them from] Sheetka to Califor[nia,] or if it is [n]eces[sary, to the] Brig he has cruising on that [coast] to tra[nsfer par]t of the cargo, 1000 more to bring a re[t]ur[n] car[go to be] prepared, if not, salt which is procured wi[th] littl[e] trouble in one of the ports on California at 125c the pood, 40 [dollars the] quintins.[29]

This freight is much better than lying idle, but it is not alltogether what the conduct of the Governor towards Mr. Hunt induced him to expect.

The commerce that has been carried on with this old Gentleman has been very advantageous to the adventurers in it.[30] The common cargoes sold here are Strong Rum, Molasses, Rice, Biscuit, Duffils, Blue cloths, coarse Sugar, &c., which the old Man used to pay well for—Rum—3$, Rice 7, . . . 50 &c and one cargo now brought out before . . . adventurers glutted the market . . . doubt brings that price.[31] He pa[ys in seal sk]ins—small ones at 75c ea. Large on[es at 1$. As the ma]rket varies in Canton for the[se] ar[ticles] . . . calculations could not be made, but it may . . . that they will always pay freight. Some [profit] . . . might also be made by purchasing sea [otters] on [the] Coast of California & exchanging . . . furs with him for . . . skins.

In the event [crossed out: this] of peace this trade will be over-

---

draft for the North West Company's purchase of the buildings and stores at Astoria. Eventually he reached New York safely. Porter, *Astor*, I, 641; Franchère, *Voyage*, p. 194.

[29] Pood is a Russian unit of weight equal to about thirty-six pounds; "quintins" is unknown, but working from the price per pound in the pood, a quintin would be about 1,140 pounds.

[30] Seton is referring to American captains, mostly from New England, whose free and easy trading methods (and ethics) often made trouble between the Russians and the Alaskan natives. Driving them out of the trade was one of Governor Baranov's aims in trying for a commercial arrangement with Astor. See A. Dashkoff to J. Jacob Astor, November 7, 1809, in Porter, *Astor*, I, 428–29. See Ronda, *Astoria*, pp. 66–86, for an appreciation of the larger dimensions of the situation.

[31] The prices given here correspond to those listed in the cargo manifest of Astor's ship *Enterprise*, when it traded on the northwest coast in 1810. Porter, *Astor*, I, 433–38.

done. There will be so many that bring out cargoes, & who must sell, that the Old man will get them at his own prices. He is perfectly aware of his being the only market, & that if you do not sell to him, you sink stock & block and he will most certainly take advantage of not only this, but of every other circumstance. What I saw of him, I would advise one steady line of conduct, of strict dealing, having every thing explained, not trusting to his generosity, liberality or honour, for be assured, if he can possibly take an [advantage] by any means, he will do it. [Those] . . . my sentiments of him, as it regards. . . .

On Saturday Evening, Augus[t 13][32] [sighte]d the Russian Settlement[33] on . . . through a thick s[mo]ke & af[te]r[w]ards boarded by . . . [Ko]diaks and Russians. The secon[d] . . . [pro]mised to send us off a pilot to [ta]ke u[s to the anc]horage ground, but did not do it. All this da[y Sunday] we have been becalmed in a thick fog, whic[h en]tirely excludes the settlement from our view, & has prev[en]ted any communication. . . . From the slight view I had of the establishment, no description can be given. A thick smoke (evidently with a view of concealing its situation (supposing us Spaniards)) had nearly made us miss it, and we were not farther than a mile from it.

From Lat. 39° 2' we have kept the coast close on board, standing off in the night time, so that it was nearly impossible for us to pass it unnoticed. Some land marks for vessels bound here are noticed in my sea journal.

On Tuesday Evening August 16th[34] came . . . the bay of Bodega in Lat. 38° 19' N. . . . position is about 18 miles to the . . . [southwa]rd of the Russian Settlement which is . . . [by ob]servation in Lat. N. 38° 28' [crossed out: North] an[d] . . . place to the settlement.[35] A small islan[d] . . . [ba]y forms a good

---

[32] This was written on August 14, 1814.

[33] This was Fort Ross, on present day Kuskov Bay, about eighty miles north of San Francisco; it was less than two years old at this time. Cook, *Flood Tide*, p. 502.

[34] This entry was written, or at least completed, at San Pedro Bay, on September 29, 1814; see below, p. 168.

[35] This outpost had been started as a collection of temporary huts in 1809; it was about thirty miles south of Fort Ross. Cook, *Flood Tide*, p. 501.

shelter from the prevailing winds. . . . southerly wind it is exp[os]ed.

. . . place what cargo Mr. Kushkoff,[36] . . . [in char]ge, requested & the remainder we take to the [vessel the] Ru[ssians] have cruizing on this Coast.

On Tuesday afternoon August 23d got under way to [make] rendezvous [with] the Ilmania, Russian Brig, & our first port of destination was St. Louis.[37] On Thursday afternoon Aug. 25th in running down the coast, as we opened the Bay of St. Louis, (which Vancouver[38] in his charts places too far north) discovered a sail lying under a high yellow cliff. As there was a fresh breeze from the NW. we immediately hauled our wind & stood off shore, at the same time showing our Colours. The stranger to all appearance lay perfectly quiet, & we seemed not to have made any stir with him. The colours he then showed were American. Captn. Northrop's Officers & Crew all declared that they knew the ship, the Albatross Captn. Smith of Boston,[39] & as information respecting the Brig we were in search of mig[ht proba]bly be procured, Mr. Hunt was induced to . . . towards the shore. When within about . . . before dropping anchor, we hailed, & . . . judged, when we answered, the Spanish . . . or La Tagle. The Helm was. . . . Brig got around on the other . . . at this time the wind . . . the . . . firing a gun for us to heave . . . his . . . the shot of the . . . under our bows, and the third jus[t] . . . , at this time the Spanish full . . . [wind]ward of us & scarcely a breath of air, all we [cou]ld do, was to back [our] top sails, & let [them] take quiet possession. . . . brought [to] anchor and the Spanish Clerk boarded us in the Whale boat, & Mr. Hunt accompanied him with the papers on board. In the evening I also went on board by desire of the Captn. & was much surprized to find a large vessel of 550 Tons 22 Brass 8 pdr. Guns & about 50 men, Spanish Letter of Marque from Lima,[40] Com-

---

[36] Ivan Kuskov was the Russian commandant in California. Ibid., pp. 500–501.

[37] San Luis Obispo.

[38] The English navigator George Vancouver.

[39] The *Albatross* had been the vessel Wilson Price Hunt chartered in Hawaii in 1813 to return to Astoria. Irving, *Astoria*, p. 336.

[40] Seton gave the name as the *Santa Catalina* in his September 29th entry; see below, p. 168.

manded by Senor Josef Cavinecio, a Gentleman of Venice. I was received politely by him, & Senor Alvarez, the clerk, who had been in the United States, & consequently had his manners & mind a little enlarged by travelling.

It was judged necessary that the Brig should be detained for the decision of the [Gove]rnor of California residing at the Presidio of. . . .[41] After an overhauling of the cargo . . . place, Mr. Hunt, Captn. N. & I [were told] in a very gentlemany & polite manner . . . vessel our residence untill the [decision of the Span]ish Govt. was known.

Mr. H. [and Captn. N. argued vig[orously a]gainst this detention, as we were not bound on the . . . & had not on board a single [article] . . . that would answer the trade of the. . . . [By the] Spanish sailors we were informed it wa[s] . . . [decided for] the Brig to go to St. Barbara,[42] & likely . . . of any fault . . . to be attached to the Senor C[aven]ecio, . . . at the mission of Purissima & the settlement of Ortega at Pt. Conception. We cast anchor in the Roadsted of St. Barbara on 2d or 3d of Septr. (the Brig in Company, a prize master with 10 men having taken charge of her since the second day of detention, & our Crew being divided between the two vessels). In the afternoon of the same day, in company with Señor Cavinecio & the Prize master, We three viz. Messrs. Hunt, Northrop & myself waited upon the Governor, Senor Josef Arguello,[43] a Captain in the Spanish army, and were received as well as could be expected from inhabitants of a country so far distant from the regions of politeness & civility. As this was merely a visit of ceremony, no business relative to the Prize was entered into. On the next [day busine]ss was commenced, & Mr. Hunt was info[rmed it was] necessary for him to live a shore, untill it was. . . . Acc[or]ding[ly] on the morning of the 5th we took [residence in] the house allotted to us, which wa[s] a[s] . . . [g]enerality of

---

[41] The *Pedler* was detained on smuggling charges. See Kenneth W. Porter, "Cruise of Astor's Brig *Pedler*, 1813–1816," *Oregon Historical Quarterly*, 31, No. 3 (September 1930), 226.

[42] Santa Barbara.

[43] Don Jose Dario Arguello, the Spanish acting governor. Marie L. Northrop, *Spanish-American Families of Early California* (New Orleans: Polyanthos, 1976), I, 40; hereafter, Northrop, *California Families*.

the Houses but whi[ch] . . . would be consigned to the . . . Capt. and his Clerk for their . . . apie[ce] building superior . . . [to which] we repaired for our meals . . . of Señor Cavinecio[44] that he [inter]ested [himself] in the clearance of the Brig & [his] treatment towards us was civil & polite. After the necessary examination, which. . . .

Thursday, 8th[45] the Brig was declared free, but as the Spanish Sailors had publickly said, that they would not give up their rights,[46] early on Friday Morning a guard of 17 soldiers with a Lieutenant & a Sargeant put the Brig in the hands of Mr. Hunt, who only laid long enough to embark two bullocks & then out to sea.

As the Spanish Vessel was bound to Panama, Mr. Hunt enquired of the Senor Cavinecio the possibility of person reaching the United States by that route. When he was told it was extremely easy & done every day, on the day before the clearan[ce of] the vessel, the voyage was proposed to me. . . . of its proving acceptable to Mr. Astor, which [although Mr.] H. could not assure me of, & as I was . . . these seas & seeing no prospect [ahead of any] thing, I gladly accepted of it. I . . . [Mr. H.] Five hundred Dollars,[47] which in . . . should not think the voyage was of . . . advise Mr. H. that expense I am . . . future day. This money I put in . . . [Senor Cav]inecio, to whom I look up to for ever[ything until arrival] at Panama.

I took up res[idence] on shore at the house of Senor Cavinecio, where we re[main]ed untill . . . , when we got under weigh & [on Monday September]26th anchored in the Bay of St. Pedro.[48]

While on shore at St. Barbara my time with some exceptions passed away tolerably agreeable. The Govr. has a large family, among them some very pretty & interesting girls. For the three last years, except these, squaw ladies have been the only beauties to

---

[44] The Americans moved ashore on September 5. Seton apparently discussed their living arrangements in the missing section, about five lines.

[45] September 8, 1814.

[46] That is, the shares granted the crew from the sale of a prize.

[47] This was the bonus which Hunt had previously given to Seton, as reported by Alexander Ross; see above, p. 150n93.

[48] San Pedro Bay was the anchorage for Los Angeles.

whom I paid my occasional devotions. Their display though of all their charms & their want of modesty, leaves the imagination no field to fancy, which let sensualists say what they please, forms one of the greatest delights of Love. The really modest looks & behaviour of these sweet girls may be supposed to have ma[de] some little impression on one situated. . . . Pity for their situation, condemned to . . . life either in a Virgin state, or share their beds [with] some . . . brute of a soldier, added greatly to [the] fee[lings I was] impressed with. I wished the . . . Fort[une] [s]mil[e] upon me, that it might be . . . by offering to share it with[h] the others in a . . . prudence whisper[ed] . . . yet your way to make . . . boisterous & even if you had [a] fortu[ne w]hat w[ould] fa[mily & fr]iends say to such a marriage wh[a]t when the . . . passage was over would. . . .⁴⁹ prejudice & bigotry added, could you trust your honour in the keeping of a Spanish woman & a Catholic; [crossed out: in spite] malgré tout cela⁵⁰ if I had been a man of fortune, I verily believe I would have committed a foolish act. But at present I am seperated, & the slight impression that was made is wearing off at the expence of a few melancholy hours &c. Barbara Arguello is the goddess whose bright eyes had nearly captivated a sighing swain. Conception Arguello a very pretty & unfortunate girl, who is remarquably unlucky, having been engaged to no less than three

---

⁴⁹ About nine lines of the journal survive only in fragments. In this portion, Seton, lonely and perhaps wondering if he would ever get back to New York, apparently thought of asking one of Don Jose Arguello's daughters to marry him. On further thought (which shows that the cause of his infatuation was loneliness—who thinks when they are in love?), he considered the reaction of his staunchly Episcopalian family and "prudence whispered." He did not have to guess at his family's reaction. In 1805, the conversion of his aunt, Elizabeth Bayley Seton, the widow of his uncle William M. Seton, to Catholicism caused a major family quarrel. Alfred's mother was one of those who most strongly objected to the conversion, especially when a cousin followed Elizabeth into the Catholic Church. Later she and her husband were reconciled with Elizabeth, shortly before the former's death. The continuing hostility of the rest of the family was one of the reasons Elizabeth moved to Maryland in 1808. Known as Mother Seton, she went on to found the Sisters of Charity in the United States and was canonized in 1975, becoming the first American-born saint of the Catholic Church. Melville, *Seton*, pp. 119–23.

⁵⁰ "In spite of all that."

strangers whom business brought to this province, & whom death deprived her of.[51]

On the 15th[52] Recd. an account [of] the English Brig Forrester, Captn. Pigot h[av]ing . . . [a]t Ortegas the day before & after hearing of this vess[el being] at St. Barbara, to have immediately de[parted. On the] 18th & 23d wrote to Mr. Hunt by certain . . . at the Rancha of Ortéga, he expecting to [stop] there for [supplies] before leaving the Coast of California. . . .

I have now [completed] my journal to date, Thursday 29th [September] on board the [Spanish] Ship St. Catalina alias [La Tagle] at the Bay of St. Pedro, Coast of California, Lat N. 33° 42' Long. W 117° 5'.

Any occasional circumstances that occur I shall note down, but as I now see Dei Gratia a prospect of soon reaching my home, I am in hopes that the time will roll on so smoothly, as not to oblige me to soil any more paper. I put my trust in Providence to conduct me safe through the sickly climes I have to traverse in my passage homewards, and without anticipating any accident I endeavour to make my time pass as agreeable as possible, which is rather dull from the strange & awkward situation, I may suppose to be in, a Protestant & an American where all around me are Catholics & Spaniards. The maxim that Lord Chesterfield endeavoured to impress upon the mind of his son, I also endeavour [to make] the basis of my conduct here, viz. Sauviter i[n] Modo Fortiter in re.[53]

---

[51] At least one of these "strangers" can be identified. Maria Concepción Arguello had accepted the matrimonial offer of Nikolai Petrovich Rezanov, an official of the Russian-American Company, and highly connected at the Tsar's court in St. Petersburg. Rezanov, a forty-two-year-old widower, may really have loved the fifteen- year-old Concepción, but he had come into the area to spy out the possibilities of a Russian expansion into Upper California, especially the area around San Francisco Bay. The marriage was postponed until permission for Concepción to marry outside her Catholic faith was obtained from both the Pope and the King of Spain. Rezanov, while returning to St. Petersburg to report, fell through the ice of a Siberian river and died. Concepción never married and eventually she entered a convent. Cook, *Flood Tide*, pp. 497–99; see also Northrop, *California Families*, p. 41, for Maria Concepción (1791-?). Whatever Barbara's feelings about Seton might have been, she did not overreact to his failure to propose; she later married another Californian. Ibid., p. 42.

[52] September 15, 1814.

[53] Translated variously, a common version would be "Gentle in manner, reso-

On Friday morning the [30th] of Septr.[54] weighed anchor from [San Pedro] Bay & on Satur[day] 1st October [arrived] at St. Juan Capistran[o,] . . . SE from the Bay of St. [Pedro]. . . . dedicated to that Saint about. . . . At this place we expect to meet [Captn. Earys],[55] the Commander of the American ship Mer[cury, tak]en by the Spaniards at the . . . St. Blas while. . . . [Earys] and some of the Crew have been detained since that time at St. Diego, a Spanish Presidio about 18 Leagues to the S & E of this position, to which place Captn. E. is to pilot this ship, the entrance of the port being intricate. There is some probability of this Gentleman going to Panama with us, it is at any rate at his option, for the Señor Cavinecio has to my knowledge offered him a passage, which I suppose he will gladly accept, for a man who has seen other parts of the world, the remaining idle in this almost <u>Indian</u> Country, must be a situation of the most irksome kind.

Captn. E. with his Clerk, Mr. Blanchard, & 3 sailors joined us here on Sunday Evening 2d Octr. when we immediately got under weigh for the Presidio of St. Diego.

We anchor[ed here] on Tuesday 4th.[56] We remained at [thi]s place untill [S]aturday 22. While here notice was [received] from the Correspondents of the Captain Cavinecio [that] renders it necess[ary] for him to touch at St. Blas, a port on the main[land Lat.] 21. 31. As the business of Captn. E. leads. . . . [57] If it is possible to quicken my voyage homeward by crossing the continent from St. Blas to a port in the Guelph of Mexico, & if the state of affairs renders it practicable, I shall endeavour to take that route, as I will

---

lute in action." Chesterfield to Philip Stanhope, Apr. 13, 1752 (O.S.), John Bradshaw, ed., *The Letters of Philip Dormer Stanhope, The Earl of Chesterfield*, 3 vols. (London: Swann, Sonnerschein, 1905), II, 510; here Chesterfield is writing of various resolutions and actions in the House of Commons.

[54] Seton completed this entry at San Juan Capistrano on October 2, 1814.

[55] G. W. Earys, or Ayres, was the captain of the *Mercury* and traded in Pacific waters. Porter, *Astor*, I, 469.

[56] Tuesday, October 4, 1814; this entry was written at San Diego on or around October 22, 1814.

[57] About six lines missing. In them, Seton noted the receipt of two letters from Wilson Price Hunt, but his précis of their contents cannot be read.

by that means avoid the pestilential clime of Porto Bello.[58] St. Blas is also very unhealthy at this season, [but] I hope by precautions to escape sickness.

Although the desire & wish of seeing my country and friends may be supposed to be the predominant passion of my soul after so long & disagreeable an absence, yet no boyish whim would prevent me if any thing advantageous should offer, from seizing it at the expence of three of four years more absence. I have not any sanguine hopes of such a circumstance taking place. It is true I have received several hints from Captn. Ca[v]inecio, who is man of large fortune & one of a [crossed out: numerous] Rich house in G[uaya]quil,[59] Lima. I have determined if [he should] offer any thing [sui]table to accept it. What I consider [suitable] is the next thing to determine. I do . . . to the charge either of a cargo or . . . settlement of the idea though . . . the [r]eal state of the maj[tter] how [ever] . . . it is, depending entirely up [on] the whims . . . Governor since Capt. . . . being on board. . . .[60] I do not know what accounts he has given him, but I am confident of one thing, that if he employs Capt. E. to take a cargo to the Govr. he will not do so well with it, as I would. No self conceit or boyish vanity makes me hazard this assertion, it is founded upon the knowledge of Governor Barenoff's opinion of Capt. Earys, & of Govr. Barenoff's disposition. Any man that carries a cargo to Sheetka, & [crossed out: when] instead of entering now & then in the debauches of the old man, keeps up a rigid formality, & steadily refuses what the old man thinks civility, will not, except he possesses other striking qualities to make up for this, do any thing advantageous with the old man.

This circumstance would appear trivial & of no consequence in commercial affairs to a merchant in any other parts of the world, but so many real examples of the truth of it have happened, that must convince the most obstinate, yet they are some Captains, in spite of the examples they have heard of, obstinately & foolishly

---

[58] On the Caribbean coast of Panama.

[59] In present-day Ecuador.

[60] About six lines missing. From what follows, Seton apparently discussed Captain Earys's dealings with Seton's drinking friend Governor Baranov.

refuse to partake of the old [man's] feasts, & [when] they fail in selling their cargo, [assure] . . . themselves by saying "damn me if . . . b[ea]st of myself for any old scou[ndrel]. . . ." A man who has not suavity enough & . . . [en]ough of the world, to conform . . . [c]us[to]ms & habits & some . . . of the peop[le] . . . [re]main some . . . serves or secure them.

As it is not my business to push my opinion of the standing & capacity of Captn. E. with Govr. Barenoff on Capt. Cavinecio, I remain an idle spectator. It is for these last reasons, that I have no sanguine hopes of doing any thing advantageous. I believe Cavinecio has a desire of doing something with the Russians, & Capt. E. is he thinks his man. Far be it from me to say or hint any thing that would injure a man who has already lost nearly the profits of 9 years of labour in these seas.

On Sunday Evening Novr. 6th[61] we anchored in the roadsted of San Blas, and found also at anchor a Spanish ship from Bengal. This place is excessively unhealthy, most of the inhabitants having removed to Tepeic,[62] a town situated about 20 leagues inland, as being more healthy. I do not know what stay we intend to make here, but have great hopes not more than 10 or 12 days. In the mean time I remain on board [ship] taking what precautions are necess[ary] to avoid [cont]agion.

The Lat. of this town 21° 3[1']. . . . It is situa[ted] one would suppose in . . . freshness of air but from . . . heat prevails in all seasons. . . . of the character of Spanish sa[ilors] . . . [acce]ptance that is very considerab[le]. . . [wi]tness last night. I . . . disputing in a gruf[f]. . . .[63] tone, to all appearance not much in anger, when one drew his knife (with which they are all provided), and instantly struck the other in the Belly, & in withdrawing the Knife, the intestines followed. The murderer concealed himself untill about 12 oClock at night, when throwing over board a stage or small raft he endeavoured to jump on it, but missing his hold & not knowing

---

[61] November 6, 1814; this entry was apparently written a few days later.

[62] Tepic.

[63] About six lines missing; in them, Seton describes the climate of San Blas and then goes on to "the character of Spanish sailors."

how to swim, he was drowned under the fore chains of the vessel. These two deaths make no talk or stir among them, they say that is their fashion of ending a dispute.

At this place we receive great news regarding the continent of Europe, which if true in a wonderful manner shows the instability of human greatness.[64] Not much is said concerning American affairs, [except] there not being peace in April 1814.

[I had the] satisfaction to find here a country[man], . . . , [of] Boston 1st officer on board the [Spanish ship from] Bengal. Tuesday morning . . . Capt. E. left us. . . .[65] unfortunate for me, the Santa Catalina remains here untill the middle of December, and I am obliged to take up my residence on shore, to the great detriment of my pocket and health. Civility is a word of whose meaning the Spaniards are ignorant. A stranger and a Protestant then may be supposed to pass his time among them not in a very pleasant manner, in fact my difficulties are much more, than a person would suppose. Prudence prevents me from uttering my sentiments as freely as I would, were I among another people. I will only add as a memento that from something the Honorable Mr. Alvarez, the confidante of Cavinecio, told me the other day, I offered myself as a common sailor to him, since I had undertaken the voyage, & was determined to proceed in some manner or other. Shame & a small portion of conscience prevented the acceptance of this offer. The sultry heats of this climate [& the] unhealthy temperament & the charac[ter of it]s inhabi[tants,] all which affect me more . . . [that I am at] times so unhappy that I wish [c]oming with Cavinecio if th[e] . . . life, the lessons I daily inc[ulate] . . . of m[an]kind may be of some v[alue] . . . the meantime—as these Gentleman. . . .

Tepeic, 20 leagues inland from St. Blas, Febuary 4th 1815 — Saturday.

My last date was from St. Blas in the commencement of Novr. last. A violent & dangerous fit of sickness has detained me in my bed almost since that time.[66]About the 20th of Novr. I learnt from

---

[64] Seton is possibly referring to Napoleon's abdication, April 4, 1814.

[65] This entry seems to have been written about November 9, 1814; the last five lines, from "1814," are largely illegible.

[66] From Seton's description of his condition in the entry for March 1815, it is likely that he contracted malaria.

Cavinecio that the vessel would be detained at least one month longer, & that it would be necessary for me to move my baggage on shore as the state room I occupied on board would be wanting for some rich passengers from Guadalajara. I immediately com[plied] with h[is req]uest, although labouring under at that . . . [of] the climate.

On shore, . . . [recommended] to me to come on to [this place] . . . more healthy, but . . .[67] get me a passport from the Commadante of St. Blas, & if chance had not assisted me, by allowing me to meet with a Gentleman of this place & of the first family, Don José Santa Maria, 'ere this perhaps I should have placed my bones in their original earth.

On 26th Novr. we reached this place, & I accompanied Don Joséf to his house; circumstances had prevented Capt. Earys from getting any further inland towards Mexico, among which was the Calenture (the current disease of the country), a cold & hot fever.[68] A small house which the family of Santa Maria's owned in the vicinity of Don Joséf was offered to Capt. E. & my[self] to live together & on the first [December arrived] there, & provided a . . . & a man to attend us. On the . . . ill with the malignancy, . . . dangerous disease of the . . . [conta]gious. Captn. E. remains . . . serious soon left. [The] only Doctor of the place visited me twice a day untill the latter end of December, about the middle of which at the crisis I suppose, he gave me up as a dead man, and said that it was necessary to confess & receive the sacrament according to the custom of their church, if I did not wish my body to be buried in the fields, a prey to dogs & vultures. As, since I have thought for myself, I have considered the form of worshipping the Almighty as a matter of little consequence, provided the Heart is impressed with a due sense of religion & of his unbounded & unlimited mercy & goodness, I complied without hesitation, confessed [the] sins that layed heaviest upon my conscience, & receive[d] [ab]s[o]l[u]tio[n. In] the afternoon reveived the . . . in ceremony which is calcula[ted] . . . & passions of thes Vulgar . . . & but to one who has witnessed th[e] . . . comfort of the Christian religion; it

---

[67] The last four lines are illegible.

[68] Calenture, a violent fever with delirium, found in the tropics.

appears more like the preparation for some puppet show than the most sacred office, that man can be engaged in.

My own feelings during the time I considered I had no chance to live, were, wicked as I am, tranquil. I placed unbounded confidence in the mercy of our Almighty Father, & I never lost the hope of being saved through the Mercy of our Saviour. From the great torments I suffered I wished the scene to be concluded; [crossed out: as] I had given Capt. E. every necessary instruction what to do with my papers, & what little money I should leave behind.

It has pleased the Almighty to restore me thus far, for which I sincerely hope he will always [find in] me a grateful heart.

On . . . of December the [Santa Catalina sailed for] Panama, & I of course was . . . bed. My thoughts were . . . and whi[ch] [co]untry, where greedy of Dollars, than a stranger would conceive. A Dollar is not absolutely worth a quarter of a one in the U. States.

On the 2d Feby.[69] arrived here from St. Blas, John O'Farrell Esq., an Irish Gentleman of fortune, married in Manilla, at present an Officer of Galoon[70] arrived a few days since in St. Blas from the Gulph of California & after 4 years absence bound back to Manilla with Dollars, three & half million, independent of private property.

I after a mature deliberation of my situation determined to reach Canton if possible, as I was in this part of the world without money, friends, &c. & to live upon Mr. Astor's friends there.[71] Althoug[h n]ot in his employ, yet I considered the sacri[fice of] my t[ime &] health & constitution I have made . . . [three] years would entitle [me] . . . support from him untill I. . . . American Employ, and is well disposed towards that nation. My situation in every respect & my desire of getting a passage on board the Galloon to Manilla, I fully explained to him,[72] and was received by him in a manner that done honour to him as a Gentleman & a Man [crossed out: of] feeling for the distress of others; he told me he would apply to the

[69] February 2, 1815.
[70] From what follows, Seton is referring to a galleon, and not a specific vessel.
[71] That is, in Canton.
[72] Presumably John O'Farrell.

Commadant & endeavour to get me a free passage but as there were 50 or 60 passengers going, this he could not assure me of; at any rate to make myself lasy, that he would insure me a passage, & invited me at the same time to come to his house & live in St. Blas, for which place he [crossed out: which place] would set out in 10 or 12 [days].

The 17th [i]nst in Company we left [Tepic and] . . . reached his house in St. Blas . . . Feby. 22.[73] I have been . . . [San]ta Maria's in apprec[iation] . . . such, as an <u>unrecommended</u> stranger had no right to expect, & I hope if ever I have an opportunity to return there, I will not be found ungrateful.

As for Capt. G. W. E. during the time we lived together, it was proved to my satisfaction that he is neither a Gentleman or man of honor. His second officer, Mr. John Blanchard of Boston, died in Tepeic, where the charity of a Spanish Gentleman had brought him sick from this place. The three other sailors (I say other sailors because Mr. B. was treated as a sailor) who accompanied us from California in the Tagle died in this port on board of her, & their bodies were thrown overboard for the sharks.

In fact it is seldom a stranger fails to feel the effects of this climate. If he escapes with [his] life, it is [at the] expence of some other disease, for . . . [although] I have no fever, & can . . . a [c]omplaint (for which I know . . .) . . . difficulty br[eathing]. . . .[74] sleeping & not exerting myself all day. My flesh is yellow, my eyes are yellow, & I am as poor as a <u>Starved Rat</u>. I trust though that the Omnipotent will allow me to revisit once more my friends, & Country.

From an English mate of a Schooner from Lima, that arrived here about the 1st inst.[75] I learn that the US. Frigate Essex, Capt. Porter, was taken off Valparaiso on the coast of Chile by H.B.M. Frigate Phabe & Sloop of War Cherub, Captains Hilyard &

---

[73] This summary entry seems to have been written sometime in March 1815 in San Blas. About three lines are missing at this point.

[74] About three and a half lines are damaged. Seton was probably suffering the aftereffects of his fever.

[75] April 1, 1815.

Tucker, after a very obstinate & bloody engagement of two hours, 120 men being killed on board the Essex. . . .[76]

At sea, April 4th 1815, on board a Pilot boat Schooner bound from St. Blas to Panama. Lat. N. 14° Long. 98° 00′ W.

The determination I had formed of reaching Canton by the way of Manilla, has been given up, owing to various circumstances, the most consequential among which, was the demand from the Captain of the Galloon of $500 for my passage; this expence my circumstances did not justify. I accordingly thought of some other means of leaving the country. My state of health [crossed out: did] would not permit of my shipping as a Seaman. I have therefore, after various difficulties & innumerable mortifications, got a passage on board [this] schooner for [Panama]. . . .[77] My sextant I sold for $80 which with 50 I had remaining of the 500 made a total of $380. Out of this, 150 as before said for my passage, leaves 230 for my expences from Panama to Home.

The difficulties I experienced in making this arrangement a stranger would not suppose. Of the only two vessels bound this season to Panama, the Captain of one of them, after I had explained the situation to which I was reduced in point of funds, & offered to put up with any inconvenience, & to give any assistance my ill state of health would permit, had the inhumanity to tell me without paying $400 for my passage, I could not embark in his vessel.

I applied then to the Captain of this vessel, Dr. Manuel Loro, & have had the happiness to succeed in my application for the [aforement]ioned sum. I cannot tell with. . . .[78] gambling in all its forms, pass away very disagreeably. The smallness of the vessel be-

---

[76] The sea fight took place on March 28, 1814; in it, the British force, commanded by Captain James Hilyer in *Phoebe* defeated, with much difficulty, Captain David Porter's *Essex*. The American vessel suffered fifty-eight men killed and thirty-one missing. Leonard F. Guttridge and Jay D. Smith, *The Commodores: The U.S. Navy in the Age of Sail* (New York: Harper & Row, 1969), pp. 242–45. About seven lines are missing.

[77] About six lines are missing. Fragments in the missing lines suggest that Seton obtained $250 from John O'Farrell, the officer from the Manila-bound galleon, in return for a draft on Astor's business associates in Canton.

[78] About six lines are missing.

ing only 60 Tons, the excessive sultry heat that prevails, & the
number of passengers also add much to the inconvenience. In what
transactions of the Spaniards I have seen of this continent, I have
observed that Men old & young are generally more corrupted,
more destitute of honour, & in fact much greater rogues than they
are with us,[79] & the women more lascivious, who think nothing of
their nuptial vow, only considering it a convenient cloak to cover
their inordinate desires, that very little distinction is made between
a kept mistress & a married woman, that they associate together &
visit one another & of course the . . . of one is communicated [to
the] other. . . .[80]

---

[79] Presumably Seton's fellow Americans.

[80] Aside from about six missing lines, this is the end of Alfred Seton's journal.
The three remaining pages in the bound book he used are blank, except for some
arithmetic sums and the word "finis." Seton, ill and, to use his own phrase, "*as
poor as a Starved Rat*" (see above, pp. 175), was still a long way from New York.
The only authority we have for the rest of the journey is Gabriel Franchère, who
clearly must have gotten the story from Seton himself: "Mr. Seton . . . went to
the Isthmus of Darien [Panama], where he was detained several months by sickness, but finally reached Carthegena [Cartegena on the Caribbean coast of Co-
lombia], where a British fleet was lying in the roads to take off the English
merchants, who in consequence of the revolutionary movements going on sought
shelter under their own flag. Here Mr. Seton, reduced to the last stage of desti-
tution and squalor, boldly applied to Captain Bentham, the commander of the
squadron, who, finding him to be a gentleman, offered him every needful assistance, gave him a berth in his own cabin, and finally landed him safely on the
Island of Jamaica, whence he . . . found his way to New York." *Voyage*, p. 195.

Appendices

APPENDIX A
LIFE ON THE OREGON*

The American Monthly Magazine, 5, No. 3 (May 1835), 215–20.

*Note to the Editors. I am ignorant, Messrs. Editors, whether you, who know, or ought to know, all things, are aware that a party of young men, in the heyday of life, left this goodly city in 1811, to rusticate on the banks of the Oregon, or Columbia River. The motives that induced this step were as various as the climes that gave birth to these adventurers:—"the love of wealth, which even in the desert has its habitance"—"the restless spirit of adventure, which no toil or hardship can restrain"—and the "mere love of danger, which to some is lure alone"—all and each lent their aid. Among those, who joined "their sweet voices to the rural music of the desert," I was an humble companion; and, albeit, more *au fait* to beaver skins than to a goose quill—have, nevertheless set down, in a listless mood, to give you a feeble sketch—of life at Columbia River.[1]

****

Genial spring has succeeded a stormy winter:—the unpleasant and dreaded part of the year, to those who are exposed, by the nature of an Indian life, to hear the moanings of the tempest, and have no shelter to avoid the storm, had passed. The mild airs of the west had brought with them the bland temperature of a more sunny clime; in short, the middle of April [1813] had come, the period fixed for our party to return to the upper country. We had, in the commencement of the winter, while near the Rocky Mountains, learned from the *gens du nord*, (the north-west people), that war had been declared, had put our goods there *en cache*, and descended to our principal establishment, Astoria, at the mouth of the Columbia River, to bear thither this important information.

Our brigade consisted of two canoes, manned by seventeen Canadians—voyageurs—John Reed, an Irishman, and myself, an American *commis* [clerk], and Donald McKenzie, bourgeois, or proprietor, who had charge of the whole. We encamped the first evening around Tongue Point, a jetting bluff in the river, some miles above Astoria: an encampment in those days, when the luxuries of a voyageur, such as tent, cassette, &c., were scarce, was a simple matter. The bourgeois selects the first cleared spot that offers, towards the dusk of the evening; the canoes are unladened and hauled up; the goods are arranged and carefully covered with oilcloths; each man, except the steersman and cook, brings in his load of dry wood; the cook lights the fire, and prepares the kettle; and should there be a good fat animal—dog, horse, deer, or bear, is of little import, provided it is only *gras*[2]—the content of the voyageur is complete;—supper ended, the pipe is lit, and setting round the bright fire, whose flickering rays are thrown on their weatherbeaten countenances, like their brethern of the fore-castle, they spin long yarns of the adventures *"parmi les sauvages"*[3]—of foaming and dangerous rapids, and last, and not least, of starvation from hunger and cold; while, as the evening wears, ever and anon, they take a dig at the kettle; for it must be indeed *jours des fetes*[4] with a regular old voyageur, if he retires without seeing the end of his mess; that once thoroughly finished, with pipe in mouth, and hood of capot drawn over his head, he wraps himself in his blanket, and under the universal canopy, forgets his cares, until the glimmering of the stars announce the approach of day, when the shrill cry of the steersman,—*debut, debut, mes amies! a l'eau, a l'eau, Camarades!*[5]

The next morning, at daybreak, our journey was commenced in earnest: the first movement, a few miles above Astoria is like a ship hauling into the stream, preparatory to going to sea. The river, for the first forty or fifty miles from its mouth, retains a width of five or six miles, interspersed with low marshy inlets, the resort, at this season of the year, of numberless flocks of "giber," some of which nightly contributed to our *chaudiere*.[6] The banks are covered with most impenetrable forest, whose luxuriance, had they been witnessed by former philosophers, would have made them chary of

promulgating to the world, the flattering doctrine, that all productions, animal as well as vegetable, deteriorate in this our western
hemisphere.[7] Majestic cedars, and towering pines, can here challenge competition with those of their boasted Europe. A white pine
tree, immediately in the vicinity of Astoria, is deserving of particular notice; it was by actual measurement, forty-two feet in circumference, and more than one hundred high. Prior to our arrival in
the country, and even to the recollections of the natives, the lightning had checked its presumption by searing its princely top; it rose
gradually, but almost imperceptively, bare of branches and free of
excrescences: the obtrusive ivy had even forborne to entwine it: it
stood, unassisted by those associations which add so much to the
colossal productions of man, a naked but gigantic column, graced
alone by the dignity of nature, and impressive only by its own sublimity![8] We successively passed the village of *Ouakekum*, those of
the *Chreluitz*, the isolated rock, called by our voyageurs, *mont des
Morts*,[9] where the dead Indian, in his lone canoe, awaits the inun-
dation which is to overwhelm all things.* We coasted the beautiful
shores of the Multnomah Island,[10] — without forgetting to pay the
village a visit, famous as it was among our voyageurs for the fat
dogs the old squaws always provided—*pour faire un excellente chaudiere*; the idea of which, *en attrapant l'isle*, always made us musical,
and the refrain—

> *Nous trouverons de quoi manger*
> *Et des jolies filles—a nos cotes—*

was joined in, with all our hearts and souls.[11] We passed Point
Belvue, where the riant landscape had induced Lieutenant Broughton in former days, under the command of Vancouver, to stop and,
in the name of his royal master, George III, take possession of the
country, which they published to the world they were the first to
discover—forgetting the existence of a certain yankee, Captain

---

Mont des Morts is a lofty isolated rock, resting upon a marshy surface on the
margin of the river. Here, beneath the shadows of the impending cliff, may be
seen the canoes of the Indians drawn up, each freighted with a dead body, fully
equipped with bow and arrows, and a paddle, awaiting for the great day to come,
when the waters shall rise and float off these dreary barques to the harbor of the
happy spirits [Author's note].

Gray—and a few miles above, we left Point Vancouver on our left, the termination of Broughton's voyage. From this spot, in the far interior, are to be seen Mounts St. Helena and Hood—mountains above mountains, with snow-capped heads, and conical forms— appearing like rugged sentinels over a savage land. The river here assumes a new character; instead of shaggy mounds, emerging from entangled woods, shelving rocks and sandy beaches alternately con- fine it: its breadth is much diminished, and its current begins to give warning of our approach to the rapids. Previously to reaching these, however, we pass the cabin of old blind Soto, a solitary fish- erman, who calls himself a white man: his story is—and his albi- gineous look seems to confirm it—that he is the son of a Spaniard: a ship of that nation, in long-by days, had been wrecked at the mouth of the river; a number of its crew reached in safety the shore; the Clatsops, who inhabit Point Adams, massacred them all except four, one of whom, whose son old Soto is, settled in the country; the others, wearied with an Indian life, went into the interior, with the expectation of finding their way to some settlement of their countrymen; but no tradition of their fate has reached the present race. The portage of the rapids, where, for about a mile, the river leaps and bounds in eddying whirlpools from rock to rock, was promptly made; each man with his shoulder under a canoe, his pacton on his back, and his gun in his hand. Two days' march above, we reached the falls;—here "crags, mounds and knolls, are confusedly hurled together."[12] The first portage, which is that of the Dalles, is about a mile and a half long: the river has here con- centrated its energies in a channel of three or four hundred feet, and sweeps, with mighty and resistless force, in a deep, rapid and silent current, through precipitous banks of solid rock; some three hundred yards above this defile, it bounds ten or twelve feet over an adamant dam, built by the hand of nature. Here the rocky shores approach each other, forming, immediately about this *chute*, on each side, indentures or bays; that on the right hand is a secluded nook, lined with rocks and crags, and made use of by the natives, who have a large village in the vicinity, as a port for their canoes, while that on the left is bounded by a naked and sandy plain, an appropriate place for an encampment, while in the neighborhood of the most hostile tribe that inhabits the Columbia.

We had made the portages of the Dalles and falls early in the afternoon, and wearied, worried, and in bad humor, for it had been banyan day with us since leaving the rapids, had finished our only meal of *poisson a sept ecorces*,[13] when, for lack of something to do, or for some other motive, our bourgeois proposed, if any would accompany him, to cross to the Indian village, on the other side, and endeavor to get John Reed's rifle. This rifle had been carried off the previous year, as a spoil of battle, by these rascals, who had, in the portage we had just made, attacked a party of seventeen men under Robert Stuart: two Indians had been killed, and old Reed narrowly escaped the fate he afterwards met, having been leveled in the *melee* by a war-club, while tugging at the cover of his gun-lock.[14] The proposition of our bourgeois was coldly received; old Reed, the elder *commis* of the party, for whose especial benefit the adventure was proposed, kept a respectful silence; the only volunteers that offered were Joe La Pierre, our cook—before whose eyes visions of fat dogs floated—and myself, who did not like to be backward in seconding any proposition my bourgeois would make. Joe took his stand in the stern of the canoe, and flourished his paddle—*en patron*—my seat was in the bow, where I pulled as regularly as the wheels of a steam-boat in motion, while our bourgeois seated himself in the centre, with all the dignity becoming the leader of such a force. In this guise we soon reached the little Indian port mentioned above. On landing, we freshly primed our rifles and pistols, saw that our heavy dirks were free in their scabbards, and drew tight the buckle of the strap that confined them to our waists. A winding path of about a hundred yards, among rocks and crags, led to the village. No notice seemed to be taken of our approach. Not a solitary being, man, woman, or child, greeted us. The dogs even, which always howled by instinct, as it were, when we appeared, kept an ominous silence. On reaching the village, a young urchin of some twelve or fourteen summers, suddenly made his appearance, and, with phlegmatic phiz, pointed to a house more large that the adjacent ones: a door, two feet wide and three feet high, which absolutely required the Sir Archy posture to effect an entrance, was the only inlet to it. We went in, in the priority due to our grades, Mr. McKenzie, myself, and Joe. We had no sooner entered than a rush, from the outside, where nothing human had a moment before been visible, filled up the narrow passage. The *coup d'oeil*[15] of the internal part was far from an agreeable one. It brought conviction at a glimpse that we had been watched, and preparations made to receive us.

The interior of the house was a parallelogram of some twenty-five by twenty feet: towards the upper extremity, a bright fire was blazing; near to it sat an Indian of some sixty winters, whom we recognized as the chief. A file of Indians, three deep, enveloped in their greasy robes, with no other part visible than their hard features, squatted in a semi-circle around three sides of the apartment. The only spot where the line was broken was the passage by which we had entered, and which was then blocked by the irregular mass from the outside. The eyes of the file were bent to the ground, and gave no token of interest in the scene. The chief pointed to the vacant side of the room opposite to the door, for us to take our seats. A stern and sullen silence prevailed, giving us time, however, to look around, and be well satisfied of having heedlessly placed ourselves in a position whence nothing but resolution and decision could extricate us.

Our bourgeois was equal to the emergency: one minute sufficed for him to decide: his prompt order was, "Keep your eyes on the chief while I am speaking, and should he give any sign to his band, shoot him, and make for the door."

The pipe was filled and handed to the chief, and was, as we were sure it would be, refused. Our bourgeois, with a countenance as impenetrable as their own own, then opened the subject of our visit: he told them, "that the white man had come into their country for the purposes of trade, bringing them blankets, axes, knives, &c., to exchange for their peltries; that their desire was to live in peace and friendship with their red brethern; that though they possessed arms, which in their hands resembled thunder and lightning, in others were useless; that the chief might know this, from his having one of the white man's guns, which was valueless to him; that he had brought over from his camp, two blankets, an axe, some beads, and tobacco, to exchange with the chief for the white man's gun, which he would show if the chief was willing to do so; that the white man's nation, though few here, were as numerous as the sands on the shore; that they were, when unprovoked, as gentle as the deer that roamed in their woods; but, when angry, as dangerous as the rattlesnake that glides among their rocks." Profound silence ruled during this speech, and continued for some minutes; once or twice the chief raised his glaring eyes, but found ours fixed on him, with the serpent's gaze. He at length arose, commencing in a low tone, but warming as he progressed, until he wound himself to a paroxysm of violent rage.

The gist of his speech was, "that his ears had drunk what the *my-ai-whoot*, (the chief), had said; but that it was spoken with the serpent's tongue; that the *pashishiukx*, (white men), had already been many moons in the country, and where could one of his tribe point to a blanket, an axe, beads, or tobacco, they had given them; that his country had no furs, therefore the white men passed his people as dogs; that the blankets the white chief had with him, as well as the young chief's gun, and the white slave, (poor Joe), ought to be left with him, as a comfort for the death of his brothers, whom a few moons since, the white men had killed; that his eyes had not yet done weeping for their death; and that the white chief had now come to deprive him of his only consolation in his calamity; that the white chief was a brother of the white men who had killed his brothers;, for his young men had that day seen the pale-faced coward who lost his gun: Our bourgeois took advantage here of a momentary pause in this amiable harangue: matters were evidently drawing to a crisis; the fiery orbs of the ruthless cordon were glaring on us with demoniacal bent, awaiting the signal of the stern old chief. We had gradually raised ourselves to our feet during the speech, had brought our rifles in a horizontal position, the barrels resting in our left hands, the muzzle of our bourgeois' within three feet of the speaker's breast, the click of the locks, as we cocked them, for a moment suffused his dark cheeks: we coolly, but promptly advanced to the door, and the Indians fell from it as a herd of deer are scattered by the stately panther.

The sun was declining as we emerged from this den. We took the precaution to keep the tops of the rocks as much as possible on our way to the canoe; and reached our camp without interruption. There our canoes were, hauled up, bottom upwards, on the beach, some ten or twelve feet asunder; the luggage was stowed at their upper extremity between them: the river formed the fourth side of the enclosure; with it our voyageurs calmly slept, to prepare them for the fatigues of the next day: without, the watch was divided between our gallant bourgeois, John Reed, and myself: the night passed off quickly, until the usual cry of *a l'eau, a l'eau, Camarades*, warned us to continue our journey.

A.

The American Monthly Magazine, 5, No. 5 (July 1835), 368–75.

NUMBER TWO

A glance at the map of the continent we inhabit, will show what regions still remain in the occupancy of the former lords of the whole—regions

> "Where thou and thine, have not as yet usurped
> Their domination, royalties, and rights."[16]

Over this vast extent, including within its limits every variety of clime and soil—the parched plains of the Orinea, and the sterile tracts of polar ice—roam one race of people. They differ in some of the minor attributes, but all possess a general feature. Apathy of character is their distinguishing trait. An impenetrable coldness of disposition is common to all. Like their own scentless flower,* told of by Captain Franklin, they are incased in ice. Our joys and our griefs, our hopes and our anxieties, are strangers to their hearts; neither time nor circumstance operate on their stoical natures. Wrapped in their panoply they have held in scorn tortures which the ingenuity of devils might envy, and set at nought the skill of the physiognomist, in reading their steady black eye and immoveable countenance. Love of country, chivalrous feeling, or deep conviction of particular religious tenets, have induced individuals, in all countries and in all ages, to submit, with undaunted demeanor, to the severest proofs man can give of the sincerity of his motives.

These isolated instances are far from forming the characteristics of any entire race. Chance has so willed it, that in my day I have peregrintated over the *Yllanos*, through which the impetuous Meta dashes with an untired current, to join the turbid Orinoco.[17] I have held converse there with the natives, who carry on *guerro hasta la muerte*[18] with the intruders on their soil—the boasting yet fiery Creole. My lot has also cast me among the natives of Norfolk Sound,[19] in the frigid zone, who are equally implacable against the trespassers on their grounds, the horde of Russian serfs, who, "of hosts, have inhospitably endeavored to make slaves;"[20] and, to my mind,

---

*Captain Franklin found, in the polar regions, a flower in full bloom enclosed in a solid body of ice [Author's note].

this apathy and coldness of character has been equally exhibited. On the Columbia River and its tributaries, I have more closely observed the Indians, before polluted by intercourse with white men, both in the soul-stirring occupations of life, and in the domestic circle, the test of character. In the former no resistless passion,

> "Too fierce to be in fetters bound,"[21]

hurries them on to acts contradictory of their national trait. The emotions of love, jealousy, revenge, ambition, insulted honor, chivalrous feelings, which prompt other men to do daring deeds, and

> "Place their lives upon a cast,
> and stand the hazard of the die,"[22]

rule with feeble sway the cold-blooded Indian. Even the desire of possessing the renown of personal courage—the strongest incentive to action, and the shortest road to honor, among all uncivilized nations—never prompts their bravest warrior openly to meet his foe, face to face. By patient endurance of the winter's cold, or summer's sun, he gains a shelter, whence he can send his unerring arrow through the heart of his enemy; or if taken in his own toils he meets the tauntings of his foe, and the torments to which he is doomed, with a countenance as impassive as that of his persecutors.

In the latter, and in circumstances in which the civilized being can only bring to his aid, and that how vainly, reason, reflection, and mighty endeavor, to qualify the escape of his emotions—the uncultured and rude Indian has added proof upon proof, that he requires not wisdom to modify feelings which do not exist.

In the direct calamity of social life, when the fell destroyer makes his appearance, and strikes with his irrevertible dart the father of a family, the mother of helpless infants, or the children that have wound themselves round our hearts, we in vain look for these evidences of feeling which one would suppose inseparable from our nature: a mournful dirge, the loss of a few locks of hair, or the sacrifice of some living thing, to the manes of the deceased, are the chief tokens of grief they exhibit. The sorrow that will not be comforted, when the mind reflects on the deprivation, the tears which flow from the very fountain of the soul, when ties like these are rent asunder, the lacerating emotion of despair which penetrates our bosoms, when death has set his chill stamp on such loved objects—find no resting place in their heart of hearts. These impulses, which makes us

"Weep our sad bosoms empty,"[23]

are the concomitants of nations both rude and civilized. The absence of them in the constitution of our aborigines is not to be attributed to their uncultured and barbarous state, but to that particular coldness of character which marks them a distinct race.

What you want, however, Messrs. Editors, is incident, illustrative of a voyageur's life, and Indian character, and therefore there is enough—*satis jam satis*[24]—of vague dissertation. Like the *Amphytrion ou l'on dine*, I must be the hero of my own tale, who so amiably talks of his neighbor, and

"Whose heart accordeth with his tongue,
Seeing the deed is meritorious—"

you may be pleased to consider me an impersonality.[25]

Our *cache*, which I told you in my former communication had been made on hearing the news of the war, was on the banks of the Shahaptin River, a few miles above its junction with the Camoenum.[26] We had, early in the fall of 1812, ascended the former as far as it was practicable to drag the canoes, with a view of establishing a trading post, which might unite the requisites of procuring furs, and the *de quoi manger*.[27] The sterile country through which the Shahaptin poured, promised little for our first object, and the other, which was equally necessary, our bourgeois thought could be best attained by building our winter quarters near the confluence of the Shahaptin and Camoenum rivers, and among the Shahaptin[28] nation, quiet and peaceable folks, who devoted themselves to the rearing of numerous herds of horse, with which they supplied their more turbulent and warlike neighbors, the Tashepas of the Camoenum on the one side of their grounds, and the Courtenois and Flatheads on the other.[29] These nations were in the annual practice of crossing the mountains to hunt the buffalo, and to make war with the Blackfeet Indians. Our huts were built in the beginning of September, and of the drift-wood of the river. When it was decided in the end of December, to carry the news of the war to the seacoast, deep holes were dug under the floor of one of the huts, there cannily and carefully our wares and merchandise were deposited, the clay with which the interstices of the roof were stopped was let in, and the buildings were burnt. We trusted that, like Cesar's wife, not only intacta, but unsuspected. This was our *cache*. I gave you an account of our return voyage (after having been to the seacoast) as far as the falls of the Columbia, in pursuit of these goods.

Previously to arriving at our destination, rumors met our ears that the restless and villainous Tashepas, whose roving disposition had made them somewhat conversant with the proceedings of white men, had been poking about our premises for weeks; until at length our *moveables*, which we thought so warily concealed, had been uncovered to their eager eyes; and that the "bowels of their mother earth" had been rifled of treasures which might have been better hid. Our arrival here found the rumors true—not a "remnant of packthread, or a shred with which a beggar might patch a garment, but was scattered about." The avaricious and covetous Tashepas had pillaged the whole. Lengthy and rueful phizes abounded, when confirmation of our misfortune, as strong as holy writ, was forced upon us. We were naked of effects to trade the *de quoi* with the natives. It was useless to say to them, "Uncharitably with us have you dealt; therefore now give us your fat horses, to make a *plat cote* for our *roti*." Our only resource, like Snowdon's knight at Coilantogle ford, was in our arms, and like him we were constrained to use them.[30]

Mr. Reed, with two men, was sent to Mr. Clarke's establishment, on the Spokan River, to give him notice of the loss, and to carry him dispatches from Astoria. The remainder of our party, seventeen in number, were employed in endeavoring to get back our goods from the plunderers. In this we were more or less successful. Several villages of the Shahaptins were searched, but few of our wares found. These people united in saying that a band of the Tashepas, whose dwellings were on the banks of the Camoenum, in a small savannah hedged in by rocks and precipices, and where fearful rapids above and below forbade the approach of canoes, were the robbers. The chief of this band might number seven or eight lustres;[31] he had all the characteristics of a prairie Indian, tall, straight, lean, high cheek bones, sharp features, and piercing black eyes.

The aborigines of wooded countries, whose communications are chiefly by water, seem adapted by their figure to the country they inhabit—as equally are those of prairies or open countries. From the rapids of the Columbia to the seacoast, (a belt of about one hundred and fifty miles), an almost impenetrable forest covers the country; then commences the prairie country, which extends nearly to the Rocky Mountains.

The natives in the south-west district are all of short stature, seldom exceeding five feet one or two inches; broad backs, deep chests, and nervous arms, are common to all, as equally are short, crooked, and bow legs. While in the open country, the sculptor might, haphazard, take any individual, and the chance would be in his favor, that he had a form from which he might model his best imaginations of symmetry and grace.

During our sojourn of the previous fall in his vicinity, the above-mentioned chief had been in the habit of visiting us more frequently than any other of the Indians, sometimes alone, and sometimes with half a dozen or more of his band. He was, in the commencement, a favorite with the Canadians, who had given him the sobriquet of *Le Grand Bobillard*, a better acquaintance, however, had, previously to our going to the sea, caused them to change it, to the more appropriate one of *Le Grand Coquin*.[32] Circumstances had made a kind of familiarity between him and myself. In his visits, at the commencement of our residence in his neighborhood, we would often take our guns—for he and most of his band had them—retire a short distance from our Comptoir, and there exercise ourselves in shooting at a mark. The ammunition on these occasions hung at my side, and in loading his gun, I generally managed, although he watched the progress minutely, with my thumb on the spring of the powder-horn, to let in at least a double charge, sometimes much more; and as my rifle bullets rolled down his wide and smooth-bored north-west Indian fusil without much friction, we used to wind them with grass to make a tight fit. One thing was sure, in his firing, which he always did with great deliberation and steadiness, viz., that if the mark was not marked, of which the probability was small, his shoulder would be, and that not lightly. The unvarying certainty with which my bullet went straight *au blanc*,[33] owing to the superiority of my gun, caused him to betray the only emotions I ever saw him exhibit. Sometimes we would mount our horses, and "fetching mad bounds," rush headlong in our utmost contention, to gather up an arrow, stuck in the ground, without checking our speed.[34] The recklessness of youth, when not by "cares, or fears, or age oppressed," made me his equal in feats of horsemanship. I knew him, however, from a circumstance which took place in a visit to his village, (about four days' march, and to which Mr. M'K. had sent me with three men, a short time before we went to the sea), for a treacherous knave.

We ascertained one day that a band of the Tashepas, (not that of the Grand Coquin), who had participated in the plunder of our *cache*, were encamped some fifteen miles above us on the Shahaptin River. We embarked to pay them a visit. On approaching their encampment, which was done from the opposite side of the river, about one hundred yards wide here, some twenty-five Indians, with guns in their hand, were discovered on the banks, immediately in front of their lodges. A dozen vigorous strokes of the paddle brought us under them. Our bourgeois rapidly swung on shore, and ordered me to follow with the men. An angular path led up the bank: at the turn, halfway up, there was a small platform; the men were in a moment drawn up there. The Indians were at the other extremity of the path, some twenty feet distant. We could see from the protuberance in their cheeks, that their bullets were in the mouths, ready, in Indian fashion, for a fight. Our bourgeois was among them examining each and every gun, and emptying it of its priming. This done, we told them we had come to the country to supply them with arms and ammunition, and thereby enable them to hunt successflly the buffalo, and be on an equal footing with the enemies the Blackfeet. That we did not wish to fight; but were prepared to do so to get back our goods, which, like the cowardly Shoshonies, they had stolen in the night. That now the young chief would smoke with them, while he examined their lodges. He told them to sit down, and ordered me to bring a pipe; each took a whiff or two and then passed it to his neighbor—and while this was doing, the bourgeois with his aid, (Joe La Pierre), ransacked their lodges. He succeeded in recovering some three or four pactins, with which we re-embarked, and fired a salute, to show the natives, who were mostly young men, without any prominent chief among them, that we were brimful of fight. We went and encamped four or five hundred yards above, on the same side of the river, and on the banks of a brook which paid its tribute here to the Shahaptin, after winding its short and meandering course through cotton-wood trees and willows, whose green and luxurious foliage induced such cool and pleasant shade, and contrasted so strongly with the naked and arid scenery around, that our voyageurs could not withstand its seductions, notwithstanding our close vicinity to unfriendly neighbors. They, however, broke up at once their transitory encampment, and wended their weary way to their own firesides among the crags and precipices of the tumultuous Camoenum. We remained here three or four days, and were joined by a large band of the friendly Scietogas,[35] on their way to the mountains. A day after this junction, I had wandered some distance from camp, near the head of the little brook we were on, looking for gibier, and unsuccessful, was breasting the opposing hill, building *chateaux en Espagne*[36] when suddenly, on the brow, Le Grand Coquin, with his band of forty or fifty men made their appearance. They were all mounted and in their war costume—deer skin leggins and moccasins, buffalo robes wrapped round their loins and resting on their saddles in front; their faces and bodies painted in various colors; their heads fantastically adorned with feathers; a round shield made of buffalo bulls hide, and buried in the ground until it had shrunk to a sufficient thickness, hung on their bridle-arm; and immediately in front of it rested their guns. Without the usual greeting, Le Grand Coquin abruptly demanded the place of our encampment. I pointed to the trees at the foot of the hill, and told him I would mount behind him and show the way. Behold me, then, on the crooper of his warhorse. No loving arm, however, was around him thrown—bolt upright, with knees firmly fixed—the left hand holding my rifle, as it rested on the charger's back in front of me, and right arm full— I felt I had him to advantage; yet ever and anon, as you may even suppose, I made my heels familiar with the gallant war-horse's ribs. One or two gutteral grunts were elicited, as group of trees after group were passed. At length the blue smoke of our fires met his eagle glance. Our bourgeois was reclining under a temporary tent made with the canoe sails. The men were in groups of two or three, in the shade of some wide-spreading willow, variously employed, but all chattering and smoking. The guns were stacked against the luggage, which, with the canoes, were arranged in the usual manner, to form a sort of bulwark. The Scietoga camp was about a hundred yards distant; their chief, with a few of his young men, was then sitting on a log and smoking, near to the bourgeois' tent. The trampling of the war-chief's band made no commotion in the camp. The keen and knowing eye of the bourgeois recognized them at once, and divined their purpose. He gave no symptoms of surprise, or even of knowledge of their presence. Like statues, they remained for some time not greeted and unnoticed. At length the Grand Coquin addressed the Scietoga chief. He urged him, (after first bringing to mind their mutual friendly relations), to join with his band, and extirpate the pale-faced traders; he pointed out our defenceless and unprepared position, the paucity of our numbers, and the ease with which we might be destroyed; he mentioned our guns, kettles, knives, ammunition, &c., which would be the reward for the deed—in a word, adduced many arguments to entice the friendly band to become treacherous guests—happily in vain. After due deliberation, the Scietoga chief replied, that peace and friendship existed between the white men and his people, and therefore they would not mingle themselves in such an affair; that the white men had, many moons since, come to his country hungry and destitute, (alluding to Mr. Hart's party[37]), that he had given them to eat, and sped them on their journey; that since, many more white men had come, bringing with them such articles as were useful, and that he considered the trading-posts the white men were establishing in the country advantageous, because, in a short time, all his young men would have guns like their enemies, the Blackfeet, who had become armed from white men trading with them; that it was true, the chief present, with his young men, could be destroyed, but that the whites were now numerous, and would no doubt revenge the deed. He repeated again that his heart was warm towards the white men; that he had delayed his journey a day to smoke with them; and that he would not consent, while he and his band were present, that harm should come to them. After the Scietoga chief had finished speaking, the band of Le Grand Coquin remained in their statue-like posture for four or five minutes, then suddenly wheeled and left our camp. It was the last time I saw Le Grand Coquin. John Reed, in the succeeding year, went with a party in his vicinity, and they were all massacred.[38]

In the afternoon, the Scietoga chief, on whom the scene had apparently made no impression, for he did not allude to it, told us, that his young men were to continue their journey, and that we would find a pleasant encampment about twenty miles below, on the opposite side of the river, and among the Shahaptins. We bade the old man a cordial farewell, and took his friendly counsel. We went and encamped on the indicated spot, which was immediately on the river, where the bank was precipitous and lofty. The area of our encampment was enclosed by a semicircular line of earth, of about three and a helf [*sic*] feet high, and appeared as if regularly constructed by men similarly situated to ourselves.

NOTES

1. The lines set off by quotation marks within this paragraph are unidentified.

2. "Fat."

3. "Among the savages."

4. "Feast days."

5. That is, "get going, get going, my friends, embark, embark, comrades." Literally, "begin, begin, my friends, to the water, to the water, comrades."

6. Gibier, "ducks or geese"; *chaudière*, "kettle."

7. This notion was spread most energetically by the French naturalist Comte George Louis de Buffon in the late eighteenth century and contested most energetically by Thomas Jefferson; see the latter's *Notes on the State of Virginia* (1787), especially "Query VI: A notice of the mines and other subterraneous riches; its trees, plants, fruits, &c."

8. Cox claimed that this tree was forty-six feet in circumference measured at a height of ten feet; it stood immediately behind the fort at Astoria and was called the king of pines, "*Le Roi des Pins*," by the Canadians. *Adventures*, p. 71.

9. Respectively: Wahkiakum, modern Cowlitz, Coffin Rock.

10. Sauvie Island.

11. "To make an excellent kettle [or stew]"; "on approaching the island [or the land]; we will find something to eat; and pretty girls at our sides."

12. This is from Walter Scott's *The Lady of the Lake*, Canto I.xiv.272–273: "Crags, knolls, and mounds confusedly hurled / The fragments of an earlier world."

13. Literally, the fish of seven layers, the Canadians' term for salmon taken

in the fall (rather than the spring) when it tended to be dry and flaky. Supposedly, one went through seven layers and still got nothing good to eat. Franchère, *Voyage*, p. 97; Ronda, *Astoria*, p. 207. The earlier reference to "banyan day" probably was an extension of the name of the Hindu sect of that title whose rules forbade the eating of flesh. Hence, a banyan day was one with no meat, a lack which the dry salmon did little to remedy.

14. See above, pp. 95–97, for this; it is also described by Franchère, *Voyage*, pp. 118ff.

15. Literally, "the stroke of an eye"; Seton probably meant something on the order of a quick glance.

16. *The Life and Death of King John*, II.i.175–176: "Call me not slanderer; thou and thine usurp / The dominations, royalties and rights."

17. *Yllanos* is probably the Llanos, an area divided between present day Colombia and Venezuela; the Meta River forms part of the boundary between the two countries, as does the Orinoco, the major portion of which is in Venezuela, the country through which it flows into the Atlantic Ocean.

18. "War even to the death."

19. Off Sitka Island, on the southern coast of Alaska.

20. Unidentified.

21. The full line reads: "Passions too fierce to be in fetters bound." It is from John Dryden, "Aureng-Zebe," Prologue, 9, James Kinsley, ed., *The Poems and Fables of John Dryden* (New York: Oxford University Press, 1962), p. 165.

22. *The Tragedy of King Richard the Third*, V.iv.9–10: "Slave, I have set my life upon a cast, / And I will stand the hazard of the die."

23. *Macbeth*, IV.iii.2.

24. "Enough is enough."

25. Amphitryon, "where one dines," is a character from classical mythology, the husband of Alcmene, killed in a war against Erginus. This particular line may be from Molière's *Amphitryon* (1688): "*Le veritable Amphitryon est l'Amphitryon ou l'on dine.*" III.i; "The true Amphytrion is the one where one dines [or who gives dinners]". The full and correct reading of the other quotation is: "But that my heart accordeth with my tongue, / Seeing the deed is meritorious." *Henry VI, Part II*.III.i.269–270.

26. That is, the Snake (Shahaptin) and the Clearwater (Camoenum) Rivers; this is the post described in the journal on p. 104.

27. "Something to eat," provisions, probably game.

28. A branch of the Nez Perce Indians.

29. Seton is either misremembering the tribal names or, like many whites, he never got them straight; the former tribe were the Tushepas or Flatheads while the "Courtenois" were the Kootenais tribe.

30. Seton probably meant *plat côte* which, loosely translated (recall that he probably learned most of his French from the voyageurs), could mean meat course, thus, meat for our spit. "Snowdon's knight" was James Fitz-James, actually King James V of Scotland, then masquerading as a lost hunter, who was

forced into a fight with Rhoderick Dhu, the chief of the Highland Clan Alpine, in Walter Scott's *The Lady of the Lake*, Canto V.xii–xv. Coilantogle Ford is on the River Teith, two and one-half miles southwest of Callendar. *Gazetteer of the British Isles*, 9th ed. (Edinburgh: Bartholemew, 1943; repr. 1970).

31. Lustre is an antique word for a five-year period, thus Seton may have meant that the chief was approximately thirty-five to forty years old.

32. In French, *bobard* is a tall story or a lie, thus *bobillard* would be a teller of tall stories or, less charitably, a liar; *coquin* is a knave or rascal.

33. Literally, "to the white," presumably to the bulls-eye of the target.

34. "Fetching mad bounds, bellowing and neighing loud." *The Merchant of Venice*, V.i.73. The quotation in the following line is unidentified.

35. Another branch of the Nez Perce tribe.

36. That is, "castles in Spain"; daydreaming, in other words.

37. Seton has given the wrong name; he means Wilson Price Hunt, the leader of the party who came to Astoria overland from St. Louis.

38. This incident occurred during the winter of 1814–1815, about the confluence of the Snake and Boise rivers in present-day Idaho. The only survivors were Pierre Dorion's Indian wife and children who made their way back to Fort Okanogan with the assistance of friendly Nez Perce living on the Walla Walla River; Cox, *Adventures*, pp. 151–54.

APPENDIX B
ASTORIAN REMINISCENCES:
THE CAROUSALS OF COUNT
BARANOFF

The New York *Mirror*, XV (September 9, 1837), 84–85.

"The place at that time was the residence of Count Baranoff, the governor of the different colonies: a rough, rugged, hospitable, hard-drinking old Russian. . . . Mr. Hunt found this hyperborean veteran ensconced in a fort which crested the whole of a high rocky promontory. It mounted one hundred guns. . . . Here the old governor lorded it over a corps of sixty Russians, beside an indefinite number of Indian hunters. . . . Over the coasting captains, the veteran governor exerted some sort of sway—it was the tyranny of the table. They were obliged to join him in his 'prosnics,' or carousals, and drink 'potations pottle deep.' 'He is continually,' says Mr. Hunt, 'giving entertainments by way of parade, and if you do not drink raw rum and boiling punch, as strong as sulpher, he will insult you as soon as he gets drunk, which is very shortly after sitting down to table.' " (*Astoria*, II, Chap. 27) [Author's Note]

There are some incidents in our lives which seem to elude the ebb of time, and, in spite of the whirlpool of more interesting events which sweep around our memory, remain fresh and unimpaired. Such are the recollections of my first *prosnick*, or drinking feast, with Count Baranoff, governour of the Russian possessions on the northwest coast of America; and, as illustrative of life in gone-by days, may serve to fill a column in the New-York Mirror.

In the beginning of April, 1814, the few Americans belonging

to Mr. Astor's company, left Columbia River, in the brig Pedler,
bound for the Russian settlements on the north-west coast; the ma-
jority of the party set out on the same day on their journey across
the continent, through the posts of the North-west Company, and
under their protection—thus deserting interests which had been
cherished by treasure and blood. Our brig was manned by the crew
of the ship Lark, wrecked on her passage to Columbia River, near
the Sandwich Islands. *Her* captain was our sailing-master: and
Mr.—*our* captain. H. and myself were the recruits embarked at
Columbia River.[1] After being detained for several days for a leading wind over the bar, we got safely to sea. The staggering breeze
which drove us rapidly on our way, soon dissipated the moody
thoughts this irksome delay and change of habit had engendered.
With the usual proportion of snow-storms, squalls and gales, for
which this navigation is distinguished, we arrived at Norfolk
Sound, in the first days of May,[2] and rounding the little island in
front of the fort, saluted Count Baranoff with nine guns.

Of this roystering old Muscovite Mr.—had some knowledge.
Two years previously, he had visited and sold him the Beaver's
cargo. Certain of his characteristicks did not find grace in Mr.—'s
eyes. The predominant one of getting royally drunk, and insisting
on his guests being equally so, before business could be commenced, was, at any rate, no feather in his cap. Whether in self-
defence the old gentleman found it necessary to do so, or whether
it was from pure love of the *cretur*, is not for me to say. He may
have found the Boston captains, as others have, too many for him
when they were sober—and the punch, (by which name he dignified his mixture of three-fourths burning arrack and the remainder
Yankee rum), tend to obfuscate their cuteness, and keep his own in
its native brightness. Let this be as it may, the law was positive.
Besides these deep-drinking habits, there were other attributes of
character, not remarkable for amiableness, inasmuch as he was a
hard-headed, perverse, and absolute old gentleman. When anything had gone wrong with him, during the last forty years, he had
thwacked and belaboured his lieutenant-governor, captains and sub-
alterns; and happy were they if the banging was the only consequence—for, if obliged to pent up his humours, and bide his time,
the results were more serious. He had an innate prejudice against a

cold-water man, while his heart warmed toward a free-drinking, careless wight, who would enter into his prosnicks with gusto. His long exercise of absolute despotism had not totally eradicated every trait of gentlemanly feeling—those were occasionally exhibited, but they were few and far between.

Mr.—paid the usual complimentary visit, soon after we anchored—told of the disastrous winding up of the Pacifick Fur Company, and the consequent dissipation of the embryo plans of furnishing him exclusively his supplies—all which the old gentleman took very coolly, but entered with more interest on the matter of a *prosnick* he proposed giving next day to Mr.—and the young Indians he had on board. With whatever disagreeable anticipations Mr.—, who was a gentleman, with gentlemanly habits, might have looked forward to this jollification, they were not participated in by H. and myself. Our residence in the Indian country had not made us remarkable delicate in the choice of our edibles: and, for the drinking part, in the presumption of our years, we thought with Sam Patch,[3] that some folks could do some things as well as some other folks.

The following day, rigged in our best, we landed in the little cove formed by the jutting precipice, on the summit of which were the governour's quarters. The Kodiak village of one or two hundred Indians, open on one side to the water and palisadoed on the other three, with here and there a bastion, lay straggling around. Along the base of the precipice, tending inward from the shore, and where the descent was more gradual, ran one line of these palisades, through which a gate opened to a flight of broad steps, and up to a platform, where were mounted some three or four brass guns, and sentries posted. Rising from the far end of this platform was a much longer flight of steps leading to the area above, and crowned by the governour's domicil. This area was inclosed by a second row of palisades, and covered by cheavaux-de-frise. Guns, large and small, were ready here to pour out destruction to any who approached with hostile intent this sanctum sanctorum. The imperial banner, emblem of dominion in so many fair realms of Europe and Asia, fluttered here, too, in the noon-day breeze—and, floating high above meaner things, spread its protecting shadow over this rugged American mount. Here, also, elevated in the air, look-out boxes, with each its watchful sentinel, peered over the surrounding country, and wo betide the unlucky wight who failed to give notice of any moving object.

Not the solitary canoe, with silent paddle, could steal over the secluded bay—not the subtle Indian, with stealthy pace, could wind around the precincts, his ghostlike way, unknown to the governour. Perched here in his eyrie—without a cabinet to discuss measures—without a congress to vex him—without a nest of waspish newspapers stinging him here and there—this responsibility-taking old potentate imbibed with satisfaction his punch, and practised his remedy—a stout hickory stick—without let or bar, from any grumbling caitiff.

The inequalities of the mount were filled up with store-houses, barracks, etc. On the apex the governour's house stood alone. It was raised one story from the entrance—a narrow staircase led up to his apartments, consisting of a long room, with partitions at each end, dividing off his sleeping-chamber and office, each of which was well garnished with military weapons. From the point of entrance there was a descending passage leading to a billiard-room, bathing-room, kitchen, etc.—a sloping side to the precipice had admitted of this construction.

Punctually as the sun declined from his zenith, we entered the principal apartment. The type of royalty was seated on a sofa at the upper end of the room—chairs were ranged around, and a dining table, invitingly spread out, was not the least interesting object. As he shook us cordially by the hand, and uttered in the *lingua franca* of the place, *Poshweehalti*—welcome—he actually looked amiable. The hale old nobleman at this time numbered about sixty years, and was in person of middle stature, with a goodly protuberance in front. His face, round and full, seamed by years and exposure, gave little token of his lion character. His features were common—keen gray eyes, which appeared to read those on whom they were bent, and partaking of a mixed expression—sometimes glaring with fierceness, and sometimes casting a bland regard, were the only redeeming ones. Long military boots—dark inexpressibles[4]—white vest, with an exuberance of lace ruffle flowing from his bosom—a bottle-green coat, of a military cut, from which dangled a medal—and wide ruffles flaring from the cuffs, completed the outer man.

The table was soon covered by several good-looking dishes, the steam of which was potent. Grasping his badge of authority, the stout cane, the governour advanced and begged us to be seated. The Lieutenant-Governour, Lashinski, by name, and one or two other dignitaries, were our attendants. The dinner was composed of various dishes of fish and wild-fowl, cooked in divers ways, in the shape of stews, ragouts and pies—the sauce piquant, of which, was good train oil.[5] This being the first Christian dinner we had seen for many years,[6] met due honour from H. and myself; plateful after plateful of all, and each, disappeared with celerity. The old gentleman was pleased with the vigour of our attack, and in the fulness of his heart, more than once uttered his satisfaction. Wine, rum and arrack were the dilutents of this Hyperborean repast. Whatever the governour drank, we drank; not from any slavish desire of pleasing him, but from the supposition that he knew what was best.

As we warmed with the feast, H.'s amusement and mine was to get the lieutenant-governor in a scrape, for it actually did our hearts good to see the second in command caned. We thought of McD., our second at Columbia River, as typified in his person.[7] We therefore alternately shouted "Lashinski," pointing to our empty glasses; and as we were on opposite sides of the table, he had to leave his seat to wait upon us, while each time he passed the old bear, he got a whack for his want of attention; and before we had done, the perspiration rolled from his head to his feet.

Everything has an end, and so has a good dinner. The governor now proposed to drink our punch, a signal for a regular set-to in the billiard-room—we adjourned thither. A big urn, filled, not with piping-hot water, but with piping-hot punch, was introduced. A tumbler or two of it told us we were gone men, if it could not find some other passage than down our thorax. There was no frill on our leather shirts, and we preferred scalding the out rather than the inside.

We commenced playing at pool, each man depositing in a pocket of the table a silver dollar as his stake. The players were the governour, his nephew, Lashinski, one or two other dignitaries, H. and myself. It so happened that in the first game the contest for the money lay between the governour and me, and a favourable chance presenting itself, notwithstanding numerous shakes of the head, and other signs of disapprobation from the jackals, I struck the old lion in the pocket, and so pocketed the dollars. He made me a low bow, with all the politeness of a gentleman of the old school, though looking, in spite of his efforts, like a chafed bulldog.

After a long pull at the punch, and a confounded hot bath, we returned to our game, and to my no small advantage, the governor made me his partner. We thus continued *punching* it and *pooling* it, until some of us could no longer hit a ball. When we reached this happy state, old Blowhard doffed coat and boots, and made ready for a dance. Large as he was, he cut a queer figure; however, he led the van in a legitimate gallopade, around and around the billiard table, kicking up his heels, and frolicking like an old cart-horse; we all followed in his wake, whooping, hallooing, shouting and cutting all sorts of capers. Many were the intervals we were obliged to stop and drink punch. The old one was a good one to go, but became blown at last. He pulled up, and at his invitation, H. and myself seated ourselves by him. The others kept up the pace; and ever and anon, when there was any inclination to go at ease, or want of vigour in the whoop, whack came the remedy.

The count, in the meantime, was undergoing a process which soon qualified him for a prolongation of the revels. Evaporation was going on rapidly with him; wine, rum and punch rolled in streams from his pores, and in half an hour he seemed as good as new again. The punch, in lieu of tumblers, was now filled in pint bowls—the vacuum was shortly supplied, and the old Sponge was quickly soaking again.

Three or four file of soldiers, with muskets and fixed bayonets, about this time entered, and stood stiff and rigid on each side of the door. A score of naked Indians, armed each with a knife, and be-daubed in various colours, next made their appearance. These seated themselves in a circle, with the exception of one, who moved slowly around within it, chanting in a low, monotonous tone. In the chorus he was joined by the whole gang; his tones gradually became more rapid, and the chorus more energetick. At length they were all on their feet in motion, and every now and then approached H. and myself, flourishing their knives almost within reach of our eyes, and screeching and howling like so many madmen. We had seen better-looking Indians in their own wilds, without the presence of armed soldiers, playing with more grace similar wild anticks, and could look therefore with unblenching eyes on their mimick warfare. We, too, could sing the war-song and dance the war-dance, and excited by the scene, we unrigged ourselves in a trice. Some jars of train oil, and bags of feathers, were ranged on one side of the room. We emptied one of these gravy-pots over us, and took the same liberty with a bag of feathers, and with jack-knife in hand, played our parts in the orgies. The old man was pleased; the inferiour dignitaries had to follow suit. The punch circulated most rapidly. Indians and all were roaring drunk; the frantic revels were at their height. Seated on a bench, supported by the wall, and flour-ishing his stick, the old governour kept us to our work around and around the billiard-table, shouting and bellowing as long as he could make himself audible; his voice at length dwindled to a growl, in which the only word to be distinguished was *puncham*; his eyes twinkled, he tottered in his seat, and then fell lumpus on the floor, regularly sewed-up—a consummation, though often devoutly wished for, few had the satisfaction of witnessing. Notwithstanding our vapour baths, in what guise, or how, and when, we got aboard, we know not. The next morning we found ourselves there, and ascertained that Mr. —, had, with his usual forethought, made an early escape from the toils of this hard-drinking old potentate.

NOTES

1. Mr.— was Wilson Price Hunt; H. was Seton's fellow clerk and good friend John C. Halsey. He seems to have forgotten that Russell Farnham was also aboard.

2. The *Pedler* actually arrived on April 22; see above, p. 156. Norfolk Sound is on the west coast of Sitka Island, off the panhandle formed by southeastern Alaska; Baranov is honored there by a park named after him as well as an island.

3. Sam Patch (1807–1829) was a daredevil who gained a national reputation by diving into rivers from great heights, including the Niagara River from Goat Island. *Dictionary of American Biography*, XIV, 291–92.

4. "Inexpressibles" is a humorous term for breeches or trousers.

5. Train oil was oil obtained from the blubber of whales, or from seals, wal-ruses, or other marine animals.

6. It is fair to recall that Seton had left New York City on the *Beaver* in October 1811.

7. Duncan McDougall.

Bibliography

Primary Material

Manuscript Collections

DeWitt Clinton Papers, Columbia University Library Special Collections.
Albert Gallatin Papers, New-York Historical Society.
Elizabeth Seton Papers, University of Notre Dame Archives.

Books and Government Documents

Bradshaw, John, ed. *The Letters of Philip Dormer Stanhope, Earl of Chesterfield.* 3 vols. London: Swann, Sonnerschein, 1905.

Brown, Everett S., ed. *William Plumer's Memorandum of Proceedings in the United States Senate.* New York: DaCapo, 1923. Repr. 1969.

Chalidze, Valery, ed. *John Jacob Astor: Business Letters, 1813–1828.* Benson, Vt.: Chalidze, 1991.

Colnett, James. *A Voyage to the South Atlantic and round Cape Horn into the Pacific Ocean for the purpose of extending the Spermaceti Whale Fisheries and other objects of commerce* . . . . London: The Author, 1798.

Coues, Elliott, ed. *The Manuscript Journals of Alexander Henry and of David Thompson, 1799–1814.* 3 vols. New York: Harper, 1897.

Cox, Ross. *The Columbia River.* Edd. Edgar I. and Jane R. Stewart. Norman: University of Oklahoma Press, 1957.

First Annual Report of the Superintendent of the Insurance Department of the State of New York. Albany: Insurance Department, 1860.

Franchère, Gabriel. *Journal of a Voyage on the North West Coast of North America During the Years 1811, 1812, 1813, and 1814.* Ed. W. Kaye Lamb. Trans. Wessie Tipping Lamb. Toronto: The Champlain Society, 1969.

Longworth's American Almanac, New York Register and City Directory.

Message from the President of the United States, communicating the letter of Mr. Prevost and other documents, relating to an establishment made at the mouth of the Columbia River, (January 23, 1823). Washington, D.C.: Gales & Seaton, 1823.

Payette, B. C., ed. *The Oregon Country Under the Union Jack: A Reference Book of Documents for Scholars and Historians.* Montreal: Payette Radio, 1961.

———. *The Oregon Country Under the Union Jack—Postscript Edition.* Montreal: Payette Radio, 1962.

Rollins, Philip Ashton, ed. *The Discovery of the Oregon Trail: Robert Stuart's Narrative of his Overland Trip Eastward from Astoria in 1812–13.* New York: Eberstadt, 1935.

Ross, Alexander. *Adventures of the First Settlers on the Oregon or Columbia River.* Ed. Milo Milton Quaife. Chicago: Donnelly, [1923].

Syrett, Harold, ed. *The Papers of Alexander Hamilton.* 27 vols. New York: Columbia University Press, 1961–1987.

Periodicals

"Biographical Sketch of the Late Alfred Seton, Esq." *The United States Insurance Gazette*, N.S., 9, No. 49 (June 1859), 65–68.

Blue, George Vere. "A Hudson's Bay Company Contract for Hawaiian Labor." *Oregon Historical Society*, 25, No. 1 (March 1924), 72–75.

Boit, John. "A New Log of the Columbia." Edd. Worthington C. Ford and Edmond S. Meany. *The Washington Historical Quarterly*, 12, No. 1 (January 1921), 3–50.

Bridgewater, Dorothy Wildes, ed. "John Jacob Aster [*sic*] Relative to His Settlement on the Columbia River," *Yale University Library Gazette*, 24, No. 2 (October 1949), 47–69.

"Captain Black's Report on the Taking of Astoria," *Oregon Historical Society*, 17, No. 2 (June 1916), 147–48.

Douglas, Jesse, ed. "Matthews' Adventures on the Columbia," *Oregon Historical Quarterly*, 40, No. 2 (June 1939), 105–48.

Elliott, Thompson C., ed. "Sale of Astoria, 1813," *Oregon Historical Quarterly*, 33, No. 1 (March 1932), 43–50.

McDermott, John Francis, ed. "Hospitality at the Punch Bowl: An Astorian's Recollections of an Evening with Count Baranoff." *Pacific Northwest Quarterly*, 48 (April 1957), 55–58.

"On the Fur Trade and Fur-Bearing Animals," *The American Journal of Science and Arts*, 25, No. 2 (January 1834), 311–29.

Seton, Alfred. "Life on the Oregon." Ed. Fred S. Perrine. *Oregon Historical Quarterly*, 36, No. 2 (June 1935), 187–204.

SECONDARY MATERIAL

Books

Barrett, Walter [pseud., Joseph Scoville]. *The Old Merchants of New York*. 5 vols. New York: Carleton, 1863.

Campbell, Marjorie Wilkins. *The North West Company*. New York: St. Martin's, 1957.

Chevigny, Hector. *Russian America: The Great Alaskan Adventure, 1791-1867*. New York: Viking, 1965.

Chittenden, Hiram M. *History of the American Fur Trade of the Far West*. 3 vols. New York: Harper, 1902.

Columbia University Alumni Register, 1754–1931. New York: Columbia University Press, 1932.

Cook, Warren L. *Flood Tide of Empire: Spain and the Pacific Northwest, 1543–1819*. New Haven: Yale University Press, 1973.

Day, A. Grove. *Hawaii and Its People*. Rev. Ed. New York: Meredith, 1968.

Dulles, Foster Rhea. *The Old China Trade*. Boston: Houghton Mifflin, 1930.

Gazetteer of the British Isles. 9th ed. Edinburgh: Bartholemew, 1943. Repr. 1970.

Guttridge, Leonard F., and Smith, Jay D. *The Commodores: The U.S. Navy in the Age of Sail.* New York: Harper & Row, 1969.

Haeger, John Denis. *John Jacob Astor: Business and Finance in the Early Republic.* Detroit: Wayne State University Press, 1991.

Hoffman, Eugene A. *Genealogy of the Hoffman Family: Descendants of Martin Hoffman.* New York: Dodd, Mead, 1899.

Irving, Washington. *The Adventures of Captain Bonneville.* Edd. Robert A. Rees and Alan Sandy. Boston: Twayne, 1977.

———. *Astoria, or, Anecdotes of an Enterprise Beyond the Rocky Mountains.* Ed. Richard Dilworth Rust. Boston: Twayne, 1976.

———. *Astoria, or, Anecdotes of an Enterprise Beyond the Rocky Mountains.* Ed. Edgeley W. Todd. Norman: University of Oklahoma Press, 1964.

Josephy, Alvin M., Jr. *The Nez Perce Indians and the Opening of the Northwest.* New Haven: Yale University Press, 1965.

MacKay, Douglas. *The Honourable Company: A History of the Hudson's Bay Company.* Indianapolis: Bobbs-Merrill, 1936.

Melville, Annabelle M. *Elizabeth Bayley Seton, 1774–1821.* New York: Scribner's, 1951.

Merk, Frederick. *The Oregon Question: Essays in Anglo-American Diplomacy and Politics.* Cambridge: Harvard University Press, 1967.

Nevins, Allan. *History of the Bank of New York and Trust Company, 1784 to 1934.* New York: Arno, 1935. Repr. 1976.

Northrop, Marie L. *Spanish-American Families of Early California: 1769–1850.* 2 vols. New Orleans: Polyanthos, 1976.

Pleasants, J. Hall. *The Curzon Family of New York and Baltimore.* Baltimore: Privately Printed, 1919.

Porter, Kenneth W. *John Jacob Astor: Business Man.* 2 vols. Cambridge: Harvard University Press, 1931.

Rich, E. E. *The History of the Hudson's Bay Company, 1670–1870.* Records of the Hudson's Bay Company 21, 22. London: The Hudson's Bay Record Society, 1958–1959.

Ronda, James P. *Astoria and Empire.* Lincoln: University of Nebraska Press, 1990.

———. *Lewis and Clark Among the Indians.* Lincoln: University of Nebraska Press, 1984.

Ruby, Robert H., and Brown, John A. *A Guide to the Indian Tribes of the Pacific Northwest.* Norman: University of Oklahoma Press, 1986.

Seton, Monsignor [Robert]. *An Old Family, or, The Setons of Scotland and America.* New York: Brentano, 1899.

Smith, Philip Chadwick Foster. *The Empress of China.* Philadelphia: Philadelphia Maritime Museum, 1984.

Swainton, John R. *The Indian Tribes of North America.* Washington, D.C.: Smithsonian Institution, 1952.

Van Alstyne, Richard W. *The Rising American Empire*. Chicago: Quadrangle, 1960. Repr. 1965.

Williams, Stanley T. *The Life of Washington Irving*. 2 vols. New York: Oxford Univesity Press, 1935.

Wilson, Allen Gay, and Anselineau, Roger. *St. John de Crèvecoeur: The Life of an American Farmer*. New York: Viking, 1987.

Articles

Barry, J. Neilson. "Washington Irving and Astoria." *Washington Historical Quarterly*, 18, No. 2 (April 1927), 132–39.

Drumm, Stella. "More About Astorians." *Oregon Historical Society*, 24, No. 4 (December 1923), 335–60.

Gough, Barry M. "The 1813 [British] Expedition to Astoria." *The Beaver*, Outfit 304.2 (Autumn 1973), 44–51.

Howay, F. W. "The Voyage of the *Hope*: 1790–1792." *The Washington Historical Quarterly*, 11, No. 1 (January 1920), 3–28.

Kime, Wayne R. "Alfred Seton's Journal: A Source for Irving's *Tonquin* Disaster Account." *Oregon Historical Quarterly*, 81, No. 4 (December 1970), 309–24.

Kytr, Hobe. "The Lady is Changeable. Catch Her When She is Angry." *Sea History*, No. 61 (Spring 1992), 46.

MacGregor, Alan Leander. " 'Lords of the Ascendent': Mercantile Biography and Irving's *Astoria*." *Canadian Review of American Studies*, 21, No. 1 (Summer 1990), 15–30.

MacLaren, I. S. "Washington Irving's Problems with History and Romance in *Astoria*." *Canadian Review of American Studies*, 21, No. 1 (Summer 1990), 1–13.

Minto, John. "The Influence of Canadian French on the Earliest Development of Oregon." *Oregon Historical Society*, 15, No. 4 (December 1914), 277–82.

Porter, Kenneth W. "Cruise of Astor's Brig *Pedler*, 1813–1816." *Oregon Historical Quarterly*, 31, No. 2 (June 1930), 223–30.

Thompson, A. W. "New Light on Donald Mackenzie's Post on the Clearwater, 1812–13," *Idaho Yesterdays*, 18, No. 3 (Fall 1974), 24–32.

UNPUBLISHED MATERIAL:

Kime, Wayne Raymond. "Washington Irving's *Astoria*: A Critical Study." Ph.D. diss., University of Delaware, 1968.

Myers, Andrew Breen. "Washington Irving, Fur Trade Chronicler: An Analysis of *Astoria*, with Notes for a Corrected Edition." Ph.D. diss., Columbia University, 1964.

INDEX

41, 44, 45, 47, 48, 59, 61, 62, 63, 69, 73, 76, 98, 99, 125
Nipesang Indian, 134
Nipissing Cree Indian, 145; *see also* Grand Nepisengue, Nipesang Indian
Nodoway River, Missouri, 15
Nootka Sound Controversy, 11, 18
Norfolk Sound, Alaska, 155, 156, 189, 202
North West Company, 1, 13, 14, 16, 17, 19, 100, 107, 108, 113, 116, 125, 126, 127, 128, 129 (purchase of Pacific Fur Company assets), 130, 131, 132, 133, 137, 142, 145, 148, 149 (terms of sale and Seton's judgment on purchase), 158, 202
Northrup, Captain Samuel, 150, 155, 164, 165

Oahu (Hawaiian island), 67, 68, 74, 80, 81
Ochotz, *see* Okhotsk
O'Farrell, John, 174–75, 176*n*77
Ogden, Josiah, 3
Ogden, Nicholas G., 150
Okanogan River, 17
Okhotsk, Siberia, 156
Oregon, 1, 4, 10, 19
Oregon, Missouri, 15
Orinoco River, 189
Ortega, Point Conception, California, 165, 168
Ouakekum, *see* Wahkiakum
Owyhee Indians, *see* Hawaiian natives

Pacific Fur Company, 1, 3, 5, 7, 12, 14, 15, 17, 19, 100*n*48, 111*n*78, 128, 129 (sale of assets to North West Company), 130, 135, 137, 145, 149 (terms of sale and Seton's judgment on purchase), 203
Palouse River, 115

Panama, 166, 169, 174, 176
Patagonia, 60
Patch, Sam, 203
Pavion, Riviere du, *see* Palouse River
Pedler (ship), 148, 149, 150, 155
Phabe, SEE *Phoebe*
Phoebe (Royal Navy frigate), 142, 175
Pigot, Captain William, 157, 159, 161, 168
Pillet, Francis P. (B. C. Payette), 89
Plata, Rio de la, 36, 38, 39
Plumer, William, 13
Point Adams, Oregon, 184
Point Vancouver (on Columbia River), 184
Porter, David (U.S. Navy captain), 175–76
Porto Bello, Panama, 170
prosnic, 157

Raccoon (Royal Navy sloop), 142, 143, 158
Ramsay, Jack (Lamasee), 18, 93*n*16
Reed, John, 95, 96, 102, 106, 107, 108, 110, 111, 112, 113, 182, 185, 188, 192, 197
Rhodes, Benjamin, 59, 60, 67, 68, 75, 84, 85
Rio de Janeiro, 35, 39, 142
Rocky Mountains, 94
The Rocky Mountains; or Scenes, Incidents, and Adventures in the Far West (1837), Washington Irving, 6 (also known as *The Adventures of Captain Bonneville*)
Ross, Alexander, 11
Russian-American Company, 7, 10, 11, 14, 111*n*78, 156

St. Blas, *see* San Blas
St. Diego, *see* San Diego
St. Louis, Missouri, 10, 12, 14, 15, 16, 94
Saltus, Nicholas, *see* Cook, Charles